S0-BCV-831

THE HEAVENLY KINGDOM

Aspects of Political Thought
in the Talmud and Midrash

Gordon M. Freeman

University
Press of
America

THE JERUSALEM CENTER FOR
PUBLIC AFFAIRS/
CENTER FOR JEWISH
COMMUNITY STUDIES

LANHAM • NEW YORK • LONDON   JERUSALEM • PHILADELPHIA • MONTREAL

Copyright © 1986 by

The Jerusalem Center for Public Affairs / Center for Jewish Community Studies

University Press of America,® Inc.

4720 Boston Way
Lanham, MD 20706

3 Henrietta Street
London WC2E 8LU England

All rights reserved

Printed in the United States of America

Co-published by arrangement with The Jerusalem Center for
Public Affairs/
Center for Jewish Community Studies

Other than for the purposes of scholarly citation or review, no
part of this book may be reproduced or transmitted without
permission in writing from the publisher.

Library of Congress Cataloging in Publication Data

Freeman, Gordon M.
The Heavenly Kingdom : aspects of political thought
in the Talmud and Midrash.
Bibliography: p.
Includes indexes.
1. Politics in rabbinical literature.   2. Covenants
(Jewish theology)   I. Title.
BM496.9.P64F73   1986   296.3'877   85-26483
ISBN 0-8191-5139-4 (alk. paper)
ISBN 0-8191-5140-8 (pbk. : alk. paper)

All University Press of America books are produced on acid-free
paper which exceeds the minimum standards set by the National
Historical Publications and Records Commission.

ACKNOWLEDGEMENTS

This work was been a project of joy and personal fulfillment. The idea was conceived at the beginning of my studies in political theory. Almost no material was available that examined Jewish covenant concepts in a political context.

My professors, John Schaar and Sheldon Wolin, helped me along in this pursuit early in my studies. They critically read some early, quite immature papers on covenant. Dr. David Lieber, President of the University of Judaism, also critically appraised those papers and offered useful suggestions.

While pursuing a Masters Degree in government, Nahum Sarna, presently of Brandeis Unversity and Gisbert Flanz of New York University, contributed to my understanding of biblical political thought, the former suggesting biblical and Greek contrasts, and the latter providing a context of political thought in which to write about biblical covenant.

Although the road seemed long at times, and the work abandoned to attend to other needs, upon my return to it, Professors Norman Jacobson and Leslie Lipson were constant sources of stimulation and encouragement. They appraised the sources insuring that I maintained the original intention, to place covenant studies in a political context.

Professor David Daube's contributions have been invaluable. His painstaking critical appraisal at each step of research and writing helped to remove glaring generalities, inconsistencies and inaccurate statements. His breadth of knowledge, acumen and mastery over so many distinct fields constantly provided a model of exhaustive scholarship. Finally, Dr. Daniel Elazar, whose pioneering in this field has been invaluable in making significant contributions concerning issues of Jewish political thought and covenant thought, has been a constant source of support and encouragement.

Needless to say, I take personal responsibility for any errors or faulty judgements this work may include. However, it is incumbent upon me to thank the above-mentioned persons who have helped me along the way.

The congregation in which I have served, B'nai Shalom, has patiently listened to numerous political explanations of biblical and rabbinic sources. It has encouraged my study and has provided a testing ground for the development of many of the ideas found in this work.

I must acknowledge the Taubman Foundation and the Littauer Foundation for their support in making the preparation of this manuscript possible. Especial thanks in this regard also goes to Mr. Marc Freeman who provided similar support.

Finally and most significantly, Susan, my wife, and Sara, Rachel, Elana and Eve have been a constant source of joy and love. They helped me to persevere.

CONTENTS

INTRODUCTION

Heretofore, political thought has been studied in works whose conceptual systems were evident. Such thought has been analyzed in the context of the specific author: his life and times, the suppositions and presuppositions he makes, and the principles he establishes. Usually such thought has become a manifestation of the Western world and part of our cultural heritage, utilizing thought patterns which are similar to those of the scholar who approaches it.

The present writer assumes that anywhere a political entity exists political questions will be asked in order to justify or attack the imposition of power on the individual living in the community. These questions may or may not be common to all political entities.

However, various cultures, exemplified by different thought patterns, will ask political questions in ways that are appropriate to them. Each culture will pose questions in its own inimitable way. Since Western scholars are usually not familiar with the culture, the language, or the very thought patterns of another culture, political thought of non-Western cultures largely has been ignored.

Such political thought, by its very nature, is not easily transmitted across cultural boundaries. This difficulty is exacerbated if the culture is no longer extant. Transmission must be accomplished through an arduous process of translation. The translator must place himself in two worlds, his own (i.e., Western thought) and the culture that he is studying.

The culture that will be examined in the present work is that of rabbinic Judaism. The origin of this culture probably can be traced back as far as the fourth century B.C.E.[1] It continued until the final compilation of the Talmud which occurred in the sixth or seventh century C.E. Most of the sources examined in this work can be dated to the second through fourth centuries, C.E.

Although the transmission of this culture was basically oral (especially in its earliest stages) written works are available. Such works as the *Talmud*[2] (a compilation of Jewish law and lore), and various collections of *midrash* (line by line interpretations of the biblical text)[3] will be the basic source material for this work. The languages of these works are Hebrew and Aramaic.

1

The scope of the material is vast. This study will concentrate on the concept of covenant as understood in rabbinic literature. Much of the material is an elucidation and interpretation of the biblical event at Sinai. The Sinai experience (Exodus 19:1; 19, 20; 23) Deuteronomy 5:1-6.3) marks the beginning of a covenant community. The biblical text deals with the formal acceptance of the covenant. We will expect an illumination of the covenant concept and an understanding of the meaning of membership in the covenant community.

The rabbis envisioned the realization of the covenant when everyone would become a rabbi, i.e., each person would rule himself by learning the meaning of the Torah, binding himself to it, thereby submitting to God's rule. While this vision is articulated in theological terms, its primary concern, elucidating legitimate authority, is political.

Leo Strauss distinguishes between political philosophy and political theology. The authority of the latter is based on divine revelation while the former is based on the human mind alone.[4] In this context the sources here examined can be called political theology. Revelation is assumed. The rabbis have authority because they participate in the study of God's revealed word. There is no attempt to prove or demonstrate the veracity of this assumption. Yet it is the cornerstone of their outlook.

While the main theme of western political philosophy is the regime rather than the law, there is not a term to be found in the Bible that could be translated, 'regime.'[5] Since the law is regarded as having human authors, it is the task of political philosophy to examine the cause of the law, i.e., the regime (*politeis*). With a choice of conflicting types of regimes (constitutions) the problem approached by political philosophy is to determine which is the most appropriate for any given situation.

Strauss points to the choice of form over matter in political thought. While the fatherland is regarded as matter, for example, the regime is the form; the best regime should be preferred over the fatherland. In Jewish thought this relationship would be equivalent to that between Israel (fatherland) and Torah (regime).[6] Torah is preferred to the land or nation.

Greek thought, whose goal was basically esthetic, i.e., the quest for harmony, understood the problems of the polity in terms of form and structure. If the proper form could be constructed then harmony could be achieved. Rationality, the highest goal, was understood to mean the ability to place each part in its proper category.

Harmony was not as significant in Jewish thought since its goal was not esthetic. The concern was not regime. Any structure could be good or bad depending on the quality of the relationship between the governed and the governor. People did not necessarily have a specific space to occupy, a category or jurisdiction from which they could not leave. Quite the opposite was the case. Each was so dependent on the other that there could not be any specific category or space to which anyone could be limited.

Covenant was to be the explication of the specific relationship. As we shall see, it assumed a mutual dependency. No one could exist alone, yet individuality was not to be lost. To dwell apart meant that one's existence had significance neither for the self nor for the community. The covenant described how individuals could relate to each other.

The covenant community found its meaning and purpose through its connection with an external force which transcended it. This force gave it legitimacy. The exclusive relationship with this force made the community and the individual unique. The shared experience of relating to such a power fused it by giving it a specific identity. This covenant relationship became the basis of the community for all those who shared its perception of the world and adopted its myth.

There are two types of relationships that the term, covenant, describes. Both have origins in the Bible: the gracious covenant and the mutual covenant. The mutual covenant was emphasized by the prophets and later the rabbis. In brief, it assumes that the existence of the governor has no meaning without the existence of the governed. Mutual interdependency and responsibility are characteristic of this type of covenant. The political ramifications of the mutual covenant are obvious. The transcendent authority cannot abstract itself from the community or the individual. Unless the relationship is intimate and personal it will not impinge on the life of the covenant partner. Implicit in this relationship is the need for trust based on the knowledge and expectation of each covenant partner. Thus, the vocabulary of the mutual covenant abounds with terms like faithfulness and faithlessness, loyalty and disloyalty. The metaphor of the mutual covenant is marriage. Each partner is answerable to the other. The relationship is a dynamic one.

The gracious covenant was emphasized by Christianity. Here transcendent authority tends to be parental, beneficiently imposing its will on the passive child. The recipients of this grace do not merit it and must be thankful for it. Undeserved love is the motive of the parent whose intentions are not always known or knowable. There is a mystery as to how one becomes a member of this type of covenant community. It is sustained by the grace of God. The political implications of the covenant of grace lie in the nature of authority and the relationship to it. It is the nature of parental authority to accept the child with love. He will also know what is best. The child is unable to understand the reasons for the love: it is beyond his comprehension.

Along the way, in the history of this concept, covenant became a

3

means of claiming legitimacy of the group rather than in realizing a relationship. Polemic between Jews and nascent Christianity and later between various Christian groups perverted the purpose of the covenant. While it was always used either to support an existing regime or as a basis for a claim challenging legitimacy by a competing group, the Christian-Jewish covenant polemic took on a new significance. Each group stated that it was the inheritor of the true covenant, the real Israel.

Later the contract theorists broke out of this circle of claim and counter-claim by rejecting the very validity of the covenant, at least in political terms. They returned to Greek thought declaring that sovereignty was derived from the people (*demos*) rather than from some external source, e.g., God. The assertion of the connection with a transcendent power was roundly denied by the contract theorists. The king did not have sovereignty granted by God. He ruled by the consent of the people. The king could no longer claim that he represented God's authority on earth. John Locke, in his refutation of Filmer's defense of the divine right of kings, was careful to assert that the dominion granted by God to Adam (Genesis 1:28) was granted to all of mankind. It was a dominion over the world, not over other men (*The First Treatise of Government,* IV:40). The ruler did not represent God's authority but man's own sovereignty which was surrendered upon entering the community.

Both covenant and contract seem to have a similar purpose, to explain the origin of the community and the motivation which caused individuals to join it. They both reflect a change that occurred in history or myth. Before the community was formed each person lived independently. Something happened or there was a shared realization that the individual could not cope with life outside a communal condition.

There is a fundamental difference between contract and covenant besides the role of the transcendent power. The contract is relevant only in the relationship of the individual to the community. If he is not part of the community, he is not engaged in the contract. The covenant relationship with God can be significant to the individual even without the community. The individual can still maintain his agreement with the transcendent power even if there is no community. Although covenant does seem to explain the origin of the community and give it meaning, meaning continues without the community as long as there is some relationship between the individual and the transcendent force.

The covenant concept, while assailed and attacked, never experienced a political death. It slowly recovered from its blows. Instead of asserting itself openly, it lurked in the background disguised by various masks. The polemical aspects of covenant, the legitimizing of claims by declaring a connection with an external force, was still utilized. In the arena of political ideas these forces were secularized and defined in terms of history, nature, class struggle, etc. The other characteristic of covenant, the concept of mutuality, also asserted itself in political thought. One example is the concept of the collegium organization of peers in organization theory as distinct from hierarchy.

This study is meant to be a contribution to political thought. While we cannot label the material under discussion philosophy since rabbinic material lacks an apparent coherent structure, we are still concerned with political issues, e.g., the basis of the community, the relationship to authority, and the legitimacy of authority. We can examine the language of the literature in order to explicate the issues under discussion.[7]

These concepts are not definable in an objective sense. They are dependent on the common usage by society to which the theorists address themselves. Often common terms are carefully defined in order to fit a specific system of discourse.[8] In rabbinic literature the people are addressed directly, for much of the material is from lectures and sermons and reflects a certain popular character. We can interpret a text by determining how commonly-held concepts interweave with each other and take on specific political meaning.

Sheldon Wolin, whose work is concerned with the elucidation of political philosophy, points out that the language of early political thought rarely went beyond common everyday language. Not until Plato and Aristotle did terms become more specialized and abstract. The everyday language of conversation was repackaged in careful definitions that become almost technical and specific so that the author could present a consistent systematic view of the world.[9] Except for the legal material in rabbinic literature, such precision did not seem necessary to the rabbis. The language they used could be readily understood by their audiences.

Wolin points to the inherent limitations of theorists caused by the categories they use.[10] Such a limitation can certainly be applied to the rabbis. The organic rather than systematic type of thinking was possible because it was limited within the context of a relatively closed society which shared the same categories.[11]

It is difficult to discover the various political views of rabbinic literature due to the lack of a philosophical approach to the questions. Historians and Jewish scholars familiar with Jewish texts are usually not sensitive to political questions, nor do they possess a political vocabulary sufficient to analyze texts and place them in their appropriate political context.

Because a study of rabbinic political thought has not been forthcoming there is a noticeable gap between Greek political philosophies

5

and early Christian thought. To read the literature one would think that Christian thought is a result of *Creatio Ex Nihilo*. While the present study does not deal with the specific Jewish influence and content in Patristic or even New Testament literature it has as one of its purposes the presentation of material in order to bridge this gap. A few examples of the apparent unawareness that something existed between the Greeks and Christianity might be useful. On early Christian thinkers, Wolin writes the success of Christianity over Hellenistic and late classical philosophies was its presentation of a new "ideal" of community drawing its constituents into " . . . meaningful participation."[12] He cites the unity of belief as a contrast to classical ideals.[13] He later characterizes early Christianity as alienated from politial rule.[14]

The unity of belief to which Wolin refers comes from Old Testament concepts of the exclusive covenant with one God which sharply differentiated Israel from polytheistic systems. The community was sanctified and given purpose through this exclusive relationship; alienation from political rule was a direct outcome of an understanding that only God's rule was legitimate. Human rule was an expedient at best.[15]

Wolin contrasts the Christian concept of time moving towards a climax to the classical cyclical view, having broken the closed system: each moment was now considered as irreversible and progressive.[16] This conception comes directly from Jewish sources as exemplified by messianism, looking to a future when God's rule would be recognized by the entire world.[17]

Wolin explains that there is no place for *fortuna* in Christianity. In its place is divine providence. There is no place for the political hero as in classical thought; in its stead is the servant of God.[18] Concepts of divine providence and the leader as God's servant are directly from Old Testament and rabbinic concepts, neither of which he cites.[19]

Roger Smith attempts to give political significance to theological language.[20] However, he does not understand the very sources of the language he is trying to analyze; there is not one biblical citation in the entire article.

In an analysis of Augustine's City of God, Rex Martin explains that we do not have enough information to understand Augustine's concepts of nature, justice or state and government, for there seems to be a break in the link with the earthly city.[21] While he refers to the source of some of Augustine's concepts as Jewish, he does not give any of the references which would have made Augustine more understandable. Augustine could have been making certain assumptions, e.g., that his audiences were familiar biblical concepts, that they themselves would have provided the link.

Further, he cites Augustine's rejection of "... classical idealization of the state ..." and calls his City of God "... anti-politics."[22] Yet he does not explain that the City of God was similar to the rabbinic concept of the kingdom of heaven, which had been adopted but Christianized, i.e., the kingdom will be the result of a community of faith rather than a community of Torah.[23]

We can attribute these types of problems in the literature of political theory to a lack of the availability of biblical and rabbinic source materials analyzed in a political context. Ignorance of the sources as well as the need for special training to be able to deal with the texts has led to an almost perfect silence in regard to them.

It is important to state explicitly what this study does not include. First of all, we are concentrating on political concepts. Historical background is utilized only for the purpose of placing the material in its proper time frame. Second, there is hardly any reference to Philo, Josephus, or any Hellenistic Jewish writers. While there certainly is not a paucity of such material, the principle points of the present study can be worked out without Philo. The theology of Philo had little or no influence on the rabbinic thought.[24] For the same reason apocryphal and pseudophygraphal and apocalyptic literature has not been considered.[25]

Western political thought has been concerned with the role and function of authority, the place of political knowledge and the origin of society and its purpose. Political authority according to some (e.g., Plato) transcends the polity while to others it is enmeshed in the community itself (e.g., John Locke). Authority can be defined as consisting of those who have exclusive knowledge (e.g., Plato and Machiavelli) or as an exclusive expression of the will of the masses. Political authority can exist independent of the people it rules or can be dependent on the consent of the governed. We have a wide range of concepts from which to choose. The student is confronted by a virtual department store variety of authority images. Yet there is a common thread running through most of them which can be traced to ancient Greek thought: authority is a function of the regime. The design of the regime will determine the limits of political authority. While the legitimacy of the regime might be dependent on its claims to some transcendent principle, concept, or idea (history, class, deity or nature), the question of its typology and structure seems to predominate for the most part. Find the structure and the political problem at hand can be solved.

The question assumes that there is some form to discover. Whether it be hierarchical or decentralized we can literally see it. Political writing seems to be a translation of visual images into words. Relationships are geometrical; one reads of the line of authority and the space it occupies. The proper angles can be drawn to find the most efficient system to accomplish the task of maintaining the polity. This visual vocabulary extends to the explanation of social origins. We see a primitive collection of individuals, the political troglodytes, who join together in order to achieve security and protection or to perform some cooperative tasks. Society is either natural and the very meaning of human existence or unnatural. But it can only come into being when each person gives up some of his selfhood, his individuality. In order to enjoy the blessings of the polity, one simply cannot act out his own life independent of others. A person living in society is different from those who live without its confines. There are limits, self-imposed or imposed by the group or its designated authority. The vocabulary is visual; one is either in or out, and if in, he has a place to occupy. The thrust of political thought is to attain a political esthetic where a modicum of harmony is achieved. The degree of that harmony and its esthetic quality is dependent, in turn, on the picture that the specific theorist has in his mind. He begins with a vision of nature, history or a political eschatology. The problems of the polity either are a result of its process of becoming (having not reached its completion, e.g., Hegel and Marx) or its clash with nature's primeval harmony.

Knowledge takes on a political and visual quality as well. The purpose of political thought is either to put the pieces together into some pattern that matches the specific image or discover the process of the world to determine if the polity is in harmony with that music of the spheres. He who has the knowledge ought to have the power to transform the vision into reality. We learn from Plato that the philosopher-king is thrust between his vision of reality and the frustration of the shadows of political existence. Thomas Hobbes, the geometrician, has taken his vision from the heavenly spheres and is frustrated by the lack of order which has resulted from the astronomical ignorance of the laws of nature.

With rabbinic thought we are confronted with similar political questions. Yet the vocabulary is so different because of the distrust of images and pictures. God, himself, cannot be envisaged. The vocabulary is aural/oral rather than visual. What is heard and transmitted is of utmost significance. The individuality of each person, community and generation allows a variety of perceptions of the original message. Knowledge of the words that brought the community into being constitutes the claim to authority. Political writing is a commentary on the messsage as it is received by the writer.

Authority and authorization in such a context is open to anyone who can receive the message and transmit it, i.e., to everyone who can hear and speak. It is interesting to note that a deaf-mute has legal disabilities in Jewish law, especially in regard to being a witness in court, that a blind person does not share. Rather than placing limits on the types of people who can have authority, the ideal is the universalization of authority. This phenomenon is not to be confused with mere consent. Everyone should learn to be able to become his own authority.

The community is founded by an authority who needs someone to hear his words in order to attain significance. All those who share the experience of receiving the message become members of the community. The authority reveals his will and intention, i.e., he instructs. Those who receive the instruction are thereby authorized to rule themselves.

The focus of the first part of this study is an explanation of the contrast of Greek and Rabbinic epistomology which led to differing perceptions of political phenomena. The political vocabulary of the rabbis is elucidated as well. The second part places the rabbinic material in a developmental and historical context. In the third part primary sources are presented demonstrating the rabbinic understanding of political concepts.

NOTES

1. Its roots can be traced to biblical thought. See Max Kadushin, *The Rabbinic Mind* (second ed.; New York: Blaidsell Publishing Co., 1965, p. 298 f. (Hereafter cited as *Mind*)

2. The *Talmud* consists of the *Mishnah,* compiled and edited in about the year 200 by Rabbi Yehudah Hanassi. The interpretation (called *gemarah)* of the *mishnah* was carried out in academies in Palestine and Babylonia, thus the Palestinian Talmud (*Talmud Yerushalmi*) and the Babylonian Talmud (*Talmud Bavli).* It is the latter that became dominant.

3. There are two types of *midradshim:* legal (*halachah),* and lore (*hagadah).* There are numerous collections of *midrashim,* many of which are no longer extant.

4. Leo Strauss, *What is Political Philosophy?* (Glencoe: The Free Press, 1959), p. 13.

5. *Ibid.,* p. 34.

6. *Ibid.,* p. 36.

7. Sheldon S. Wolin, *Politics and Vision* (Boston: Little, Brown and Company, 1960), p. 14.

8. *Ibid.*

9. *Ibid.,* p. 15.

10. *Ibid.,* p. 21.

11. See below, "The Organic Thinking of the Rabbis."

12. Wolin, p. 97.

13. *Ibid.,* p. 106.

14. *Ibid.,* p. 98f.

15. See below, "Covenant and Community" and "The Character Political Authority."

16. Wolin, p. 124.

17. See below, "The Rabbis and/or Philosophers."

18. Wolin, p. 127f.

19. See below, "Covenant Between the Leaders and the People," and "The Legitimacy of the Leader in Relation to God."

20. Roger W. Smith, "Redemption and Politics," *Political Science Quarterly,* LXXXVI, No. 2 (June, 1971).

21. Rex Martin, "The Two Cities in Augustine's Political Philosophy," *Journal of the History of Ideas,* XXXIII, No. 2 (April-June, 1972), p. 204.

22. *Ibid.*, p. 216.

23. See below, "Kingdom of Heaven."

24. George F. Moore, *Judaism in the First Centuries of the Christian Era,* Vol. I: *The Age of the Tannaim* (Cambridge: Harvard University Press, 1925), p. 357.

25. Solomon Schecter, *Aspects of Rabbinic Theology* (New York: Schocken Books, 1961), p. 5. R. Travers Herford, *The Pharisees* (Boston: Beacon Press, 1962), p. 186 ff) explains that while the rabbis might have been familiar with this literature, they did not use it because it did not include *halachah,* which is difficult to accept because there are certainly biblical books that do not include *halachah.* More to the point, he states that the message of much of this literature is despair of man's ability to create God's kingdom on earth. See especially, *Ibid.,* p. 191.

PART I.
GREEK AND RABBINIC THOUGHT: ENCOUNTER AND AFTERMATH (A COMPARATIVE STUDY)

CHAPTER 1: GREEK THOUGHT PATTERNS LEADING TO PHILOSOPHICAL CATEGORIES

The thrust of the Greek philosophical enterprise was to attempt to set the gods outside of experience.[1] They dwell in some far-off place with little or no connection with the world.

The purpose here is to briefly trace how philosophy developed from Greek religious ideas. A comparison between rabbinic and Greek thought will bring into relief quite different tendencies. Even though the culture of the rabbis and Greek civilization as reflected in the literature of each certainly had some contact, the consequences of each were unique. There was not wholesale assimilation on the part of the rabbis into Greek philosophical systems, in contrast to the Greek influence on other cultures. This is not to say that Greek culture had no effect on the rabbis. A summary of that influence will be given. However, the seemingly total lack of a Greek philosophical system in rabbinic thought is certainly well known and has even impeded research.

The fact that research into Greek influence on rabbinic thought has been so difficult, that the elements of that influence so hard to sort out, is significant in and of itself. Most scholars agree that the problem lies in the almost thorough Judaization of Hellenistic thought. The Jews displayed a tendency opposite every other culture that confronted ancient Greece. Instead of assimilating its own thought into Greek patterns, that which was useful in Greek thought was carefully selected and transformed into Jewish thought. At times the transformation is so complete that it is difficult to recognize its origins.

The concept of fate, destiny (*moira*), plays an important role in early Greek literature. In Homer *moira* rules both men and gods. It is spatial rather than temporal for it constantly refers to an "allotted portion", i.e., the part allotted to each man and god in the world.[2]

In Hesiod *moira* seems to be understood in a temporal sense, i.e., the fates precede the gods.[3] Yet it is temporal only in the sense that it has prior control in distributing the jurisdiction of each of the gods. Because they come later in time, they cannot control their allotted portion.

Fate is not necessarily benevolent: It is not concerned with man's interest or wishes.[4] Neither is purpose or design attributed to fate, for both are to be found in the human/divine sphere. *Moira,* in contrast, seems not to act willfully except when its boundaries are trespassed.[5]

Without individual purpose except the "... provincial ordering of the world..." *moira* represents the elements of necessity and justice in the universe.[6] One's destiny is determined from on high; his proper place in the world is beyond his control. He is allotted his portion and, in order to remain in harmony with the universe, must not attempt to go beyond it.

There is a significant change in the concept of *moira* in the *Iliad.* The gods take over fate by distributing their own areas of jurisdiction through the drawing of lots. The gods give up their willfulness and accept their assignments as distributed by *moira.*[7] The resulting jurisdiction is sanctified by the great oath of the gods. This oath is a contract that establishes the order of the universe and its separate jurisdiction.[8] Later it is Zeus who controls the distribution process. A change has occurred from the impersonal *moira* to become personalized in a god.[9] Cornford labels this change an act of legislation.

As the dispenser of fate responsible for the distribution of power, Zeus is considered the law-giver. The very word for law, *nomos,* is derived from *nemein,* to dispense.[10] Our modern understanding of constitutional law and the concept of distributive justice, i.e., placing everything in its right order, is most likely derived from this primal Greek concept of Zeus' role. Conceived spatially, each party to the contract, each participant in government, whether ruler or citizen, has a proper place in society; he plays a part in an ideally harmonious whole.

In contrast, justice and law in biblical thought are temporally oriented. God does justice (*osay mishpat,* Psalm 146:7), i.e., he is the originator and the continual source of justice. He does not have to take over a pre-existing distributive system by force like Zeus. Contracts are not made to guarantee one's space in the system. Rather, covenants are made to guarantee a relationship throughout the passage of time. The relationship is not a definition of categories, each maintaining his own sphere of influence. The oath is taken, not to insure that parties do not overstep their bounds; the oath establishes the obligations each has to follow as covenant partners.

The purpose of biblical relationships is to cross boundaries, to be present, immanent, for the parties of the covenant to be aware of each other, to be dependent on each other. The experience of the relationship is its very validation.

We can appreciate this contrast by considering the Greek concept of law-giving. It is a task accomplished once by single person. The *nomoi* become a written constitution that is sacrosanct and unchanging. The very act of law-giving redistributes power and jurisdiction.[11]

There is a difference between the act of dispensing (Greek: *nemein*) and the act of giving (Hebrew: *notayn*). The former assumes that someone has enough power to carry it off. Everyone receiving a portion of the power is passive (they have already lobbied for their share before the final results have been established). It is a heavenly distribution, transcending human reality and control.

The latter can be best epitomized by the present tense liturgical accounts of giving the Torah; the Torah is given continually throughout time to be received by every generation. The giving is inexorably linked to receiving; the interdependency of the relationship is primary. The act of receiving is positive and dynamic. It is the consequence and the cause of Israel's merit. By receiving the Torah Israel has merit; but Israel also had to have merit before the act of giving is initiated. In contrast, the Greek concept of law-giving, while the consequence of a political act (prior condition of lobbying), gives the recipient a separate power. It defines the place of the recipient and separates him from the dispenser. After the power is received, each retires to his own jurisdiction. The relationship is concluded, the link between powers coming to an end after the dispersal; the gods become angry with those who over-reach their accepted bounds.

Education is the instrument to train people in the laws, i.e., the place of each element in society to insure harmony. Greek philosophers perceive education as a means to elicit man's greatest potential.[12] The very function of the state is education to harmonize society with the pre-determined fixed law.[13] Greatness was attributed to Solon, the law-giver, for he was able to moderate society and the polity.[14] Everyone was to know his place and not go beyond his own sphere.

The very model of separate spheres, of careful self-definition through education, was the image of the Olympian god. He had no congregation to which he could relate. He was separate from the world; only external, contractual relationships resulted from his dispensing power. The purpose of worship underscores his role: sacrifice was seen as a gift or bribe in return for expected benefits.[15]

There was no communion or bond with these Olympian dieties. The mystery cults of Diogenes, which formed a church-like organization, were probably a reaction to the utter break with the gods, satisfying a human need for contact with the deity. In these cults the god was regarded as the collective representative, or *daemon,* of the community. The cult-community was transfixed seeking to be joined to the god. In order to accomplish this union each member had to lose his own individuality.[16]

According to Cornford the Olympian gods became more and more transcendent until they no longer had any significance for the people.[17] They were so confined to their own sphere they could not become men; but man could not become a god either.[18] Having bought off the gods through sacrifices, the *polis* had established its own power. The gods were no longer needed.

Plato took the next logical step in demythologizing Greek religion, by advocating the replacement of the rule of gods by reason, i.e., the human mind. Greek religion developed into philosophy because the gods had finally been drained of everything they had to offer men. Sovereignty was in the *demos*[19] which had already paid for it through propitiation.

From The Mystics To Plato

The mystical tradition of the Greeks is time-oriented in contrast to the static spatiality of Olympic religion.[20] However, it is the cyclical time of returning eons of history.[21] The repetition of the cycles had a certain determined quality, i.e., one could not break out of the time system.

Dike, the notion of righteousness, replaces *moira* in Greek mysticism.[22] In Plato's *Laws* (904E) *dike* is used in the sense of the reward of the soul according to its deeds.[23] To be righteous is to be in harmony with nature. Although the methods are different, the goal is essentially the same as that of the Olympic religion — to attain a harmonious society. To the mysteries all of nature is connected together through *dike's* influence.[24] Olympianism, on the other hand, taught the separation of gods and men, presenting a dichotomy between human society and the rest of nature; *dike* was limited to political structure and order.[25]

In the Diogenes cult all life was perceived as a unity enduring a cycle of death and rebirth. A collective soul was imminent in the group, yet synergistic. With the Orpheus cult came a shift toward heaven; orgiastic cultic worship was replaced by sun worship. It also included the emotional experience of obtaining truth through union.[26] Pythagorean mysticism emphasized *theoria,* objective rationality, which was to influence life's purpose — the pursuit of wisdom (*philosophie*).[27] It aimed at achieving an end to bodily emotions.

Unity of life, harmony with nature and the goal of losing individual identity to achieve oneness with the group are the primary teachings of the Greek mystery religions. The mysteries were a reaction to the compartmentalization of Olympianism and its lack of emotion and warmth of community.

Cornford implies that Platonic thought is derived ultimately from the mystic concept of *dike*. He certainly looks for harmony rather than rule of law. Instead of encouraging separate spheres of power and interests, Plato, in his *Republic*, attempts to demonstrate that the state should adhere to an ideal model that is found in the natural cosmos. Just as the cosmos reflects principles of justice, so that if so modeled, the state will rule in like manner.[28]

Plato saw a dichotomy between law (*nomos*) and nature (*physis*). Plato chose nature.[29] The philosopher was trained to use his intelligence to rule, not by *nomos*, but by wisdom.[30] Goodness was defined as the right kind of knowledge to achieve wise rule. The purpose of the *Republic* was to determine how to arrive at such goodness.[31] The good man was the result of the good state. Plato set it as his task to define the good state.

Not everyone had the capacity of becoming a philosopher. Hence, a hierarchy was developed so that each could find his own place according to his ability.[32] The philosopher, at the pinnacle of the hierarchy, was to know the essence of justice, beauty and temperance to implant it into the very lives of his subjects.[33]

The specialization that would result in the just political system was to insure that each person fulfill the responsibilities of his own station without meddling in those of another station.[34] The image presented is an esthetic ideal. Justice is harmony, every element fitting properly in place. Paradoxically, it is an extension of the concepts of *moira* and *nomos*, yet defined in terms of *dike* and *physis*. The integrity of the community depends on its unity. The old Olympian system of lobby politics through the rule of custom and conventional law (*nomos*), is attacked, for it led to disharmony. The philosopher must transcend the law created by man through interest politics and compromise. Plato was trying to fight the individualism that resulted in interest politics to form a union of souls seeking harmony with nature.[35]

The Platonic state was conceived as an analogue, a construct of the human mind.[36] Underlying the model created by Plato was his basic concern, the dichotomy between law and morality, i.e., external rules versus the ideals upon which order depends.[37] Education in the Platonic polis functioned as a sort of political socialization process, leading to an internalization of the group's norms of temperance, self-control, beauty and wisdom.[38] To guarantee stability, the philosopher could not change the polity arbitrarily.[39] Rather, he is to preserve it as a static body adhering to its primary ideals.

In his *Politicus,* Plato teaches that the only true state is that which is ruled by statesmen who possess knowledge.[40] Knowledge becomes the unifying factor of the state. There is no need for law or consent — these are the source of political confusion; they are antithetical to the achievement of harmony. Consent is based on individuality (and the assumed freedom of each party to an agreement). Acquiescence is the expected response.[41] Consent is irrelevant since the people cannot possibly evaluate the art of the statesman, who by nature of training and knowledge, has transcended the mass.

Acquiescence due to the statesmen is the consequence of trust in his knowledge. In contrast, the state based on law is based on distrust in government.[42] In the *Laws*, Plato substitutes mind (*nous*) for nature (*physis*) and places it above law (*nomos*).[43] Mind becomes synonymous with nature. Lack of reason is not natural. Natural rules create harmony within nature. Reason takes the place of Zeus. It is impersonal, much as Pythagorean mysticism, a wisdom without bodily emotion.[44] In the *Republic* (Book III), Plato attempts to demythologize and deanthropomorphasize the gods to make them perfect beings without needs or appetites, the very image he projects of the philosopher-king. Man can become like God by practicing virtue.[45] The just society is static, unchanging; so God does not change, for he is perfect.[46]

The role of knowledge as the unifying factor of the good society in Plato, is superficially similar to Torah in rabbinic thought. The rabbis did not attempt to transcend Torah as the philosopher transcended the *nomos*. Torah (teaching as distinct from *Halachah*, the legal material which is included in Torah) is the way to discover God. It is revelatory, and each person has access to the divine will by studying Torah.

The concept of nature (*physis*) is absent from rabbinic thought which regards history as non-cyclical and as a record of God's acts. The rabbis have faith that God keeps his promises. The solutions to the problems of the community and the individual are to be ascertained by studying Torah and acting accordingly. In contrast, the faith of the Greeks is dependent on a nature which is immutable and unchanging. For the Greek, the source of his problems is disharmony with nature.

The rabbinic solution assumes the individuality of each person, linked to the community through the shared experience of revelation. However, that experience is itself individual. According to Plato, man must transcend himself to find harmony with nature. According to the rabbis, man must keep his promises so that a relationship of trust obtains between the individual and God and between the individual and others in the community. The model used is the relationship between persons, especially marriage.

16

Both Plato and Aristotle, true to their culture, found time inimical, destructive and evil, far inferior to space, matter, which was considered eternal.[47] Jewish thought in both the Bible and rabbinic tradition celebrated time over space.

Aristotle, Epicurus and the Stoics

Aristotle continued Plato's demythologization. God became an abstraction without matter, pure without change, static, not moving, removed from any activity or energy.[48] This ultimate end can only contemplate itself. To condescend to enter worldly affairs would remove its attribute of perfection. While God could enter into any relationship with an imperfect world without denigrating his own perfection, the world was expected to demonstrate love for God by following God's example by monastic contemplation.[49]

God is separate from his world, having nothing to do with it, without needing even the love of his world. Yet the world must love God and desire to attain the divine. The life of reason is divine. To attain divine perfection the individual must transcend society, becoming self-sufficient, without needs.[50] The end is the demise of the social order and life itself. Pure reason is the loss of ego to find union with God.

In *The Politics*, Aristotle declares the *polis* to be natural, prior to the individual (not in time but in nature),[51] for in nature the whole is prior to the part (the part assumes ᴧhe whole).[52] The *polis* is to be self-sufficient. To be human is to dwell in the *polis;* outside of its bounds dwell beasts and gods.[53] The self-sufficiency of the polis is attained by limiting its size so that people can know each other personally.[54] Self-sufficiency, independence from external sources, seems to be the key to Aristotle's understanding of God, the individual and the *polis*. But self-sufficiency has a different meaning in each of these spheres. God is perfect, removed from the world. The individual can strive to be like God; he has the potential. Wolin has demonstrated that Aristotle's concept of the *polis* is much wider than that of Plato. Political conciliation is included in the concept of judgment, i.e., politics requires a special type of judgment that includes the opinions of members of society.[55] What Aristotle has taken from his theology and applied to his politics is the concept of the self-sufficient whole. From this concept we can understand that, in reality, the *polis* does not need God except as an object of worship in some sort of civil religion.

In the evolution from religious concepts to philosophy, the meaning of God changes. Perhaps the Greeks had different images of themselves reflected in their changing concepts of God. Plato was not sure where God belonged in this system. Aristotle's motionless God, while not quite totally removed, dwelt in spheres as far away as possible from the human condition.[56]

For Epicurus gods were ageless beings indifferent to events occuring in the surrounding worlds.[57] He tried to construct a world that would free men from the fear both of the gods and of superstition. The world was a machine, not affected by either malevolent or benevolent divinity. His aim was to attain happiness and intellectual pleasure by escaping the world, thus becoming liberated from desire, need, pain and passion which were regarded as limiting.[58]

The Stoic's God was so involved in the world he could not transcend it.[59] Conceiving of a universal brotherhood, a world state, the Stoics considered everything as deriving from one God who ruled the universe. This power was an all-wise destiny which decreed what was best for man.[60] The universe was designed by God who obeyed his own law. Since everything was predetermined, there was no free will. Pantheistic in tone, the philosophy conceived of God as part of the world. All men were spiritually equal since they had the same origin.

Of all the philosophies, Stoicism seems, at first glance, to be similar to the Judaism of the rabbis. The immanence of God, the divine origin and equality of all people, the vision of universal brotherhood, all appear similar to biblical prophecies and rabbinic commentaries. Indeed, if we were to trace a connection we might find that Zeno, hailing from Phoenicia, may have had some contact with Judaism.

However, the surface similarities dissolve when we probe a little deeper. The pre-determination of the Stoics, a logical consequence of their thought, was not represented in most rabbinic thinking. There was, to be sure, a realization that certain aspects of life were largely pre-determined. However, attributed to Rabbi Akiba is the declaration that man has free will as well (*Avot* 3:19). God is immanent yet he is also transcendent. The basic conceptual framework is temporal rather than spatial — God is not confined to a certain space, but changes his relationships depending upon human response.

The point to be made from this excursus into Greek thought is its spatial quality. Looking to an esthetic model, harmony, it searched for the proper regime that would fit this pre-determined model. There is little sense of dialectic of process which denies the static quality of the ideal, unchanging model; this search for perfection limited the concern for understanding the dynamic quality of political life.

NOTES

1. Frances M. Cornford, *From Religion to Philosophy* (New York: Harper and Brothers, 1957), p. 158f.
2. *Ibid.*, p. 16
3. *Ibid.*, p. 18
4. *Ibid.*, p. 20
5. *Ibid.*, p. 20f.
6. *Ibid.*, p. 21f.
7. *Ibid.*, p. 22
8. *Ibid.*, p. 23
9. *Ibid.*, p. 24
10. *Ibid.*, p. 27
11. *Ibid.* It is interesting to note that the act of lawgiving assumes a change from the status quo. But this change is usually not recognized.
12. Ernest Barker, *Greek Political Theory* (New York: Barnes and Noble, Inc., 1960), p. 42
13. *Ibid.*, p. 44
14. *Ibid.*, p. 49
15. Cornford, p. 114; Walter R. Agard, *The Greek Mind* (Princeton: P. Van Nostrand Company, Inc., 1957) p. 18. Agard speaks of the relationship between the gods and man as a ". . . business relationship."
16. Cornford, p. 114
17. *Ibid.*, p. 115
18. *Ibid.*, p. 118
19. Barker, p. 50
20. Cornford, p. 160f
21. *Ibid.*, p. 167. This is Thucydides' concept of time.
22. *Ibid.*, p. 160f.
23. *Ibid.*, p. 172.
24. *Ibid.*, p. 182.
25. *Ibid.*
26. *Ibid.*, p. 199.
27. *Ibid.*, p. 200.
28. *Ibid.*, p. 183.
29. Barker, p. 79f.
30. *Ibid.*, p. 129.
31. *Ibid.*, p. 169.
32. *Ibid.*, p. 196. This compartmentalization is Olympian.
33. *Ibid.* Barker, in a critical note, page 199, points to the discrepancy between the attempt to fashion everyone in the likeness of the philosophers, and the inability of most to become philsophers. Also, if most persons are not philosophers, how would they have the wisdom to obey the philosophers?
34. *Ibid.*, p. 203.
35. *Ibid.*, p. 204.
36. *Ibid.*, p. 205.
37. *Ibid.*
38. *Ibid.*, p. 227.
39. *Ibid.*, p. 237.
40. *Ibid.*, p. 320.
41. *Ibid.*, p. 327f.
42. *Ibid.*, p. 331.
43. *Ibid.*, p. 350.
44. Cornford, p. 36f.
45. Plato, *The Republic*, X, 414.
46. *Ibid.*, II, 180; see also Thorlief Boman, *Hebrew Thought Compared With Greek*, trans., J.C. Moreau (Philadelphia: The Westminster Press, 1960), p. 192.
47. Boman, p. 128.

48. Cornford, p. 261.
49. *Ibid.*
50. *Ibid.*, p. 263.
51. Aristotle, *The Politics,* I, 2, 12.
52. *Ibid.*, p. 13.
53. *Ibid.*, p. 14.
54. *Ibid.*, IV, 4, 14; see also, 3, 10.
55. Wolin, pp. 59-62.
56. Harry A. Wolfson, *Religious Philosophy* (Cambridge: Harvard University Press, 1961), p. 270.
57. *Ibid.*, p. 271.
58. W.W. Tarn, *Hellenistic Civilization* (3rd ed. rev. by the author, ed. G.T. Griffith; Cleveland and New York: Meridian Books, 1952), p. 329.
59. Wolfson, p. 271.
60. Tarn, p. 331.

CHAPTER 2: THE PROCESS OF RABBINIC LITERATURE

The inherent problem with the type of analysis of Rabbinic literature that Max Kadushin attempts to accomplish is that we cannot know how the rabbis really thought. All we have is the literary remains which ranges over a long period of time (at least five hundred years), from different places and under the influence of specific historic circumstances from revolution and war to accommodation to a variety of political regimes and religious environments. The material has been edited and obviously selected as well, thus reflecting the concerns of the group of editors (who also worked at different times and in different places). These factors lead the reader to realize that no statement can be made as to the dates of any rabbinic material with any degree of accuracy. They are simply unknown because the texts come after the events and are often quoted by a line of rabbis over generations.

What Kadushin calls the Rabbinic mind is hard to assume, since there are too many factors that come into play that mitigate against a specific mind-set that we would be able to abstract from literary remains.[1]

However, we know that these rabbis were certainly involved, if not facilitators and actors themselves, in various types of political dramas. They had to confront political issues that were the concern of the Jewish communities where they lived and in the course of external factors that affected the Jewish people. Yet there are no political theories or political analysis *written in the Greek philosophic mode* found in the Hebrew Bible or in rabbinic literature. We *cannot* assume from this absence that they were not concerned with political matters. In fact, if we can learn anything from generations that existed under similar circumstances later in time, much of the literature was, perhaps, purposely written in a non-political mode. Language changed because more basic issues than political organization were involved. The very basis of the community and legitimacy of authority were being questioned. The integrity of the Jewish people was challenged as well.

These are all issues of political process; yet the method and language do not follow a reasoned, structured approach. Rather, as we read this literature we are struck by its reactive nature. Its language is polemical. Its choice of words is careful in that it immediately appeals to entire frames of reference. Key words were used eliciting responses that vindicated the Jewish political process. Using Kadushin's method of analysis we discover that philosophic categories are not appropriate to Rabbinic and even biblical thought.[2] Rather than definition, i.e., placing the object, value or concern at hand in its proper "category" by demonstrating how it differs from

21

all other objects, Rabbinic thought does not attempt to define. The exception is found in legal categories when it is important to apply the proper law to the case at hand, or to understand the limits of the application of a specific law.

The type of material to be examined in the present work is *agadah*, the non-legal aspect of Rabbinic literature. The word, *agadah*, is derived from the root meaning, "to tell". Its origin seems to be a technical expression used by the school of Rabbi Yishmael which finds meaning in a biblical text through exegesis upon which interpretation is based linked to the text.[3] The *agadah*[4] became a means to broaden the application of the biblical text while maintaining its basis on the text itself.[5] The biblical text is understood to be the subject of the interpretation. Originally there was no distinction between the usage of the expression, *magid* (from which *agadah* is derived), in legal and non-legal material. It was used for both, since the methods of elucidating the text were the same.[6] Only later was this expression applied exclusively to lore.[7]

Agadic study took place in the academy and the synagogue. When the Torah was read in public in the synagogue it was interpreted often in a homiletic fashion. The interpretations helped to sustain the nation and insure the continuity of the tradition from one generation to the next.[8] The *agadah* was a means to be able to introduce new concepts through old texts, thus linking the present with the past.[9] The *agadah* also offered a free outlet for interpretation, for there was little restriction upon its creativity.[10]

Agadah does not seem to be systematic.[11] However, lack of system should not be construed as lack of consistency. A feeling of consensus in rabbinic literature lasts throughout the many centuries of its development despite cataclysmic historic events and internal schisms,[12] dispersal through many lands and the lack of a national center.[13] Solomon Schechter warns that it is impossible to discover an orderly system of rabbinic thought. Not only are there problems with the texts that have survived (which frequently are mere fragments), but there is a tendency to read into the texts, to fill in the conceptual gaps, so to speak, to find system where there is none to be found. Such attempts at reading into the text sometimes have apologetic or polemic motivations but is essentially not a record of what the rabbis said or meant. Schechter even suggests that the very lack of system might have been intentional.[14]

Rabbinic literature is organic, i.e., the understanding of a term or concept is dependent on its context. One idea has no meaning without its relationship to others. The idea changes its nuance as it relates to other ideas or concepts. Without defining, i.e., setting limits in a spatial sense, the concepts seem to be living organisms that are unable to survive without proper nourishment and environmental conditions.

Rabbinic literature can be traced through the Pharisees and scribes to the Bible in an organic continuum.[15] After analyzing each part of the organic complex, Kadushin finds that in interpreting the Bible[16] the rabbis read in their own organic complex.[17] This complex had a wider range than that of the Bible due to the variety and length of the historical experiences of the people.[18]

The very source of the oral tradition is the Bible.[19] The Bible, especially the Pentateuch, was most likely interpreted from its inception. The application of written law to living situations, in itself, is interpretation. The rabbis perceived the Bible as a whole for the purpose of interpretation. Each biblical passage was understood in terms of all other biblical passages, and the meaning of each could be found in the relationship with other passages.[20]

The organic complex of the rabbis should not be construed as more abstract than that of the Bible. If anything, the rabbis were less abstract, e.g., the use of anthropomorphism in describing God is more profuse in their writings.[21] There seems to be no creed or established theology since Rabbinic thought is unsystematic and attempts to avoid the abstract.[22] The Jewish historian, Salo Baron, contrasts the methods of the rabbis (Pharisees) with those of the Sadducees and attributes the resiliency of the former to their temporal quality.[23] Rabbinic literature was not philosophic or speculative but rather the outcome of religious experience. The object of inquiry was not the object as it existed but rather its significance in its relationship to the perceiver. Experiences of God were temporal in that they were composed of God's relationship to the people in history. These experiences could be national or individual, dramatic or prosaic.

The value complex as reflected in the literature seemed to be responsible for the very coherence of the community.[24] It was universally shared and understood by all members of the community. To be a member was to be plugged in, so to speak, to the value complex. While communal values were shared by each individual, they did not become significant until they were applied to specific situations.[25]

For example, we can contrast the philosophic (structural) and organic (process) perception of God; in philosophy the conception of God is an abstraction which can have no continuous relation with the world; in religion, the conception of God gives meaning to history, comfort to the individual in sorrow, direction and purpose in life.[26] The very issue of anthropomorphism revolves around the contrast between philosophy and organic thinking. To abstract philosophy concrete ascriptions to God would seem to question his very abstract quality and perfection. Yet everything in our experience changes. God cannot, therefore, be a part of our experiences or he would not be perfect. To the rabbis, God demonstrates his concern for people constantly. They describe this concern in anthropomorphic terms and are not embarrassed in so doing.[27]

The concepts within the complex are understood in terms of each other and are interwoven with each other. The whole influences the parts and the parts influence the whole. There is no hierarchy of parts because each of the parts cannot exist by itself. Nor can the whole exist without the parts.[28]

While a glance at rabbinic literature would indicate the wide divergence of opinion among the rabbis over any given issue, the contradictions are within the conceptual complex, i.e., an emphasis of one concept over another.[29] The concept gives significance to experience. In its drive toward concretization, the concept even creates new events. It certainly determines the meaning of any event.[30] For example, the event might be a joyous experience in one's life. The recitation of the appropriate prayer which is imbued with some of the various concepts causes the concept and the event to attain new meaning. The blessing was known before the event but had no meaning, for there was no event experienced when it could be said. The event is then interpreted in light of the concept.

The terms for the various concepts are connotated or suggestive, for they cannot be defined and are not set systematically in any neat order.[31] They cannot be defined, for the idea embodied in them is not complete until actualized in speech or action.[32] The law[33] functioned as a means to realize the concepts of action.[34] The *agadah* served to concretize the concept in speech.[35]

The concepts represent the value of the community and distinguish it from other communities.[36] The very interpretation of the biblical text was not concerned with the Bible as literature but as a repository of community values.[37] Whereas the methods of interpretation might seem literary, their purpose is to reveal the values inherent in the Bible. In presenting an interpretation of a given text, the rabbis might even violate the simple meaning of the text; in so doing they were able to eschew any limits to their creative spontaneity.[38]

This relationship to the text was an attempt to overcome the dogmatic authority of the written word. By opening its horizons to interpretation the rabbis declared that divine law could be subjected to scrutiny that might change its original understanding, and this exercise was sanctioned by God.[39]

Value Concepts

Value concepts are noun forms found in rabbinic literature that function to give significance to events or situations rather than to objects or relations in sensory experience. These concepts relate to each other in an organic manner rather than through logic. Hence, they are not deductible, nor do they have any place on a pre-existent hierarchy. Their coherence is found in the dynamic manner in which they interweave with each other.[40]

The Righteous (*Tzadik*)

This value concept is a sub-concept of the concept, Israel.[41] Its obverse concept is the "wicked". Unlike other value concepts it appraises a personality trait of a person.[42] This concept overlaps with that of the learned, in that the study of Torah has an effect on conduct.[43] Some rabbis held that the righteous person can be Jewish or non-Jewish.[44] The righteous merit the experiencing of God's presence (the *shekhina*).[45] The death of the righteous provides vicarious atonement for his generation.[46]

The "righteous" is a personality which the people are to emulate. His good deeds are affected by his study of Torah. The righteous person is to be rewarded although not necessarily in this world but more likely in the world to come, thus answering the question of why the righteous may suffer.

In a society where people are free to choose their models because of a lack of political hegemony and political power, the righteous person became the model for the people. Personality took the place of office as the main source of influence for action.

Righteousness and Deeds of Loving-Kindness (*Tz'dakah, G'milut Hasadim*)

"Righteousness" and "deeds of loving-kindness" are overlapping concepts.[47] Righteousness connotes charity as well as love. It is a sub-concept of *derekh eretz*, the ethical acts between people.[48] An act of charity is significant because it connotes love.[49] A sub-concept of Torah, "deeds of loving-kindness" refers to acts that go beyond the strict requirements of the law.[50]

The presence of these two value concepts in rabbinic thought is not merely to display ethical niceties by which people are to live. Their significance lies in the realization that in order for a society to survive and have purpose, it must try to go beyond the need for individual security. The concerns of each person must be thrust aside to fulfill the needs of other persons even when it does not seem to be beneficial. Charity is regulated by commandments which must be observed to be a member in good standing in the society. In a sense its purpose is utilitarian, for it assumes that the fate of each person is bound with that of his fellow. One day one gives charity, the next day he might have to be the recipient of charity.

"Deeds of loving-kindness" is a value that goes beyond the minimum utilitarian aspect of living together in society. Its purpose is to lead to greater cohesiveness between people. Acts of loving-kindness include attending a funeral, visiting the sick, helping an orphaned bride. Such acts are to insure that individuals are mutually concerned for each other. Each person is obligated in a very specific manner to others living in the society. When those obligations are fulfilled a trusting relationship obtains, for each person would have clear expectations of the actions of others.

Such deeds (along with prayer) replaced the sacrificial cult after the destruction of the Temple, according to Rabban Yohanan ben Zakkai.[51] By acting in such a manner, the community itself could look forward to God's act of redemption.[52] The word, *hesed*, the singular form of *hasadim* (loving-kindness), referred to action that was in concert with God's covenant.[53]

Atonement and Repentance (*Kaparah; T'shuvah*)

Atonement and repentance are both sub-concepts of God's compassion. The former may be concretized in law, in particular in all acts of atonement such as participation in the Day of Atonement, a ritual means of reconciliation with God. Its cause is prior estrangement due to sin or misdeed.

The rabbis taught that man was created with freedom of choice. He can turn in either direction. Literally meaning "turning" in Hebrew, repentance is the conscious effort to turn to a good life. Not only does it involve repentance of previous sins but the striving to a holy life as well.[54]

The values inherent in these concepts are choice and love. The authority chosen by inviduals in the rabbinic world is not one who imposes his power to insure compliance. It depends on the freedom of the individual to accept that rule. However, the authority is not to be regarded as so over-powering that it does not demonstrate love when the individual rebels or sins. Punishment need not be exacted if the person turns in his attempt to reconcile himself with the divine authority. Membership in the community is not dependent on consent alone but on the personal acceptance of the authority and its direction. The authority needs to be accepted in order to rule and, hence, is willing to be reconciled.

God's Justice (*Midat Hadin*)
Measure for Measure (*Middah K'neged Midah*)
Corporate Justice
Individual Justice
Vicarious Justice

The divine attribute of justice is one aspect of the experience of

26

God according to the rabbis, the other being God's attribute of compassion; one attribute cannot be disassociated from the other.[55] Justice is the quality of differentiation, distinction, separation and transcendence, while compassion or mercy is a quality of merging, unity, symbiosis and immanence. For the rabbis God was understood in terms of these opposites. No effort was made to solve this apparent paradox.

God's justice operated in the world, deciding the fate of individuals and nations.[56] At times the attribute of justice was regarded as synonymous with God. At other times it was characterized as detached from God and personified, for example, in a dialogue between God as prosecutor and God as defender.[57] The attitude of the rabbis toward this aspect of God was one of complete trust, that God is just, even though it was difficult at times to understand his justice in specific situations.[58]

A sub-concept of God's justice is "measure for measure": for every act there is an appropriate response from God that is parallel to the act. For example, the midrashic explanation of Laban's deception of Jacob is presented in the context of Jacob's previous deception of his father.[59] There is direct recompense for people's actions. Thus the deceiver is deceived; "measure for measure" is applied to both good and bad actions.

Two phases of the sub-concept of God's justice are applicable in either situation, i.e., being part of society one suffers for the sins of others, for he is responsible by virtue of living in it even though he might be blameless as an individual. Rewards, punishments and distributive justice are the manifestations of recompense due the individual. Yet there is a justice applicable to an individual as well, outside the social context.[60]

The various applications of the concept of justice and its sub-concepts demonstrate its ubiquitous quality, interweaving with almost all of the other concepts at one instant or another. God's justice, according to the rabbis, was an explanation for both the fortunes and achievements of men.[61] The world and the individuals in it are administered by divine justice. As man exercises his innate freedom, he is constantly held responsible for his choices. There can be no escape from God's providence. Individuals and communities are to establish justice in the world; if they fail or if they are unable to establish justice completely, God steps into the breach, if not in this world, then in the world to come.

Merit (*Z'khut*)
Merit of the Fathers and Merit of Abraham
(*Z'khut Avot, Avraham*)

27

Merit of the Tribes of Israel, Merit of the Torah
(Z'khut Sh'vatim, Yisrael, Torah)
Merit of the Children (Z'khut Habanim)
Merit of I (God) (Z'khut Ani)

The concept of merits in rabbinic thought is the opposite of sin and transgression. Each person could accrue merits by obeying the commandments. According to some rabbis, the world depended on the merits that each individual acquires by his good deeds. For others it was in the imputed merits of the past that established the world. Arthur Marmorstein, examing rabbinic theology, demonstrates how the former opinion was held by most rabbis; however, the masses favored on the merits of the fathers, of the righteous, of the Torah, etc.[62] Gradually both ideas assimilated into each other. The concept of imputed merits was transformed into the personification of ideals. The merits of the individuals of previous generations became faithfulness, obedience, compassion, unselfishness and self-sacrifice.[63]

Marmorstein understands the doctrine of merits to be very close to the ideas of the Stoics, that merit keeps the world together. He states that the Stoics derived this concept from Jewish theology and adapted it to their system.[64]

Israel was given the Torah in order to have the opportunity to gain merits so that every nation would acknowledge God's might and name.[65] This concept attempted to combat the Gnostics who viewed the commandments as punishments visited on a stubborn people, for they thought that since God does not need these laws, they were senseless, without meaning.[66]

Merits may be stored up for future generations or could be used immediately for some end. Both Jews and non-Jews could acquire merits by performing good deeds.[67]

Inherent in the concept of merits is the idea that God created the world for his own sake, and no amount of merits could possibly be a recompense for all that God has done. God needs nothing, yet helps the world to demonstrate his kindness and compassion. On the other hand, the concept of merits teaches that man can improve himself and emphasizes God's justice, for man's action does have an effect on the world. It was due to the merits of the fathers[68] that Israel was redeemed from Egypt, received the Torah and was later forgiven for the sin of the golden calf, according to sources in the *midrash* and *Talmud*.[69] Indicative of this concept is that the past serves the present.

It is the mythical past on which society depends in its relationship to authority. The concept of imputed merits, whether they be of the past (fathers) or the future (the children), answers the question why authority chooses to covenant with the people at all. Present covenant is a fulfillment of previous promises that were made and is a recompense for the merits that the fathers had or the children will have as a result of living according to the Torah. The concept of merits also functions as a method by which the claims of the society are made vis-a-vis authority. It is a political demand to fulfill previous covenants. It also raises the status of the people and, as such, is suggestive of later claims feudal lords were to make upon their king.

The merits of Israel and the merit of the Torah were proclaimed as a result of polemical battles against Christians who denigrated Israel's claims of an historic relationship with God.[70] By proclaiming that the world depended on Israel's acceptance of the Torah, the rabbis declared the legitimacy of the covenant with the Jewish people. No new covenant was necessary since the ancient one proclaimed at Sinai was forever binding.

The merit of "I", that is, God, was an affirmation that the world was established upon God's merits, not dependent on demiurges or men, a refutation of Gnostic claims. The various Gnostic sects taught that the Bible was the result of an evil demiurge. The god of light or goodness (in contrast to a malevalent god of darkness) was not a concept to be found within Jewish teachings according to the rabbis who declared that God created the world and gave the Torah to Israel because of his compassion.

Holiness (*Kedushah*)

The concept of holiness originates in the concept of the Kingdom of Heaven; in order to achieve the latter one must pursue a life of holiness.[71] Holiness is considered an imitation of God.[72] In daily experience concretized in Jewish law, it meant a separation from impurity and defilement both ritually and ethically.[73] Just as God is holy, Israel is to be holy (Leviticus 14:2).

If man is able to imitate God, i.e., achieve holiness through his deeds, then the concept of God as authority over and above man loses its meaning; man is to internalize holiness. Although God transcends his creation, the ability to become holy brings man very close to God. The relationship, instead of being parental, is likened to the mutual love of spouses, or of partnership.

The Sanctification of the Name (*Kiddush Hashem*)
The Profanation of the Name (*Hillul Hashem*)

Referring to the name of God, these concepts are affirmations or rejections of God directed to the world at large.[74] This concept refers to the extreme act of martyrdom as well as to the mundane daily situation. To suffer cruelty and even death in order to keep God's commandments was to publicly make the world aware for Israel God was of ultimate significance. Yet man, even in his daily actions, could sanctify God's name.[75]

There is a sense of mission inherent in this concept. By acting as an example, ethically as well as demonstrating the willingness to make sacrifices for its beliefs, Israel was to declare to the world the sanctity of God and his existence. On the other hand, when not observing its covenant with God, Israel failed its mission and thereby profaned God's name. This sense of mission, of living and acting in dedication to a transcendant cause in order to inspire others to accept that same mission, has important ramifications for later Western religious and political thought.[76]

Redemption (*Ge'ulah*)

Redemption from servitude or oppression was one of the hopes that the Jewish people held during the rabbinic period. This concept probably helped to inspire the several wars and revolts against the Romans during the first and second centuries.[77] Manifestations are to be found in the liturgy recited three times a day.[78] The people were inspired by the story of the exodus and regarded it as a proof for their faith that God would redeem them once again from Roman oppression.

Israel's redemption would prove to the world that God continually kept his promise. Its realization would be a self-justification for the Jewish people to maintain its separate identity in a Roman Empire striving for cultural homogeneity.

Torah
The Study of Torah (*Talmud Torah*)
Commandments (*Mitzvot*)
Ethics (*Derekh Eretz*)

Torah means teaching.[79] The rabbis understood Torah to include not only the written text of the five books of Moses but the accumulated and continual process of interpretation of the Bible which was designated the oral Torah.

Both written and oral Torah have divine origin according to the rabbis, having been revealed at Mt. Sinai simultaneously.[80] Torah was regarded as the source of knowledge given by God to mankind through Israel.[81] Thus the value concepts of Torah and Israel are interrelated; the Torah, having been one of the phenomena created by God before the formation of the world, was created for the sake of Israel whose very existence depended upon it. The Torah is the manifestion of the love God shows for Israel.[82]

The Torah derives its authority from the "kingdom of heaven", a concept which will be explained below. The rabbis interpreted the biblical passages that were introduced with such words as, "'I am the Lord your God" (e.g., Exodus 22:6, Leviticus 18:2), as manifestations of the divine authority of the Torah. In order to accept the rule of Torah, Israel had to first receive the "yoke of the kingdom of heaven".[83]

The Torah was regarded as an institution and the basis of faith which was the cornerstone and raison d'etre of the existence of the Jewish people.[84] As a revealed promise it was an expression of God's will, and was the blueprint for the creation of the world.[85] The Torah was personified in rabbinic literature and was regarded as having its own separate existence.[86] As the foundation of society, the teaching of the Torah was likened to giving life to a person, equivalent to acts of charity. Studying it was incumbent on everyone, rich and poor alike. Since the study of Torah fulfilled a basic requirement of the social structure, interference with this activity was forbidden.[87] The most prestigious occupation was the study of Torah. The relationship between teachers and their students was compared with the nurturing love of parents.

The concept of *mitzvot* (commandments) was understood as a specific fulfillment of the Torah and was evidence of " . . . God's relation to man in general and his historic relation to Israel in particular."[88] Thus, for example, to deny the legitimacy of the commandment of just measure was equivalent to denying the legitimacy of the exodus from Egypt. Not to a have compassion for one's fellows was likened to throwing off the yoke of the "kingdom of heaven", i.e., a denial of the divine authority of the commandments. The obverse of commandments, sin and transgression,[89] separated men from God and constituted an act of rebellion against God by denying his authority and providence.[90]

The concept of ethics (*derekh eretz*), is broad and applicable to the range of human experience and behavior.[91] Although this concept is an aspect of Torah, it is universal and does not originate in the Torah. It is obligatory on all mankind and specifies ethical human behavior that is to be expected from each person as a matter of course and common sense.[92]

God's Compassion (*Midat Harahamim*)[93]
Prayer (*T'filah*)

God's compassion is expression in a range of personal relationships from parental love to the love between spouses. God gives the world to mankind and at the same time gives mankind the ability to sustain itself.[94] This concept interweaves with other value concepts presenting a complex understanding of love relationships. God is affected by the behavior of the individual, and as such, longs to reward him, grieving when he must punish him. The stimulus for creating the world is God's compassion, for he longs for a world in which he may demonstrate his compassion and be loved; it is similar to the relationship of an artisan to the art that he creates. The terminology in Hebrew would at first glance lead us to believe that the concept should be understood as God's grace, i.e., undeserved love. The world used for compassion, *rahamim*, is derived from the word, *rehem*, which means womb and would seem to designate the undeserved, unearned compassion that a baby receives from its mother even before birth. Although at times God's compassion does have this aspect it has been extended in the *midrash* beyond this limited understanding.

Prayer, a sub-concept of God's compassion, is an expression of the method by which people may respond to God's compassion. This intensely personal concept is reflected in instances of man's prayer, that God teaches man how to pray and that God prays himself.[95] One who prays sincerely and with intensity feels God's nearness.

The attitude toward authority expressed in these value concepts is a positive one. God relates to the world and its inhabitants, demonstrating benevolence by initiating the relationship. The very significance of God as leader is based on the need to relate. Without his creation to receive his compassion, the leader is meaningless, as a person cannot become a parent without a child. By attributing compassion to authority, the people define their own power, for they realize that by their very existence they fulfill an inherent need in their ruler. Although there is an element of grace, for the most part there is a realization of mutual dependence. If the people reject their God, that is, forget him, he no longer exists for them and hence no longer has significance for them. But the reverse is realized as well — that if God rejects the people, they have lost any reason or purpose to survive.

Man (*Adam*)
Israel
The Nations of the World (*Umot Ha'olam*)

The world was created for the sake of man according to the *midrash*, yet without Israel, God would have destroyed the world.[96] There are two opposing tendencies in aggadic literature in regard to the reason that Israel is chosen to accept the Torah. Some state that Israel was elected as an act of God's grace. In this view God had created Israel before the creation of the world because he foresaw the corruption in the world. Israel then was to be a witness of God's existence by virtue of the special relationship he had with her. Even when Israel did not keep the covenant, the direct punishment she would suffer would demonstrate to the world that there is a God of justice. Israel then is considered incidental to God's kingship and power.[97]

There were those who understood the election of Israel in terms of Israel's merits. It was Israel who had chosen God coincident with God's choosing of Israel. Israel merited God's choice. Many different reasons for this merit are given:

1. God foresaw the righteousness of Abraham and therefore chose his people;

2. Israel was chosen as a consequence of the Song of the Sea they sang praising God (Exodus 14:30-15:18);

3. God chose Israel because of their willingness to accept the Torah at Sinai;

4. Israel merited this special relationship due to her humbleness and meekness;

5. another reason offered was that because she was persecuted and had experienced oppression, the Jewish people were especially chosen by God.[98]

We can surmise that this latter view is a response to attacks by Christians and Gnostics who impugned the election of Israel for their own reasons. By demonstrating that Israel had deserved her election, the rabbis could declare to the people the reason for the separate existence of the Jewish people.

A statement in the *Mekhilta* (Friedmann edition, 36b) which is quoted several times in rabbinic literature (e.g., *Talmud Bavli Hagigah* 3a-3b)[99] presents a good example of the close spouse-like relationship between God and Israel.

> They recognized in him the king, as he recognized in them the masters of the world...Israel declares (his unity) in the words, 'Hear, O Israel the Lord our God, the Lord is *one*' (Deuteronomy 6:4); the Holy Spirit proclaims her election (in the words), '...and who was like thy people a nation that is *one* (or alone) in the earth.' (I Chronicles 17:21)

The concept of Israel is placed in the context of its role vis-a-vis the "nations of the world". Like Israel, the nations of the world can include both wicked and righteous people, indeed righteous non-Jews share in the world to come with Jews.[100] This concept designates the entire non-Jewish world as an entity that is distinct from Israel.[101] This distinction between Israel and the nations of the world can have either a positive or negative connotation depending on the context in which it is found; it does not reflect a necessarily adverse attitude towards the nations of the world.

"Israel" and "The Nations of the World" are used together to emphasize the distinctiveness of Israel, especially in regard to the special relationship with God's authority. Such distinctions legitimize the individuality of Israel. During the time such statements were made, the Roman Empire and later Christianity attempted to disparage all national differences in order to prove their universal legitimacy to world rule. In reaction, the rabbis emphasized an earlier view that the individuality of Israel was determined by God who transcends the universality of both the Roman Empire and Christianity.

The Kingdom of Heaven (*Malkhut Shamayim*) Strange Worship (*Avodah Zarah*)

The recognition and realization of the "kingdom of heaven" is a concept pointing to the hope for future fulfillment.[102] However, this concept was not apocalyptic for most rabbis, rather, they understood its potential fulfillment within human experience and history.[103] In order for it to be realized, people must make the choice to receive it.[104] His rule is manifested through his attributes of justice and compassion, his giving of the Torah, his choice of Israel, etc.

Israel acknowledges God's rule through the study and observance of the Torah which must be done constantly by each generation, by individuals and by the corporate entity. Acceptance and acknowledgement are accomplished with an attitude of love (emphasizing God's attribute of compassion), and with reverence or fear (pointing to God's attribute of justice). Breaking a commandment may indicate the repudiation of God's sovereignty.[105] Its declaration is part of the daily Jewish liturgy, and precedes the acceptance of the commandments. The first commandment is interpreted as an expression of God's sovereignty through which the rest of the commandments are significant, i.e., a commandment presupposes an authority initiating it and insuring compliance.[106] In rabbinic literature it is hoped that the day will come when all nations will accept "the kingdom of heaven".[107] The manifestation of the "kingdom of heaven" is in the acquiescence to the Torah by the majority of Israel and later of mankind.[108]

God did not become king until he created mankind which made it possible for someone to obey him as a matter of choice, thus making his kingship worthwhile and meaningful.[109] Hence, the creation of angels or beasts was not satisfying to God because they did not have the ability to make choices.[110] Thus the kingship of God is dependent upon recognition on earth. It is not secure until an entire people recognize it. Israel was to fulfill this function. In the *midrash* (*Exodus Rabbah* 23:1) God says to the angels: "If my people decline to proclaim me as king upon earth, kingdom ceases also in heaven."[111]

This kingdom is not understood in rabbinic literature as some spiritual time or place beyond the world. It is definitely of this world and can be established by people recognizing its presence.[112]

A government was not judged according to its form or structure,[113] but rather whether it acted in a righteous manner encouraging justice and righteousness.[114] The right to rule was derived from God, yet the choice of how to rule was regarded as an inherent choice of man. The form of government was not a source of inquiry. *Talmud Yerushalmi, Rosh Hashanah* 1, 3, 57a, in the name of Rabbi Eleazer ben Pedat,[115] interprets a famous Greek proverb, that for a king the law is not binding: "Ordinarily a human king issues a decree and if he chooses to, he obeys it, otherwise others obey it, but when the Holy One Blessed Be He issues a decree he is the first to obey it."[116] God, then, does not take advantage of his power; rather he, too, is regarded as having limited himself to obey his own laws, unlike the king of flesh and blood.

The emphasis on God's kingship was a consequence of historical circumstances,[117] i.e., another ruler claimed the title of God. It has been suggested that this king might be identified as Caligula (37-41) who ordered his statue erected in Jerusalem (in the year 40), declaring himself divine. Citing Rabbi Yohanan ben Zakkai's statement in *Talmud Bavli, Hagigah* 13a, as a rebuke to the self-deification of Roman emperors, Buchler understands it to mean God's kingship is here, based on the recognition of every person.

The declaration of the kingship of God over the universe was also in reaction to the pagan world which criticized the concept of an all-powerful God. Citing a legend regarding Titus, the conqueror of Jerusalem, Marmorstein[118] states that seeing the failures of the Jewish nation in politics and war, the Jewish God was perceived with contempt, for in their view, he was unable to protect his temple from Roman destruction or its people from slaughter by the Roman legions or its land plundered. In pagan thought, a people's god fought along with the people; if the people were defeated so was its god. On the contrary, according to the Jews, God was king and could not be defeated, for no other gods even existed.

Moreover, not only was this concept a reaction to pagan derision and polemic, it was also a result of skepticism among the Jewish people themselves during the latter part of the second century and the third century, a result of the defeat of Israel by Rome. Many *midrashim*[119] express the need to speak of God's omnipotence and rule in order to combat this skeptical tendency. If God's kingdom did not seem present now it would come into full existence in the future when God's unity would be recognized by all persons, thus leading to the unity of mankind under God's rule. God's kingdom for the present was limited because not all people recognized and perceived it. Rome's rule was considered incompatible with God's rule, and until Rome's power ended, God's rule would be limited in the world.[120]

The obverse of this concept is "strange worship", i.e., idolatry. To believe in many gods or to deny the Kingdom of Heaven was to deny the legitimacy of Israel's claims and refute the relationship between God and Israel and the world. The Hebrew term is *kofer* which can also be translated: to rebel. Likened to an act of political treason, for a Jew to deny the authority of God was to deny the reason and purpose of his very existence as a member of the corporate entity of Israel as well as the efficacy and divine authority of the Torah.

That all sovereignty flowed from the deity was nothing new for political thought in the ancient world. But to the polytheistic world, gods were limited. Even the chief of the pantheon could be overpowered by the fates. To understand God in universal terms, that his power was not limited, yet he limited himself by making covenants with mankind, was quite a different matter. The "kingdom of heaven" was a vision of what could be, transcending human authority. Its realization was dependent on the perception of people, i.e., it was up to mankind, in the words of the ancient rabbis, to take upon itself "the yoke of the Kingdom of Heaven".

The Exodus From Egypt (*Y'tziat Mitzrayim*)

That God brought Israel out of Egypt was a cornerstone of rabbinic thought and a dogmatic belief rather than a value concept. To deny this belief was to deny the commandments; similarly to deny the commandments was to deny this belief, so intertwined were the two.[121] However, because of the organic quality of rabbinic thought, there were several interpretations of that event included in its literature.[122]

This belief was essential because it was an example of how God kept his promise made previously to the patriarchs, and responded to the people when they complained of their servitude (Genesis 15:13-14; Exodus 2:23-25), and redeemed them from slavery. Because of this act, Israel was bound to God to keep her promise, i.e., to observe the covenant which she had accepted as a consequence of redemption. The bond between ruler and ruled was thus strengthened by mutual dependence, obligation and responsibility. The basis of God's authority to rule was the very acts he had performed on Israel's behalf.[123] The exodus from Egypt was regarded as paramount among them.

The Giving of the Torah (*Matan Torah*)

The concept, "the giving of the Torah", is to rabbinic literature what covenant is to biblical literature. This term is not limited to the Sinai episode or to any other single event.[124] According to the rabbis, one was to regard the Torah as if it was given to the individual in the existential present.[125] It is regarded as a dogmatic belief with specific consequences for those who deny or those who acknowledge it.[126] Similar to "the kingdom of heaven" (see above), to deny God's giving of the Torah was an act of idolatry.

Included in the Torah that was given at Sinai, was not only the written Pentateuch but also the unwritten or oral Torah: the rabbinic interpretations of the written text had divine authority.[127] This concept of Torah was concretized in new laws and interpretations, so that the teachings of the rabbis were identified as Torah given by God.[128]

In rabbinic literature the term, covenant, is usually understood to refer to specific covenants, i.e., the covenant of circumcision, the covenant of the Sabbath, rather than having the general significance it has in the Bible.[129] Buchler posits that covenant in the Bible is not parallel to the Torah, rather it is the agreement to keep the Torah. It is not until the Pharasic *Psalms of Solomon* 10:5 (c. 67 B.C.E.) that covenant is denoted as Torah.[130]

The biblical use of covenant is perceived either as one-sided, that this agreement is binding on Israel alone, or mutual, that every partner in the agreement is bound to its observance. With the rabbis there is a significant change: mutuality predominates.[131] Perhaps that is the reason that the terminology is transformed in rabbinic literature. The covenant concept in the Bible is *brit* (literally, covenant); for the rabbis the same concept becomes *mattan Torah* (the giving of the Torah). A giver assumes a receiver. Israel received the Torah from God. Buchler substantiates this point with a citation of a controversy found in the *Mekhilta* (edited by Lauterbach, Vol. II, p. 210), regarding the manner of sacrifice Moses made after receiving the Torah (Exodus 24:6). Half the blood was to be sprinkled on the altar while the other half was sprinkled on the people. According to Rabbi Yishmael, the sprinkling of the blood on the people was meant to bind them to the covenant (and not that God was bound to it).[132]

Opposing Rabbi Yishmael's interpretation was the regnant view that the sprinkling of the blood on the altar and on the people demonstrated that the covenant was mutually binding on God and Israel. Buchler cites *Midrash Tannaim* (Hoffman edition, on Deuteronomy 11:26) as an expression of Israel's promise not to worship other gods in exchange for God's promise not to substitute Israel for another nation.

In the Pentateuch where the central event is the exodus perceived as a fulfillment of earlier covenants with the patriarchs, God's power is greater than that of Israel. It is God that initiates all covenants. Gradually with prophetic writings there is a change: God is placed on a level closer to Israel. This can be seen especially with the metaphor of marriage that is used to explain the relationship between God (the husband) and Israel (the wife).[133]

In rabbinic literature there is a tendency to place Israel almost at par with God. Israel is not imposed upon, rather it actively receives the covenant. It is not the power of the deity that necessarily is emphasized. A subtle change of nuance has made the giving-receiving relationship a demonstration of mutual concern and inter-dependency. The giving of the Torah is the vehicle by which the ruler can rule on the one hand, while the people are willing to trust that rule on the other. It forges the link between authority and society.

This giving of the Torah is then not merely a contractual relationship but is also a recognition that neither party to the agreement has any significance or reality without it. The relationship itself creates a new phenomenon: a disparate collection of individuals, howbeit sharing common family ties, becomes a people. The deity, a transcendent power, becomes a leader of a people through whom he can make himself known to the rest of the world. The catalyst is the Torah.

NOTES

1. These problems are elucidated in many essays by Jacob Neusner, e.g., "Being Jewish and Studying About Judaism," 1977.

2. See especially, Kadushin, *Mind*.

3. W. Bacher, " The Origin of the Word Haggadah (Agada)," *Jewish Quarterly Review* (Old Series) IV (1891), p. 416.

4. *Agada* is Aramaic; its Hebrew equivalent is *hagadah*.

5. Bacher, p. 417.

6. *Ibid.*, p. 418 f.

7. *Ibid.*, p. 419. Bacher points out that *magid* was used only in Rabbi Yishmael's school, and not in Rabbi Akiba's school (e.g., *Sifra* uses *m'lamed* instead); see p. 421 f.

8. Y. L. Zunz, *Hadrashot B'Yisrael*, translated by M. Zak (Jerusalem: Mosad Bialik, 1954), p. 3.

9. *Ibid.*, p. 32 (my translation).

10. Herford, p. 80.

11. Louis Ginzberg, "The Religion of the Jews at the Time of Jesus," *Hebrew Union College Annual*, I (1924), p. 310.

12. Schechter, XXII.

13. *Ibid.*, XXIII.

14. *Ibid.*, p. 16. He does not explain this intention.

15. Max Kadushin, *Organic Thinking, A Study in Rabbinic Thought* (New York: Jewish Theological Seminary of America, 1938), p. 226. Hereafter cited as OT.

16. *Ibid.*

17. *Ibid.*, p. 221.

18. *Ibid.*, p. 227.

19. J. Newman, *Halachic Sources From the Beginning to the Ninth Century* (Leiden: E.J. Brill, 1969), p. 3f.

20. David Daube, "The Influence of Interpretation on Writing," *Buffalo Law Review*, No. 1 (Fall, 1970), p. 49.

21. Kadushin, *OT*, P. 227.

22. Max Kadushin, *The Theology of Seder Eliahu, A Study in Organic Thinking* (New York: Bloch Publishing Co., 1932), p. 17. Hereafter cited as *TSE*.

23. Salo W. Baron, *Social and Religious History of the Jews* (2nd edition, revised; New York and Philadelphia: Columbia University Press and Jewish Publication Society of America, 1958), II, 37f. Hereafter cited as *History*. But see also, David Daube, "Texts and Interpretation in Roman and Jewish Law," *The Jewish Journal of Sociology*, III, No. 1 (reprint), p. 8ff where he demonstrates that, contrary to popular belief, the Sadducees were not literalists.

24. Kadushin, *TSE*, p. 202.

25. Kadushin, *OT*, p. 1.

26. Kadushin, *TSE*, p. 45.

27. Some ascribe the term, *k'v'yachol*, as an attempt to ameliorate anthropomorphism. Kadushin, *TSE*, p. 44f, cites Bacher, who claims that this term was used as an apology when a strong expression about God is found. (The term is translated as, "as it were: or "so to speak".) Ginzberg suggests that it is used when a corporeal description of God appears. However, A. Marmorstein, *The Old Rabbinic Doctrine of God* (New York: Ktav Publishing House, Inc., 1968), II, p. 128ff (hereafter cited as *Doctrine*), states that *k'v'yachol* was used to demonstrate ". . .that the Scriptures or some parallel support convey the same thought. . ." as the rabbis. He also contends that later sources use the term more promiscuously as a means against obvious anthropomorphism as a manifestation of God's adherence to Israel; God even feels Israel's pain. It is an apologetic teaching that God has not forsaken Israel. *Ibid.*, p. 75f.

28. Kadushin, "Aspects of the Rabbinic Concept of Israel: A Study in the Mekilta," *Hebrew Union College Annual*, XIX (1945-1946), p. 69. Hereafter cited as "Israel".

29. Kadushin, *OT*, p. 187.

30. Kadushin, *Mind*, VII, and p. 47.

31. *Ibid.*, p. 2 and 29ff.

32. *Halakhah.*

33. Kadushin, *Mind*, p. 80.

34. *Ibid.*, p. 52.

35. *Ibid.*, p. 78.

36. *Ibid.*, p. 98.

37. David Weiss, "Towards a Theology of Rabbinic Exegesis," *Judaism*. X, no. 1 (Winter, 1961), p. 19.

38. *Ibid.*

39. *Ibid.*, p. 20.

40. Max Kadushin, *Worship and Ethics: A Study in Rabbinic Judaism* (Evanston: Northwestern University Press, 1964) VII. Hereafter cited as *Worship*.

41. Kadushin, *Mind*, p. 40, note 12. A sub-concept in Kadushin's system does not imply a hierarchy of concepts; rather it is related to the more inclusive concept of Israel.

42. *Ibid.*, p. 4.

43. *Ibid.*, p. 29.

44. *Ibid.*, p. 41.

45. *Ibid.*, p. 228 and note 34.

46. *Ibid.*, p. 388, note 57.

47. Kadushin, *Mind*, p. 297.

48. *Ibid.*, p. 15.

49. *Ibid.*, p. 110.

50. *Ibid.*, p. 80.

51. *Avot de Rabbi Natan*, IV, 34.

52. Jacob Neusner, *A Life of Rabban Yohanan Ben Zakkai CA. 1-80 C.E.* (Leiden: E.J. Brill, 1962), p. 143.
53. *Ibid.*
54. Kadushin, *TSE*, p. 120.
55. J. Abelson, *The Immanence of God in Rabbinical Literature* (New York: Hermon Press, 1969), p. 31.
56. Kadushin, *Mind*, p. 163.
57. *Ibid.*, p. 165.
58. *Ibid.*, p. 197.
59. *Genesis Rabbah* 70:19
60. Kadushin, *Mind*, p. 17.
61. Abelson, p. 164.
62. A. Marmorstein, *The Doctrine of Merits in Old Rabbinical Literature*, (New York: Ktav Publishing House, Inc., 1968), p. 6. Hereafter cited as *Merits*.
63. *Ibid.*, p. 25f.
64. *Ibid.*, p. 29.
65. *Ibid.*, p. 14ff.
66. *Ibid.*, p. 16.
67. *Ibid.*, p. 20.
68. *Ibid.*, p. 10f. An earlier form of this concept was, *ma'asay avot*, deeds of the Fathers. In the school of Rabbi Yishmael it was known as *s'khar avot*, the reward of the fathers.
69. *Exodus Rabbah* 1:36, *Genesis Rabbah* 28:1 and 2, *Talmud Bavli Shabbat* 42a as cited by Schechter, *Aspects*, p. 174.
70. Baron, *History*, II, p. 136ff.
71. Schechter, *Aspects*, p. 199.
72. Kadushin, *Mind*, p. 169.
73. Schechter, *Aspects*, p. 205.
74. Kadushin, *TSE*, p. 67.
75. Such as reciting the *Shema* (Deuteronomy 6:4) twice daily.
76. To act and be willing to die for a cause whether it be for Christianity, communism or democracy was largely a contribution of rabbinic thought. Polytheists would be willing to accept other gods into their pantheon. Jews could never do this and still maintain their religious beliefs.
77. This concept does not refer to redemption from sin, but political redemption. See Kadushin, *Worship*, p. 93.
78. Schechter, *Aspects*, p. 117.
79. Kadushin, *OT*, p. 27.
80. *Ibid.*, p. 41.
81. *Ibid.*, p. 80f.
82. Schechter, *Aspects*, p. 116. See *Sifra* 85b and *Mekhilta*, II, 233-242.
83. *Ibid.*, p. 118.
84. *Genesis Rabbah* 1:4. Other creations of God that were premundane include Israel, the Throne of God, the name of the messiah, hell and paradise and repentance.
85. Schechter, *Aspects*, p. 129.
86. Kadushin, *OT*, p. 64.
87. Schechter, *Aspects*, p. 231.
88. *Het.* 89. Schechter, *Aspects*, p. 230ff.
90. Kadushin, *OT.* p. 118.
91. *Ibid.*, p. 127ff.
92. *Middat Harahamim.* Marmorstein, *Doctrine*, I, p. 44. This term and its companion, *middat hadin* (see above), were first mentioned by Rabbi Meir (second century). The old Tannaitic *aggadah* did not know these terms. The tetramaton was first designated as a manifestation of God's justice and *Elohim* was designated as a God's love. Not until the statements of Rabbi Meir (*Pesikta*, Buber edition, 62a, 164a) and Rabbi Shimon Bar Yohai (*Tanhuma*, I, 34, Buber edition, 73a) do we have them reversed. Those two rabbis switched the designations as a result of heretical gnostic interpretations.

Elohim is a plural form in Hebrew grammar which the gnostics viewed as proof for their theory of demiurges, i.e., the world was created chaotically by an evil demiurge. By designated it as God's justice they demonstrated the orderliness of the world.

93. Kadushin, *TSE*, p. 110.

94. Kadushin, *Mind.* p. 141f.

95. Marmorstein, *Merits*, p. 99, cites *Genesis Rabbah* 8:5. Marmorstein understands this statement and others like it (*Song of Songs Rabbah* 77:1 and *Genesis Rabbah* 66:2) as responses to Christian and Gnostic anti-Jewish propaganda in third century polemics.

96. Schecter, *Aspects*, p. 59-60, cf. his citations.

97. *Ibid.*, p. 59f.

98. Cited and translated by Schechter, p. 48; see also Kadushin, "Israel", p. 58.

99. Kadushin, *Mind*, p. 28.

100. *Ibid.*, p. 41.

101. Schechter, *Aspects*, p. 65f.

102. Kadushin, *kTSE*, p. 58f.

103. *L'kabel malchut shamayim.*

104. Kadushin, *TSE*, p. 60f.

105. Kadushin, *Mind*, p. 21, 130.

106. *Alenu* prayer, cited by Kadushin, *Mind*, p. 192, 266.

107. Schechter, *Aspects*, p. 64, Note 3.

108. *Ibid.*, p. 65. If we were to translate such prayers into political terminology they would function as pledges of allegiance, affirmation of the preamble to a constitution, or the celebration of patriotic events in the history of a people or nation.

109. *Ibid.*, p. 81f.

110. Translated by Schechter, *Aspects*, p. 85.

111. *Ibid.*, p. 89. However, there was definitely an eschatological concept of the Kingdom of Heaven in Jewish thought. See W. W. Buchanan, "Introduction" in R. A. Charles, *Eschatology, the Doctrine of the Future Life* (New York: Schocken Books, 1960), for a survey of the scholarship on this point. Hereafter cited as *Eschatology*.

112. *Ibid.*, p. 92, citing *Talmud Bavli Berachot* 58a and *Avodah Zarah* 17a.

113. *Ibid.*, p. 93.

114. Saul Lieberman, *Greek in Jewish Palestine* (New York: Jewish Theological Seminary of America, 1942), p. 37f. Rabbi Eleazar ben Pedat lived in third century Tiberia.

115. Parallels to this statement can be found in the *Talmud Bavli Pesahim* 30 and *Exodus Rabbah* 21:1. See also David Daube, "Princeps Legibus Solutus," in *Studi in Memoriodi: Paolo Koschaker*, edited A. Giuffre (Milan: Multa Paucis, 1954), pp. 463-465 for historical background.

116. Buchler, *Studies in Sin and Atonement in the Rabbinic Literature of the First Century* (New York: Ktav Publishing House, Inc., 1967) p. 44. Hereafter cited as *Studies*.

117. Marmorstein, *Doctrine*, I, p. 169f. For sources of the Titus legend see p. 171, Note 31. The legend was that Titus entered the Holy of Holies with two harlots, tore away the curtain and challenged God. On the way home he experienced a storm and again challenged God by saying that God had power over the sea (the flood, pharaoh) but not on dry land. God responded by sending his smallest creature, a flea, to conquer Titus.

118. Cited by Marmorstein, *Ibid.*, p. 174.

119. *Ibid.*, p. 174. See especially statement of Rabbi Abbah ben Kahana in *Midrash on Psalms* 10b, edited by Buber, "The congregation of Israel stood before the Holy One Blessed Be He (and said), Master of the Universe, I am the Lily of the Depth who was placed in the depths of trouble in order to cause Me to stumble, and as the Holy One Blessed Be He draws me forth from troubles I am fresh in good deeds as a lily and sing a song before him, as it says, 'the Lord in distress, they sought you' (Isaiah 26:16)."

120. Kadushin *Mind*, p. 358f.

121. *Ibid.*, p. 73.

122. See *Mekhilta*, II, Chapter 5.
123. Kadushin *Mind*, p. 57f.
124. *Ibid.*, p. 151.
125. *Ibid.*, p. 348f. Those who deny are among those who do not have a portion in the world to come (*Sanhedrin* 10:1). See also Schechter, *Aspects*, p. 220, "...the throwing off of the yoke is classed together with the removing of the covenant made by God with Israel at Mt. Sinai...", and his citations there.
126, Kadushin *Mind*, p. 353.
127. *Ibid.*, p. 357.
128. See below "Covenant Terminology". Buchler, *Studies*, p. 16, Note 1.
129. *Ibid.*, p. 20ff.
130. *Ibid.*, p. 22.
131. Marmorstein, *Doctrine*, II, p. 29ff. This idea that the sovereign cannot be limited by covenant is also found in Hobbes, *Leviathan*, part 2, chapter 18. See also Mark Gavre, "Hobbes and His Audience: The Dynamics of Theorizing," *American Political Science Review*, LXVIII, No. 4 (December, 1974) on the use of terminology in order to persuade his Puritan audience, esp. p. 1552.
132. Hosea 2:21-22, "And I will be betrothed to you forever..."

PART II: RABBINIC COVENANT IN ITS SETTING

CHAPTER 1: BIBLICAL ANTECEDENTS

The rabbis understood that their major task was to realize and fulfill the words of the Torah, the repository of God's revelation. Their very claims to authority were based on their perceived relationship with the Bible. In order to evaluate this claim it is necessary to understand the rabbinical concept of covenant in the context of the earlier biblical covenant idea. The Bible[1] posits the covenant as the foundation of society, the result, not of natural phenomena, but of revelation. The ultimate obligation of the Israelite was not to his nation, but to God through his maintenance of the covenant. According to the terms of the covenant, God is the supreme authority whose obligation includes the protection of the community. While the Israelite king functioned on God's behalf (through personal covenants between the king and God and between the king and the people), when he acted contrary to his covenantal responsibility, the prophets, God's spokesmen, admonished him.[2]

The covenant form[3] as we have it in the Bible is based on an ancient literary form which might have had, as its source, royal treaties since the terminology and structure are comparable. Most of these ancient forms date back to the mid-third millenium, B.C. and are found in treaties of the Hittite Empire (ca. 1400-1200 B.C.E.) which formed the basis of the empire. It was through these treaties that the relations between the empire and its vassal states were ordered.

Protection was offered to the vassals in exchange for their military support. These treaties exhibit a formal structure beginning with a preamble which identified the king and gave his titles and genealogy, followed by an historical prologue which reported the previous relationships between the parties concerned. The stipulations of the treaty were followed by a provision for the deposit of the document in a shrine or sanctuary where it was to be read before the public periodically. A list of witnesses included the gods of both parties and natural phenomena (the mountains, the seas, etc.). Finally, came the list of blessings and curses.[4]

The Hittites had no specific word for covenant or contract and designated their relationships as "oaths and bonds"; the covenant was always initiated by the king of the empire.[5] These treaties were usually unilateral, although we do have some examples of parity treaties.[6] The historical prologue of the suzerainty treaties emphasized the past benevolent deeds of the king for the vassal whose action constitutes an exchange of obedience in the future for benefits received in the past, which, he acknowledges, were given graciously.[7]

The form of address in these treaties was placed in the second person, pointing to a personal relationship between the parties. The stipulations contained the detail of the obligations accepted by the vassal which included a prohibition of other foreign relationships, a prohibition of enmity against anything or anyone within the king's domain, i.e., he was not allowed to conquer other vassals of the king. The vassal was required to answer the king's call to arms (cf. Judges 21:8f), maintain trust in the king and forbidden to utter evil words against him. No asylum was to be given to refugees (who might be rebels or enemies of the crown) by the vassal. The vassal had to appear before the king at least once each year (probably at the time of the annual tribute) (cf. Exodus 23:17). All controversies between vassals were to be submitted to the king for judgement. The list of witnesses was parallel to biblical listings found in Deuteronomy 32:1 and Isaiah 1:2. The curses and blessings were similar to those found in Deuteronomy 28.

The structure of the Decalogue, of course, is easily compared to the Hittite treaties. Moses acted as the messenger of God; he himself was not a party to the covenant. The preamble identified God and an historical prologue recalled God's deliverance of Israel from Egyptian bondage. Israel obligated itself to obey the stipulations of the covenant (Exodus 19:8). A solemn ceremony followed by which the tribes and clans became bound to each other and bound to God as a people through the covenant.[8] One of the first obligations was the rejection of all foreign relations (whether they be gods or nations) which might diminish Israel's unity. The covenant was to be deposited in the ark of the covenant. This covenant form is also used in Joshua 24.

The covenant with Abraham, however, is different. Although God makes promises to him, Abraham seemed to have no obligation (the circumcision was not an obligation, but a sign that a covenant had been made).[9]

Sinai

Sinai marks a change from the patriarchal family covenant to a national covenant which no longer had to be renewed. An entire community would be conscious of it and pass the tradition from one generation to the next.[10] The Bible recounts that Israel was enslaved in Egypt. She cried out to God, who remembered his covenant with the Patriarchs and his obligation to protect his people (Exodus 2:24.25). He promised to redeem them from slavery and renew the covenant (Exodus 6:2-8), which was to be binding on God and on his people forever.

There was no need to renew the covenant with the people, since it was made for all time (Deuteronomy 29:9-14). God would always remember his promise (Deuteronomy 4:31).[11]

Here the irreducible difference between Israel and other nations in terms of relations to the deity can be found. Israel worshipped a God of the covenant, of time and history, rather than a god of nature, of space. This implied a choosing God, who rather than being part of the cycle of nature, would explicitly decide to enter into history. The relationship was based upon will and choice rather than on the physical needs of gods of nature.[12] God, with unlimited power, limited himself in order to enter into a covenant relation with Israel.[13] The covenant at Sinai was the foundation of Israel's reponsibilities as well as its beginning as a nation.

The Unilateral Covenant

The covenant established a society whose authority was God. Observance of the stipulations of the covenant, as well as general loyalty to the covenant, was to be the uniting factor of the society. God remained faithful to his covenant even though Israel continually broke it.[14] God was free from any influence that could distract him from his loyalty to the relationship. Israel, however, was often seduced by the surrounding culture. Unlike all other treaty partners in the entire ancient world, God transcended his covenant.[15] We are confronted with an insoluble paradox of a God who limited himself in order to establish the covenant, yet transcended it at the same time. Although Israel had freedom to break the covenant at will, God was bound in a way no human is bound, by his own forces which he himself had created.[16]

Covenant, Law and Revelation

Law has been defined as the "...exercise of coercive power by the community or its agents."[17] Since Israelite law like other ancient law was regarded as divinely revealed, it was built on the authority of the deity.[18] A polarity existed between the ideal authority, the source of the law, and the earthly, political authority which was to administer it (Deuteronomy 30:11-20). It was the responsibility of the latter to assure that there would be a just society. The political authority was castigated when it failed in this task.

Revelation in the Bible appears in the form of a dialogue. God speaks with the chosen person or people and expects a response. At times the response will be an argument, e.g., Abraham (Genesis 18) and Moses (Exodus 3-4); at other times the response is a plea. But there usually is a response. There is no Hebrew word equivalent to revelation in the Torah. Rather, we have a sense of communication and conversation. The most important communication, i.e., at Sinai, is characterized by its public manifestation before all the people. They must know its content before they may enter into the covenant relationship and be held accountable for its fulfillment.

In the first verse of the Decalogue (Exodus 20:1f) God introduces himself to the people. God's authority must be accepted in order that the covenant and the law be valid.[19] God's word has binding effect, not because of the content of the law, but because of its authority, which is to insure its promulgation and practice.

Parallels to biblical law in the ancient near east are to be found among the casuistic laws, i.e., those laws having the conditional style of "if...then". However, the unique style of the apodictic laws (using the statement, "thou shalt (or shalt not)...") emphasizes the direct and intimate relationship of the authority.[20] This apodictic law, because of the very nature of its style is revelatory and serves to enhance the authority of the law as well as the binding quality of the covenant on the community.[21]

Characteristic of Israelite law was the severe penalty for crimes against God.[22] Idolatrous acts were regarded as treason. The divine orientation of biblical law is manifested in the religious, ethical, cultic and civil law.[23]

Covenant and Community

Israel's experience of God's revelation established the community.[24] God ruled directly transcending, and thereby unifying disparate forces, local powers and tribal jurisdictions.[25] The rulership of God and the memory of their history in Egypt and their subsequent deliverance unified the people. The covenant also served to provide a reason for their existence by giving meaning to national history and direction to the fulfillment of their goals.[26]

The covenant also provided a new will to a previously unorganized band of free slaves (Exodus 14:3-6).[27] As the very foundation of the community, its dissolution would lead to the end of the community, according to the prophets' warning. The Bible emphasizes that the covenant obligations were accepted in unison, Israel responding with "one voice" (Exodus 24:3, 7). Its terms are binding on the community forever (Deuteronomy 5:3).

In early Israelite history there was no permanent leadership or political organization. Until the monarchy, there was no central authority. The tribes rallied around the ark of the covenant, a cultic symbol for the covenant which united them.[28]

When Joshua was about to conquer the land, he was commanded to remind the community of their covenant relation with God. The males were to be circumcised as a sign of that covenant (Joshua 5:2-3). After the victory at Ai, Joshua wrote the law as Moses had done and commanded, and he reviewed the blessings and the curses of the covenant before the entire community (Joshua 8:31-35). Before his death, he charged the leaders to keep the law of Moses, warning Israel of the consequences of idolatry (Joshua 23:6ff); then, before a convocation of the entire people, Joshua recounted the history of the covenant reminding them of their relationship with God. The community again pledged their loyalty to God and his covenant (Joshua 24).

The rise of the monarchy marks the end of the old tribal organization. Samuel, in appointing a king, reiterates that the covenant with God is still binding. The people must continue their loyalty to God who is still the ultimate authority (I Samuel 12:14-15). At the dedication of the Temple in Jerusalem by Solomon, the covenant at Sinai, as well as the covenant with David and his house, is restated (I Kings 8:23). All of Israel's military and political troubles are defined in terms of covenant breaking by acts of idolatry (cf. II Kings 17:7-12)

People and Holiness

Holiness is defined as "...hallowed, set apart..."[30] When Israel accepted God, regarded as holy, they became a people set apart, unique, holy according to biblical thought. Israel was to be a "... kingdom of priests and a holy nation" (Exodus 19:6). The entire people was to be responsible for its actions, not merely the king or priests. Israel was to be God's people, his possession, and became sanctified by observing the commands of God. Leviticus 19 defines holiness as fearing one's parents (verse 3), keeping the Sabbath (verse 3), not performing any idolatrous act (verse 4), observing the ritual and cult (verses 5-8), and maintaining a just society (verses 9-20). Israel was to be separated from the rest of the nations by its special relation with God. The observance of the commandments was to lead to the achievement of holiness (Leviticus 20:26; Deuteronomy 14:2).

The Individual and the Community

At first the communal aspect of the understanding of responsibility played a greater part than its individual aspect. With corporate responsibility came the corollary that any individual who sinned could affect the entire community. The individual participated in the blessing brought through his relationship to the community.[31] Men were unified by a common will which was received in terms of dedication to the covenant [32] hence, a sinful act might dissolve the common will which in turn could lead to the dissolution of the community.[33] With the coming of monarchy, increasing urbanization of the population, and the rise of prophecy, the individual was no longer able to be related to God through the tribal community since it no longer existed per se. He now related to God directly and owed him exclusive alliance.[34]

Covenant and Authority

The history of Israel was told in terms of the success or failure of its leaders' loyalty to the covenant. All valid authority emanated from God: leaders were messengers transmitting divine authority.[35] Prestige in times of victory went to God and never to the leaders.[36] As the king's power and prestige increased, God was regarded as more transcendent and seemed to be less relevant to the everyday life of the individual. The message of the prophets was to counter this tendency. Jeremiah, for example, empasized man's relationship to God through word, rather than through impersonal ritual.[37]

Ideally, political authority was to be synonymous with God's authority. God, as the supreme ruler, promised leadership and protection in return for exclusive loyalty on the part of the people.[38] Psalm 23 expresses the biblical conception of the ideal leader, i.e., God. There are two motifs in this psalm, of a shepherd and a host. Verse 1 opens with a picture of nomadic life which was regarded as the ideal by the prophets who saw such a life as a reflection of Israel's wandering in the wilderness with God as the shepherd and guide. The good shepherd leads his sheep (he is at the head of the flock; the sheep follow him because they have confidence in him), to good pasture where there is shade. He leads them to gentle flowing waters to that they can quench their thirst.

He turns his flock away from an evil direction — the function of the leader is to lead his people on righteous paths. In verse 3 the shepherd leads his sheep on smooth paths. Since this is a voluntary relationship, God leads, and it is up to man to follow. He so acts because this is his essence; the word in Hebrew for righteousness, tzedek, also can mean victory; thus, righteousness must ultimately be victorious. God acts in this manner because he is essentially righteous; he cannot act in any other way, even though man may not deserve it.

Although he tries to lead the flock on smooth paths, sometimes other ways are unavoidable. If the flock must go through a very dark valley where the step is unsure (the usual translation, "through the valley of the shadow of death," is incorrect), the flock need not fear because God is with it. Before this verse the psalmist uses the third person for the shepherd and the first person for the flock. When he is to walk through the dark valley the psalmist states he does not fear because, "You are with me." The moment he comes into a situation of fear and danger, his relationship to God changes from the third person ("he"), an impersonal relationship, to the second person ("you"), implying a most intimate relationship between the leader and his subjects.

The psalmist has confidence in the symbols of God's authority (verse 4, "your rod and your staff"). In verse 5 the image of the leader changes from shepherd to host who is duty-bound to protect his guest; God is his protector (as host). He spreads a meal for him, excluding his enemies. God is a generous host, as symbolized by the overflowing cup, i.e., he lacks nothing. As a result of the psalmist's confidence in God, good, instead of the enemy, pursues him (verse 6). The Bible's description of the good leader includes protection, love and trust.

Human leaders, appointed by God, were to be his agents and were to have no will of their own while leading the community. The choice of the leader was quite arbitrary. There were no special qualifications of class, power, or training. On the contrary, the leaders usually came from very low stock. He who possessed charisma which emanates from God is regarded as the leader.[39] The authorization for leadership emanated from God's "spirit". The community followed the leader as one and became one with him.[40] There were five types of leaders with this quality: the patriarch, the leaders (Moses and Joshua), the judge, the king (but not a successor, i.e., not a member of a dynasty, only the founder), and the prophet.[41]

The patriarch was really not a leader, since he had no people to lead. However, not only did he have the qualities of a leader, but he was the "father" of a people. His fatherhood was commanded by God.[42]

God placed some of the authority of Moses upon the elders so that they, too, would be able to carry out certain leadership roles (Numbers 11:18). While Joshua received the mandate of leadership from Moses, it was God who charged Joshua with authority (Deuteronomy 31:7-8, 23). At the beginning of Joshua's rule, God spoke to him and renewed their partnership (Joshua 1:1). Later Joshua's authority was demonstrated before the people by his performance of signs similar to those performed by Moses, e.g., the splitting of the Jordan River (Joshua 4:14; 3:13). God promised Joshua that he would remain with him (Joshua 1:5-9). Through his personal relationship with God, Joshua's leadership was recognized (Joshua 1:16-18). When Joshua died there was complete decentralization of authority and administration. The threat of external forces and Israel's need to free itself from foreign oppression, brought about the rise of judges who led the people to victory. But this occurred only after national repentance, when the people would again dedicate themselves to the covenant.

God appeared to the judge and told him that he was to lead the people (e.g., the appointment of Gideon, Judges 6:12). Because of the temporary nature of such leadership, there was no centrality: "In those days there was no king in Israel; every man did what seemed right in his own eyes" (Judges 17:6).

Samuel's leadership marked the beginning of a tendency toward centrality, for it was continuous and widely recognized. Perhaps this was due to Samuel's dual role as priest and prophet, thus having cultic and political authority. The shift from the temporary character of the leadership of the judge to the permanent character of the king's authority was gradual. Saul was appointed at first not as king but as chief, a role similar to that of the judge.[43]

God, as the true king, anointed, through his agent, a prophet, an earthly king, who would have enough power and authority to unify the people and fight off their enemies. In Deuteronomy we find provisions for kingship which were to be established with reluctance. The text emphasizes that God would choose the king who was to be familiar with the laws so that he would be able to judge the people and use his authority to uphold the covenant (Deuteronomy 17:14-20).

It is important to note that the biblical authors did not agree about their attitude towards monarchy. The final redaction of the Bible preserves contrary attitudes concerning ther appointment of the first king, some that are pro-monarchic and definitely anti-monarchic.

The people prevail upon Samuel to provide them with a king to free them from Philistine domination. Against the institution of monarchy because he perceives it as a challenge to God's authority, Samuel feared that the fidelity of the people to God would be eclipsed by their loyalty to the king (I Samuel 8). Saul's appointment as king was accepted by the people because he had the same charisma typical of their previous leaders, i.e., his rule was authorized by God through the manifestation of "spirit".[44]

God's personal relationship with Saul, the first king, functioned as a covenant; God promised to support and protect the leader as long as he maintained loyalty to God. After Saul proved himself in battle, he was again declared king by the people (I Samuel 11:15). The relationship between Saul and the people also existed by agreement — they accepted him as God's anointed. When Saul sinned by breaking the covenant with God, God rejected him. As soon as the "spirit of God" lifted from Saul, it rested on David (I Samuel 16:14). David, too, derived his authority from his appointment by God, who made a covenant with him (II Samuel 7:16f). David assured God of his faith and loyalty (II Samuel 7:22).

Because it was believed that David's house would rule forever, a sense of security pervaded the land.[45] The prophets did not threaten David's line with destruction even though many of the kings after David were corrupt. It was unthinkable to them that God would break his covenant with the Davidic dynasty. However, with the corruption of the monarchy it was difficult to conceive that a just God could support it.

During the eighth century, B.C.E., the prophets revived the Mosaic covenant, which was contingent on Israel's loyalty to God. The echo of Sinai resounded through the very dialogic form of their prophecies. The contrast between God's acts of benevolence in the past and Israel's disobedience would result in the fulfillment of the curse leading to the ultimate destruction of the state. Dependence on sacrificial rites rather than reliance on social responsibilities to fulfill the covenant was attacked. The sacrifices were meant to be symbolic of God's covenant relationship with Israel. Recalling Israel's history during the time of Moses the prophets emphasized the covenant at Sinai. Hope in David's dynasty would not save Israel without loyalty to the covenant.

Restricting the Leaders

Buber excludes those who were not directly appointed by God from his definition of the biblical leader.[46] He states that " . . . biblical leadership always means a process of being led."[47] The leader was to follow God's commands, and was praised only insofar as he fulfilled them. He had a personal covenant with God to uphold the covenant of the community.[48]

The leader was required to maintain his loyalty to the covenant of Sinai. Joshua was praised as a good leader because he kept the law (Joshua 11:12, 15). Before Gideon could achieve leadership he had to throw down the pagan altars in his father's house, demonstrating his loyalty to the covenant (Judges 6:25-26). After Gideon led the Israelites to victory, they asked him to be king, but he refused stating that only God could be king over Israel (Judges 8:22-23). Jeptha's sacrifice of his daughter was his demonstration that neither he nor his family had pretensions to rulership. It was a declaration that only God's rule was legitimate.

With his introduction of the kingship Samuel reminded Israel that its real king was God. The earthly king was appointed by God and ruled only because he had God's consent (I Samuel 12:12f).[49]

The meek (e.g., Saul) and the humble (e.g., Jeptha) were chosen to lead rather than the strong (even Samson, in a sense, was weak because he was easily tempted by women). Older sons, the natural heirs to the office of family Patriarch, were rejected. Abel, Isaac, Jacob, Joseph, Moses, David and Solomon were not the eldest — most of them were the youngest in the family.[50] Perhaps the eldest was not chosen because leadership was to be a result of God's command rather than of expectations based on birth order. The eldest could not claim that he was to lead because he came first. The only legitimate claims could be God's command; nothing else was acceptable.

The king was primarily a military authority with very limited religious functions. As the servant of the God of the covenant, he was to uphold and execute divine decrees (Psalm 2:10-11). He could not legislate against these decrees — there was no room for a rival human power to God in the Israelite system.[51]

While the kings had to follow the law, and to justify their acts according to the law, at times they perverted its meaning (I Kings 2:28-34 which follows Exodus 21:14; I Kings 22:5f, especially 26:27 and Deuteronomy 24:16). Even Jezebel tried to use the law to achieve her goals (I Kings 21:8).[52]

The king was still vulnerable to the criticism of the prophets when he was disloyal to the covenant. David was a successful leader because he was charismatic, having been appointed by God. By bringing the ark to Jerusalem, thus enhancing the priests' position, he was on good terms with the priesthood as well. He listened to the elders of the community, yet always acquiesced to the demands of the prophets, Samuel and Nathan. David's reign proved that it was possible for the institution of monarchy to work within the demands of a covenant community.[53] He never tried to usurp the role of the priest as Saul (I Samuel 13:9), and Uzziah (II Chronicles 26:18f). He was allowed to participate in the cult in a limited way, like Solomon (I Kings 8:5 — probably because of the special occasion of the dedication of the Temple which Solomon had built). The Israelite king had no divine functions like his Babylonian counterpart who was the intermediary between the gods and the people; this function was held only by the priests in Israel. The king's special task was to defend his people against foreign invasion.[54]

Covenants Between the Leaders and the People

Dynasties were established and sustained until the covenant was broken either by the people or by the leader. While the word, "covenant", is not customarily used, the description of the relationship between the leader and the people in terms of obligations and duties on both sides is inherently covenantal.

The relationship is always contingent on the leader's covenant with God, whose purpose and will was to be manifested through the acts of the rulers.[55] The leader was to execute God's word and represent the people in pleas for mercy or protection.[56] Moses acted in this role (Deuteronomy 5:24-28). Joshua was appointed leader before all the people in order that they would accept him, and agree to his rule over them (Numbers 27:18-23).

The leader's role as the judge of his people (which is the role of the king as well, (cf. I Kings 7:7, 3:16-28), expressed the covenant relationship that he represented; he was to judge the people according to the covenant. Hence, the codification of the Pentateuch came with the monarch which served to emphasize the primal covenant between God and the people, having precedence over their relationship with the king.[57]

Kingship was established by covenant, for Israel was bound by an oath to obey the king. God, the witness to this oath, promised to maintain the Davidic line (II Samuel 23:5).[58] David made a covenant with the people before he assumed the kingship (II Samuel 5:33, 3:21). After Ataliah (the only monarch to have usurped the throne of Judah) was deposed, a new covenant had to be made between the people and the monarch, for the Davidic line had been broken (II Kings 11:17). The covenant was renewed in a three-fold manner:

1. God and the new king renew the covenant insuring the Davidic line;

2. the people and God renew their covenant;[59]

3. the king and the people again agree that the authority is to be vested in God.[60]

Covenant and Cultic Authority: The Priesthood

The priests exercised power through their control of the temple cult and treasury and as advisors to the king. That they were not to own land according to Mosaic law might be construed as a restriction of their power.[61] The task of the priests was to keep the law, teach it (Leviticus 10:11; Deuteronomy 33:10; Ezekiel 44:23f; II Chronicles 15:3), and be in charge of the cult. The priesthood was established under Aaron and his family to serve in the tabernacle and supervise the sacrifices offered there (Exodus 28:1, 43).

The priests' role as teachers fit into the covenant scheme. It was the priest who, as the cultic mediator between the community and God, was to explain the covenant and its demands to the people.[62] In contrast to the prophets, the priests emphasized that God was to be approached mainly through the cult under their control, thus demonstrating preference for formal worship over intimate personal prayer.[63] While the prophets worked to have the law and covenant internalized in the hearts of the people, the priests emphasized a piety expressed ritually as well as ethically.[64]

Through ceremonies and rituals, the priests attempted to maintain the remembrance of the covenant.[65] They protected the sacred teachings and the ethical content of the religious life of the community. In their emphasis on God's otherness, they tended to be conservative and perceived a static quality in the permanent order of the world.[66] Often they came into conflict with the prophets who demanded radical change in the behavior of the people. The ritual, according to the prophets, had become an end unto itself, instead of a reminder of the covenant.

Covenant and the Prophet

The prophet was God's spokesman[67] and representative. With the continual concentration of political power in the king came a gradual weakening of reliance on god. The kings, for the most part, did not experience divine revelation, for they probably did not perceive any need to seek God's aid. God's will was then expressed through the words of the prophets.

The difference between the prophet and leader was that while at times divine power filled the leader propelling him to outward action utilizing the force granted through his office to execute his will, the prophets did not have institutionalized force at their disposal. While we have an expression of inward experiences, especially with the later prophets, they often used quite violent means to fulfill their goals.[68] Since these inward experiences brought them to understand God's will and inspired them to preach what they had learned, the prophet was regarded as God's agent attempting to insure the manifestation of God's will.

The prophetic political outlook had to conform to religious standards, i.e., a determination of the relation between a specific policy and God's will as expressed in the covenant. It assumed that God had ordained everything and that Israel must submit to his will to be loyal to the covenant. The prophet perceived that he stood before a dissolving community attempting to save it from destruction. He pointed to the covenant, which was to be regarded above all other loyalties. He never complained against the structure or function of political authority. He never preached against kingship, but against specific acts of kings which turned the people away from the covenant.

The prophetic announcements of doom and destruction were conditional upon the actions of the people: if there was a sincere return to the covenant, disaster could be averted.[69] The prophetic message was not new to the people. It spoke of the continuing covenantal relationship with God.[70] The prophetic exhortation to keep the covenant was based upon a long traditon of covenant content and its

observance. The prophets castigated the people for breaking covenant promises.[71] In II Kings 17:13 it is explicitly stated that:

> The Lord had warned Israel and Judah, by
> means of all the prophets, every seer, saying, turn
> back from your evil ways, and keep my command-
> ments and my statutes, in accordance with all the
> law which I commanded your fathers, and which I
> have sent to you by means of my servants, the
> prophets.

Kings, Priests and Prophets

The specific forms of government were evidently not a concern to
biblical authors. The judge rose to save the community from its enemies and then receded. The monarchy was established only for military purposes, i.e., to centralize the community so that it would be
able to effectively deal with its foes on a long-range basis. Before the
onset of the monarchy, the structure of government was so loose, that
most scholars are amazed that the community was ever able to survive not only military threat, but threat of cultural assimilation as
well.

The monarchy crystalized the form of government into one institution limited in scope. The king was severely admonished if he
overstepped his jurisdiction. The monarch always had to remember
that he acted only to help protect the community so that it could
carry out its covenantal responsibilities. But the institution of monarchy led to increasing political centralization that was much more limiting than the temporary centralization under the judges. In order to
enhance the king's control, tribal boundaries were replaced by a
royal administration that crossed old borders. Provincial governors
were appointed by the king and hence were loyal to the central government.

The king was largely secularized over time. He hardly participated in the cult and had no status in the ritual which was jealously
guarded by the priesthood. Unlike his predecessors, he was not
appointed directly by God (unless he was the founder of a dynasty),
and had no direct relationship with God.

The theology of the Davidic covenant and priestly conceptions of
the role of the cult largely supported the monarchic system. The
priests regarded themselves as intermediaries between man and God
who was transcendent. People could relate to God through the cult,
i.e., through the priests. The king's position was secured through the
concept of God's covenant with David insuring the dynasty forever.

As a consequence of these two theological concepts, the covenant
of Sinai receded. The theology of the Sinai covenant had emphasized

God's immanence and direct relationship with the people as well as the continual responsibility of the community to maintain the covenant. By relying on the king and the priesthood to fulfill these responsibilities, the people felt no need to adhere to the covenant. The added security of God's unconditional guarantee to the Davidic dynasty further eroded the power of the Sinai covenant.

However, many other factors had served to erode community consciousness. Increased urbanization (especially from the eighth through sixth centuries, B.C.E.) and the centralization of the government and cult in Jerusalem led to a weakening of national identity. The gap between the rich and the poor increased with absentee landlords and impoverished tenant farmers, many of whom fled to the city as they lost their lands, there forming an urban proletariat.

The royal policy of alliances with various nations and the increase in trade resulted in a cosmopolitan atmosphere in Jerusalem which fostered a fascination with foreign cultures and cults. Fetishistic practices flourished, symptomatic of a society experiencing change, looking to the outside, not for a new faith but to fulfill the desire to become more cosmopolitan.

In contrast, the Sinai covenant had emphasized that each individual, no matter what his social status, had the *same* obligations vis-a-vis the covenant. Each was responsible for the observance of the terms of the covenant whether he be king, priest, rich or poor.

With increasing urbanization came a growing awareness of individuality, manifesting itself in the weakening of communal responsibilities. Each man pursued his own gain without respect for others. However, the prophets, in decrying this tendency, were paradoxically the most outstanding examples of individuals standing up against the entire community. On the one hand, they stood apart from the community, castigating, warning and admonishing. On the other, they were full members of their community, pleading to God to save it from destruction.

Recognizing that a return to the old order was no longer possible, the prophets sought to create a new order, a new covenant (Jeremiah uses this very term), that would internalize the pre-monarchic covenantal forms and responsibilities. Previously, the individual was to lose himself by totally identifying himself with the covenant community. Jeremiah realized that a new covenant was necessary which would imprint the Sinai covenant in the heart of every individual. There was to be no hierarchy which might compete with the authority of one God. The very legal structure was egalitarian. The prophets preached against any legal privileges because of rank or social status. Everyone had the same rights and obligations in relation to the covenant.

NOTES

1. All references to the Bible refer to the Old Testament: i.e., the Jewish canon of the Bible. The material on the biblical concept of covenant is extracted from Gordon M. Freeman, "Political Theory in the Bible: A Study of Covenant (unpublished Master's dissertation, Department of Government, New York University, 1966).

2. George E. Mendenhall, *Law and Covenant in Israel and the Ancient Near East*, (reprinted from the *The Biblical Arhaeologist*, XVII, No. 2 (May, 1954), and No. 3 (September, 1954) by the Presbyterian Board of Colportage at Western Pennsylvania, 1955) 5a. Hereafter cited as *Law*.

3. James Muilenberg, "Form and Structure of the Covenantal Formulation," *Vetus Testamentum*, IX (1959), p. 365.

4. George E. Mendenhall, "Covenant", *The Interpreter's Dictionary of the Bible*, I, p. 714.

5. Mendenhall, *Law*, p. 31.

6. *Ibid.*, p. 28f.

7. *Ibid.*, p. 32.

8. *Ibid.*, p. 37f. But see Dennis T. McCarthy, *Treaty and Covenant, Analecta Biblica*, XXI (Rome: Pontifical Biblical Institute, 1963), p. 166f. He states that the Sinai event in Exodus 19 lacks the essential blessings and curses of covenantal forms.

9. Mendenhall, *Law*, p. 36.

10. Brevard Childs, *Memory and Tradition in Israel* (London: SCM Press, 1960), p. 43.

11. Martin Noth, *The History of Israel* (New York: Harper and Brothers, 1958), p. 49.

12. Yehezkel Kaufmann, *Toldot Ha'emunah Hayisraelit*, 4 vols. (Jerusalem: Mosad Bialik, 1960), I, p. 5.

13. W. Eichrodt, *Theology of the Old Testament*. Trans. J. A. Baker (Philadelphia: The Westminster Press, 1961), I, p. 287.

14. Paul Ramsey, "Elements of a Biblical Political Theory," *Journal of Religion*, XXIX, No. 4 (October, 1949), p. 260.

15. *Ibid.*, p. 265.

16. As contrasted to the gods who were bound and limited by external forces, e.g., fate.

17. Mendenhall, *Law*, p. 3. Biblical Antecedents

18. Gerhard von Rad, *Old Testament Theory*. Trans. O. Stalker (Edinburgh: Oliver and Boyd, 1963), I, p. 95.

19. H.S. Nahmani, *Human Rights in the Old Testament* (Tel Aviv: Joshua Chachick Publishing House, 1964, p. 48f.

20. William F. Albright, *From the Stone Age to Christianity* (New York: Doubleday and Co., 1957), p. 268; Alt, *Der Gott der Vaeter* as quoted in Martin Buber, *The Prophetic Faith* (New York: Harper and Bros., 1960). p. 54.

21. Buber, *The Prophetic Faith*, p. 55, (*melekh* used in the quote means king).

22. *Ibid.*.

23. Eichrodt, p. 74f.

24. Buber, *The Prophetic Faith*, Chapter 5.

25. Nahmani, p. 93.

26. G. E. Wright, *Biblical Archaeology* (Philadelphia: The Westminster Press, 1957), p. 55.

27. J. Pedersen, *Israel: Its Life and Culture* (London, 1959), II, p. 286.

28. John Bright, *A History of Israel* (Philadelphia: The Westminster Press, 1959), p. 143f.

29. Buber, *The Prophetic Faith*, p. 15.

30. *Ibid.*, p. 48.

31. Pedersen, II, p. 263.

32. *Ibid.*, I, p. 165.

33. *Ibid.*, II, p. 417.

34. George E. Mendenhall, "The Relation of the Individual to Political Society in Ancient Israel," *Biblical Studies in Memory of H.C. Allerman* (New York: Augustin Publishers, 1960), p. 100. Later Christian Protestant thought also emphasized the direct

relationship with God (rather than through a church hierarchy). We must remember that one of the great influences on Protestant thought was the Old Testament, the study of which was encouraged by Protestant leaders. This concept of direct relationship affected Protestant political perceptions of authority. Locke, for example, emphasizes the necessity of consent. Political authority is not legitimate unless it has the consent of the governed. Direct relationship with God was emphasized by the rabbis who also came to the same conclusion, i.e., agreement of the people was needed in order that God's authority be manifested in the community. See, for example, *Mekhilta*, II, p. 229f.

35. *Ibid.*, p. 101.

36. *Ibid.*

37. Buber, *The Prophetic Faith*, p. 164.

38. Wright, p. 78f and Martin Buber, "Biblical Leadership," *Israel and the World* (New York: Schocken Books, 1948), p. 128. Hereafter cited as "'Leadership". This is especially evident with early leaders such as Moses, Joshua, Samuel, etc.

39. Pedersen, III, p. 34.

40. *Ibid.*, p. 40.

41. Buber, "Leadership," p. 127.

42. *Ibid.*, p. 127.

43. Bright, p. 169.

44. Eichrodt. p. 443.

45. Mendenhall, *Law,* p. 46.

46. Buber, "Leadership," p. 122.

47. *Ibid.*, p. 132.

48. Jacob Agus, *The Evolution of Jewish Thought* (New York: Abelard-Schuman, 1959), p. 20.

49. Buber, "Leadership," p. 124.

50. Eichrodt, p. 439.

51. S. Yeivin, "The Administration in Ancient Israel,: *The Kingdom of Israel and Judah*, Edited by A. Malamat (Jerusalem: Israel Exploration Society, 1961), p. 58.

52. Eichrodt, p. 443ff.

53. I. Mendelsohn, "Canaan-Israel," *Authority and Law in the Ancient Orient* (supplement to *Journal of the American Oriental Society,* no. 17 (1954), p. 27.

54. Pedersen, III, p. 39.

55. Eichrodt, p. 192.

56. Mendenhall, *Law,* p. 15. Biblical Antecedents

57. *Ibid.*, p. 45f.

58. Actually, the people reiterates its dedication to God's covenant at Sinai. Since God had not broken the covenant, he was not directly involved in this covenant reaffirmation.

59. John Gray, *I and II Kings: A Commentary* (Philadelphia: The Westminster Press, 1963), p. 523.

60. Nahmani, p. 140.

61. Jacob Hoschander, *the Priest and the Prophets* (New York: The Jewish Theological Seminary of America, 1938), p. 70.

62. Eichrodt, p. 407.

63. *Ibid.*, p. 416.

64. Hoschander, p. 69.

65. Eichrodt, p. 433.

66. Harry Orlinsky, *Ancient Israel* (Ithaca: Cornell University Press, 1954), p. 143.

67. Max Weber, *Ancient Israel*. Translated and edited by H. Gerth and D. Martindale (Glencoe: The Free Press, 1952), p. 319. See also David Daube, *Civil Disobedience in Antiquity* (Edinburgh: The University Press, 1972), p. 64, 105.

68. Hoschander, p. 143.

69. Eichrodt, p. 300.

70. R. E. Clements, *Prophecy and Covenant* (London: SCM Press, 1965), p. 23f.

71. Mendenhall, *Law,* p. 19.

CHAPTER 2:
THE LANGUAGE OF COVENANT
AND ITS TRANSFORMATION

While covenant, in its operational sense, functioned to insure the legitimacy of individual partners while binding them in relationship, it must be emphasized that the covenants were exclusive. The main characteristic of this relationship was that it excluded other possibilities. For example, in the marriage covenant, specific conditions were set limiting like relationships with others. To enter such a relationship outside those conditions of the covenant would mean that the covenant had been breached. A series of negative consequences would then flow as a result of the breach.

Political language reflects the exclusive nature of covenant. Language is the communicative connection that creates community; communities can be perceived as established within language boundaries that exclude others not using the same language. Language then becomes the code, the means of mutual recognition to determine those within and outside the community. Each community has its own *shibboleth* which separates, through language, citizens from aliens, home-born from strangers, members from non-members.

Of course there are many other determinants of community — shared experience (history) and observances to name but a few. However, since covenant traditions originate and find their meaning in literary documents, it is well to examine how covenant language operates to bind community as well as polemicize to exclude and define those beyond its secure boundaries. The polemic had many purposes. First, it functioned to legitimize the community; that is, it answered the question why a specific community should maintain its identity rather than assimilate and cease to exist as a separate entity. The very language of covenant justified the existence of the polity. It also defined the community by determining who was to be included and who was not. Finally, covenant laguage used polemically tended to socialize individuals into the community context, bolstering morale by defining meaning in terms of membership.

Polemic of Covenant Terminology

While the faith of Talmudic Judaism was based on the Bible,[1] there were changes in the terminology used for the covenant concept. Such changes reflect a shift in the historical conditions and a refined application of the implications of the covenant.

The Bible is concerned with national survival and hegemony. The various political systems from Judges to Kings deal with the problems of a nascent state confronted with the real threat of foreign invasion and conquest. The integrity of leadership and its policy were measured in terms of the covenant. After the first destruction of the temple, the prophetic message was clear. Israel could survive without a state and without a political system as long as each member of the community adhered to the covenant. The second commonwealth was established and it, too, fell (70 C.E.). The Roman Empire seemed invincible. Political independence was not possible, yet the Jewish people could still survive.

With the traumatic discovery that reliance on a messianic pretender to defeat Rome would not succeed in fulfilling Jewish dreams of political independence, the rabbis in the second and third centuries did their best to salvage the saving remnant. These rabbinic leaders were faced with a people dispersed throughout the world, lacking the religious center of the temple to unify them. With political hopes dashed, the resulting depression could have led the people to seek other means of religious expression. Syncretistic cults, Greek mystery religions, the youthful Christianity and the various Gnostic sects competed for Jewish souls. Without a king, high priest, or messiah, there seemed to be no religious authority to which the people could turn.

The rabbis attempted to fill the gap by establishing themselves as the legitimate inheritors of the priests and the prophets. New conditions required an adherence to the national belief system without land or compulsion. The rabbinic answer was the same as that of the prophets after the destruction of the first commonwealth: adherence to the covenant would guarantee the revival of the Jewish people.

Indoctrination of religious beliefs and practice was to be accomplished through the universal study of God's Torah, the content of revelation. Although this program probably had its beginning even while the second temple still stood, competing authorities (cult and apocalyptic messianism) served to undermine it. Now that these other forces had failed, study of the Torah remained as the only legitimate method to guarantee the integrity of the people. The very change in covenant terminology expressed this awareness. In biblical literature the term for covenant was b'rit, a word which may have derived from either of two roots. Conceivably, it might be a parallel to the similar root in Arabic meaning, "to eat." The making of a covenant in the ancient near east was often accompanied by a covenant meal, a cultic ceremony at which sacrifices were offered to the deity, and the covenanting partners partook of the sacrificial offering. The other possible derivation could be from the root in Hebrew, "to cut." When a covenant was made the expression was usually stated in terms of "cutting a covenant," which probably referred to the act of cutting the terms of the covenant in some solid object, i.e., stone, so that the covenant would be permanent.[2] Even though this term might not be used in a specific context, the concept itself was recalled in other terminolgy. The word, *edut*, testimony, is a parallel expression. Also, words denoting oaths, the decalogue, etc., all refer to the covenant at Sinai.[3] Similarly, the Greek term, *symbolion* (from which our word, symbol, is derived) referred to the pieces of a ritually divided sacrifice that covenant participants used as a sign of their new relationship. The Latin term, *foedus,* (from which the word, federal, is derived) has a similar meaning that indicates cutting and binding.

Other covenant terminology emphasizes the operational character of biblical covenant. For example, *hesed*, meaning covenant love, describes the covenant relationship and its reciprocal and mutual nature. *Hesed* then, as a covenant term, was not used in the sense of gracious or arbitrary love.[4]

A case could be made that the verb, to speak (*dvr*) could mean to make an agreement or pledge based on an Akkadian parallel use of the term. In that sense, every time the text says *vay'daber*, usually translated as "and he spoke," should be understood as establishing the term or conditions of a covenant agreement.[5]

Martin Buber's studies of covenant also point to the operational function of biblical covenant terminology, emphasizing reciprocity. The "blood of the covenant," for example, links constituency and authority in a mutual manner. He points to the exclusive nature of covenant as a means of connecting God and Israel. The covenant cited in Isaiah 61:6-8, later used as a basis of the polemic between various groups claiming to be the new Israel, was originally used operationally, according to Buber, simply extending and applying the sense of universal priesthood found in Exodus 19, that all Israel will have a direct relationship with God.[6] Whereas the term, "new covenant" in Jeremiah 31:31-34 also forms the basis of later polemic, originally it was an operational term perhaps describing the hope for a complete socialization of the covenant so that there would no longer be a need for coercive force to maintain it.[7]

In rabbinic literature the term, *b'rit*, was used in a limited sense. it had the following four meanings:

1. circumcision;

2. indication of a Jew (*ben b'rit*) in contrast to a non-Jew;

3. reference to the written Torah as distinct from the oral Torah; also, it was used in the context of biblical quotations;

4. use as an expression of the truth of a statement, i.e., that of a fulfillment of a promise (as an oath).

1. In the Bible, the circumcision of Abraham (Genesis 17:9-14) is regarded as a mark or sign of the covenant God makes with him and his descendants. In rabbinic literature the circumcision itself is called *b'rit* or *b'rit milah* (the covenant of circumcision).[8] This use of *b'rit* at times is used to distinguish Jews from Christians and Jewish Helleni-

zers, the latter sometimes taking pains surgically to remove the signs of circumcision because of shame.

2. As an indication of the difference between Jew and Non-Jew, the term, *ben b'rit*, son of the covenant, is related to its reference to circumcision.[9]

3. The written Torah (Pentateuch) is separate from the oral Torah which the rabbis declared was given at the same instant in time.[10] As we will see below, the rabbis had to defend the legitimacy of their oral tradition. They claimed that their traditions were Torah even though they were not written at Sinai.

> Rabbi Levi bar Hama said in the name of Rabbi Shimon ben Levi: What does the passage, "And I will give to you the stone tablets and the Torah and the commandments which I wrote to teach them" (Exodus 24:12) (mean)? Tablets: these are the Ten Commandments. Torah: this is the Pentateuch. Commandments: this is the Mishnah. What I wrote: these are prophets and writings. To teach them: this is the Talmud to teach you that all were given to Moses from Sinai.(*Talmud Bavli Berachot* 5a; see also *Megilah* 19b in the name of Rabbi Hiyah bar Aba in the name of Rabbi Yohanan.)

> The laws (*hukim*): these are the interpretations (*midrashot*); The judgements (*mishpatim*): these are the laws (*dinim*); The Torah teaches that two Torahs were given to Israel, one written and one oral. Rabbi Akiba asked: Did Israel have but two Torahs, were not many Torahs given to Israel, (e.g.,) "this is the Torah of the whole-burnt offering," "this is the Torah of the meal offering," "this is the Torah of the guilt offering," "this is the Torah peace sacrifice," "this is the Torah in the case of the death of a person in an enclosed place". "which the Lord gave between him and the people of Israel": Moses merited being the agent between Israel and their father in heaven. "On Mount Sinai by the hand of Moses": teaches that the Torah, its laws (*halakhah*) and details (*dikduk*) and explanations (*perush*) were by the hand of Moses at Sinai. (*Sifra* 112b on Leviticus 26:46)[11]

The rabbis also claimed that their Torah was the equivalent of the *b'rit*.

> Covenant means Torah, as it is said: "But for my covenant of day and night." (Jeremiah 33:25) (*Talmud Bavli Shabbat* 33a).

> Great is circumcision, since, without it heaven and earth would not endure, as it is written: "But for my covenant of day and night" (Jeremiah 33:25). This conflicts with Rabbi Eleazar who said: Great is the Torah, since without it heaven and earth would not endure, as it is written: "But for my covenant of day and night". (*Talmud Bavli Nedarim* 32a).[12]

The dual meaning of the term, *b'rit*, in the general sense of covenant or specifically circumcision, becomes the crux of the polemic between rabbinic Jews and "covenant" sects which did not require circumcision (e.g., Christians).

4. People would swear by the *b'rit* as a form of popular oath.[13] A "covenant cut at the lips" expressed the effectiveness of a statement, the fulfillment of what had been said.[14]

The very multiplicity of the uses of this term as well as the paucity of sources where it is found (in relation to the vastness of rabbinic literature) in contrast to the many references the terms, "Torah" and "the giving of the Torah", is significant. That most of the references refer to circumcision might indicate a limitation. One reason there was a reluctance to use *b'rit* in its pervasive biblical sense could be that Christians claimed that they were the true inheritors of the covenant through the coming of Jesus. We know of sects and Jewish groups that used covenant terminology largely avoided by the rabbis. The latter substituted Torah for other covenant terms. For example, various Jewish sectaries, such as the Qumran sect and the Damascus sect of covenantors, used *b'rit* in their literature. The biblical covenant formulations appear repeatedly in their documents.[15]

The use of covenant in Apocryphal literature, New Testament and the Septuagint follows a similar pattern.[16] The New Testament uses the Greek word, *diatheke*, for covenant which is the exact word used in the Septuagint translation of the Jewish Bible. The term actually refers to a last will and testament and, like most translations, does not completely fit the word, *b'rit*, as covenant.[17] In fact, *diatheke* finds its way into Jewish law as a technical term for a will.[18] The point here is that *diatheke* is not understood as the equivalent of *b'rit* in rabbinic literature. Evidently the New Testament usage is a direct borrowing from the Septuagint. The same Greek word is used in the Apocryphal literature to describe *b'rit*. The Septuagint translators were hard pressed to find an equivalent to *b'rit* and settled upon *diatheke*, although this meaning is quite rare in Greek literature itself.[19]

B'rit and its Greek "equivalent," *diatheke*, were employed by various sects to demonstrate a renewal of the covenant of Israel, that they were the new Israel, replacing the Jewish people in this role.

Because of their sins, the Jews had been punished and rejected by God. It is the new group who now receives God's covenant.

The rabbis were careful to limit their use of *b'rit* most frequently utilizing the term as a reference to circumcision; the claims of those groups, that they were the inheritors of the covenant, was not legitimate because they did not require circumcision.

In substituting Torah for the covenant, the rabbis were demonstrating that by their study, interpretation and application of the Torah to life the Jewish people was the only group continuing and living according to the original covenant. The use of *b'rit* specifically as covenant was no longer necessary, since the covenant had once and for all bound God and Israel. Even though the Jewish people might have sinned and been punished, they were not rejected. The Jews were still bound to the covenant, as God was still bound to his covenant with the Jewish people, the Israel of the Bible. Renewal of the original covenant was not necessary.

We have seen that Torah was regarded as the equivalent of *b'rit*.[20] In the Septuagint Torah is translated, *nomos*, law. But throughout the Jewish Bible, in the prophets, wisdom literature and in Ezra, Torah means teaching in a general sense.

C. H. Dodd points to the Greek translation of Torah into *nomos* as a failure to relate its meaning. Torah for the Jews is the essence of religion, while *nomos* (law) does not express that essential quality at all. *Nomos* is custom which hardens into what is called law which does not even imply a legislative authority. "It is rather an immanent or underlying principle of life and action."[21] *Nomos* expresses the means to differentiate right and wrong as an eternal principle.[22] In contrast Torah is divine revelation or divine teaching, appealing "...to the heart, mind, and will."[23]

The apocryphal books of *Ben Sira* and *Barukh* identify *hokhma*, wisdom, with Torah which has the same sense as teaching.[24] Josephus uses wisdom in the same way, to refer to the *knowledge* of the laws and the interpretation of the Bible.[25] The rabbis, influenced perhaps by Hellenistic thought, used *hokhma* and identified it with Torah.[26]

In this sense of wisdom and teaching, Torah became the one element that united the community. Adherence to Torah, accomplished through prayer, study and observance, was what all Jews shared throughout the world. The rabbis referred to the event at Sinai as *matan Torah*, the giving of the Torah. This term and its equivalent (the Torah was given, the giving of the Torah, etc.) are found throughout rabbinic literature,[27] and appear in a wide variety of contexts.[28] Torah is dichotomized into written and oral Torah (*Talmud Bavli Shabbat* 31a; *Sifre* 145a). The Torah is even personified as a seeker after God's compassion for Israel (*Song of Songs Rabbah* 4:a6). It acts as a witness (*Lamentations Rabbah* 24). It cries before God

(*Esther Rabbah* 3:9). The expression, "Torah from heaven," refers to the revelation at Sinai.[29]

While writing was probably introduced to Israel by Moses (there is no indication of it earlier),[30] it was so innovative that "...the Bible repeatedly emphasizes that it was done by God himself (Exodus 24:12; 33:15-16), or by Moses upon the order of God (Exodus 17:14; 34:27; Deuteronomy 31:19)."[31] The written Torah was a holy relic reposing in the Ark of the Covenant.[32] But for the people at large oral instruction was the mode of Torah tradition. The written Torah acted as a witness, the oral instruction of the people developed into a tradition parallel to the written Torah. The learning of the covenant was accomplished through memorization, knot symbols and mnemonics as well as by writing.[33]

In *Mishnah Avot* 1:1 a chain of tradition is recorded. "Moses received the Torah from Sinai, handed it to Joshua, who handed it to the elders, the elders to the prophets, the prophets to the men of the great assembly..." etc., to the contemporaneous rabbis.[34] Even though the Torah had already been written, it had to "...be confirmed by witnesses of oral transmission," i.e., by the chain of tradition.[35] While this might seem strange to the modern reader, where oral traditions must be confirmed by written documents, in Jewish law the "oral tradition...was treated as the testimony of a witness."[36] The oral tradition was understood to be as ancient as the written one and functioned as a contemporaneous witness to its veracity.

Challenge and Response to Sectarian Groups

There were many different groups that were regarded by the rabbis as separate sects challenging the legitimacy of the oral tradition, i.e., rabbinic Judaism. We have seen how significant the uses of terminology were in emphasizing those claims. Whether sects of Gnostic, apocalyptic or Christian thought, they were all comprised of Jews challenging the authority of the rabbis and their interpretation of tradition. Israel, they claimed, had been rejected by God. They (the specific sect) were the new Israel with whom God had made a new covenant.

Often these sects set out to find potential new members, Jews and non-Jews, to proselytize and convert. Their good, new and glad tidings were not to be kept to themselves. Rather, they felt the responsibility to save the world so that everyone could be redeemed. They felt compelled to attack the old Israel when prospective converts would point to the Jewish people and ask how these new groups could claim to have the covenant when the very inheritors of the old covenant were still present in their midst. In rebuttal, the sectarian would point to the apparent rejection of Israel by God. For surely, if God still loved Israel, he would not have allowed her to be defeated in such a disastrous manner. The new sect claimed to have captured God's favor in place of the Jewish people.

The attack against the Jewish people had yet another motivation. The strategy of the sect would be to attempt to convert the Jewish people to its teaching. If widespread Jewish support was forthcoming, then it would give the new teaching legitimacy and respectability. If God's chosen people accepted the new teaching then it would be as if God's covenant was transferred to it. However, in attempting to maintain the integrity of rabbinic Judaism, the rabbis rejected the teachings of such groups. The wrath of the rejected sectarians was harsh. They would take advantage of any place of power to exact punishment agains the Jewish people. There were others who, while not Jewish themselves, were sympathetic to Judaism and the Jewish people. These were recognized by the rabbis as "fearers of heaven" — semi proselytes, who understood Judaism and perhaps observed some of the rituals, but were not ready for one reason or another to formally convert to Judaism. Some even attended local synagogues.[37] To the rabbis however, a sectarian, a *min*, was a heretical Jew, who rejected the divine origin of both the Torah and its oral traditions; a belief which held the covenants together; to believe otherwise would cause one to fall outside of the community.

> Rabbi Yohanan and Rabbi Yudan ben Shimon: one said, if you observe that which is oral as well as observing that which is written I will cut a covenant with you; and if not I will not cut a covenant with you. Hurana said: if you observe that which is oral and observe that which is written you will receive reward; if not you will not receive reward. Rabbi Joshua ben Levi said: all of these, Torah, *Mishnah*, *Talmud*, lore (*agadah*) and even that which will be taught in the future has already been said to Moses from Sinai. (*Talmud Yerushalmi Megilah* 4:1, see also *Talmud Yerushalmi Peah* 2:6).
>
> "Because he despised the word of the Lord"; This (refers to) one who says the Torah is not from heaven, even if he said all the Torah is from heaven except for this verse that was not said by the Holy One, Blessed be He, but by Moses on his own (i.e., not authorized by God). And even if he says, except for this one single point, or the rule from the simple case, how much the more in a complex case (*kal v'homer*) or the rule of comparing word contexts (*g'zerah shava*) he is included (in those who will be

cut off) "because he has despised the word of the Lord." (*Talmud Bavli Sanhedrin* 99a on Numbers 15:31).[38]

The response of the rabbis to the sectarian challenge was varied. Primarily, there was a determined declaration that the cause of Israel's troubles was her sins. Israel was being punished, but that, in itself, explains how God is maintaining his covenant. He certainly would not chastise an unwanted child; he would merely cast him out in rejection. It was comforting to Israel to be told that it was God and not the might of the Roman Empire which brought on Israel's calamity.[39] The reverse of this explanation was also believed, that Israel's righteous deeds would bring redemption. In other words, Israel's destiny was in her own hands. It is important to note that each Jewish group claiming legitimacy used similar polemical arguments but supplied their own explanation of how redemption would be effectuated.

The Christians tried to demonstrate that the Jews were not chosen to begin with. They claimed that they were the spiritual descendants of Abraham. *Sifre* on Deuteronomy 32:9 section 312 (and parallels) is an answer to Paul's own *midrash* in Romans 4:4f that God chose Abraham.[40] The *Sifre* emphasizes that God chose Jacob, and Jacob chose God; the relationship is mutual, reciprocal. In the passage from Romans, Paul declares that God chooses Abraham, but reciprocity is not involved; it is a covenant of grace.[41]

In *Genesis Rabbah* 38:13 the *midrash* takes pains to cite a legend to demonstrate that Abraham chose God by the way he lived before God spoke to him. Abraham merited the covenant. The tendency of the rabbis, for the most part, was to reject the covenant of grace as it had been rejected previously by the prophets, even to the point of anachronistically reading into the life of Abraham legends that pointed to his righteousness before God chose him. The Sinai covenant with its concept of inherent reciprocity became the primary covenant form. The *Sifre* passage followed the same covenant pattern: God chose Jacob, and Jacob chose God; the covenant relationship is reciprocal. Jacob deserved the covenant, an explicit rejection of the covenant of grace, i.e., that the recipient received the gift of grace because of God's love.

In the *Epistle of Barnabas*, chapter 14, another challenge was presented to Israel. Since Israel had rejected God by worshipping the golden calf, God in turn rejected Israel. The commandments were Israel's punishment.[42] The golden calf incident was cited in answer to the problem of the status of Israel in relationship to the Christians after the coming of Jesus. The *Sifre* passage answered this challenge by citing an unambiguous quote (Deuteronomy 14:2) that God chose

Israel again after the golden calf, and that the commandments were not given in punishment. What is emphasized here is that choice is made on the basis of merit rather than grace, because Israel chose God at the same time that God chose Israel.[43]

Chapter 16 of the *Epistle of Barnabas* referred to the destruction of the Temple as further proof of God's rejection of Israel. In reply, the *Sifre* passage quotes Jeremiah 10:16 to the effect that God's promise would continue into the future. Israel's suffering was a sign of chastisement rather than rejection.[44]

The rabbinic polemic against the Christians occurred after the year 90 C.E. as a direct response to the publishing of Paul's letters (between 90 and 100).[45] The polemic was directed against the acceptance of the "heavenly voice" (*bat kol*) as proof of an argument of Rabbi Eliezer ben Hyrcanus in the academy (*Talmud Bavli Bava Metzia* 59b), although the heavenly voice had been accepted earlier in the disputes between Hillel and Shammai. It has been suggested that the reason for Rabbi Eliezer's excommunication was due to his insistence on allowing evidence from a "heavenly voice," whereas the court denied the validity of such evidence.[46]

The Christian claim of new evidence from heaven and the presence of miracles to substantiate the messianism of Jesus was met by the rabbis by denying the very validity of miracles and "heavenly voices" in their courts. The oral tradition was open to anyone who wished to learn it. It did not depend on heavenly voices. Seen as an explicit threat to the oral tradition of the rabbis, anyone who could claim a heavenly voice could disrupt the work of the academies in trying to explicate the text. The rabbis held that the tradition which gave continuity to the community would be destroyed.

With the rise of Pauline Christianity which refuted the binding character of *halakhah* came the response that the entire *halakhah* had to be accepted as a requirement for conversion. Even though this requirement had been made in the past, there seems to have been a much greater stress upon it after that time.[47] By stressing the spiritual life of the patriarchs who lived before the Torah was given, Christian writers could demonstrate that the Torah itself was not permanent.[48] On the other hand, the rabbis, stressing the importance and permanence of Torah, compared its study to divine revelation at Sinai.

> Rabbi Yehudah said in the name of Rav: At the time that Moses ascended on high he found the Holy One, Blessed Be He, sitting and tying crowns to the letters. He said: Master of the Universe, is there lacking in your hand (what is the purpose of these crowns)? He said to him: One man will come in the future after many generations, Akiba ben Yosef is his name, who will be able to derive heaps

of laws on each jot. Moses said: Master of the Universe, let me see him. He said to him: Turn around. Moses went and sat at the end of the eighth row and was unable to comprehend what they were talking about and became ill at ease. When a certain subject came up one of Akiba's students said: Rabbi, from whence do you derive this? He said to them: It is a law of Moses from Sinai, and Moses was comforted (*Talmud Bavli Menahot* 29b; see also *Bamidbar Rabbah* 19:4).

"This day. . ." Was that the same day that the Torah was given to Israel? Was it not forty years later? But this comes to teach you that Torah is dear to all those who study her: every day is like the day the Torah was given at Mt. Sinai. (*Talmud Bavli Berakhot* 63b on Deuteronomy 27:9).

In this sense, the study of Torah itself was regarded as an act of redemption: God kept his promise of rewarding the Jews with his presence, when they study the content of revelation, i.e., the Torah. Just as Christians saw the Christ figure as one who came to redeem the biblical promise, for the Jew the act of Torah study brought redemption of the ancient promise embodied in the written text.

The rabbinic concept of covenant emphasized the Sinai covenant as opposed to the covenant of the patriarchs. A primary motivation for this emphasis was a response to the Christian challenge. The parting of the ways over the difference in choice of covenant theories was to be significant in the subsequent development of each religion.

Polemic and the Claims of Revelation

The *midrash* and *Talmud* took pains to find proof texts in the Torah to emphasize that the entire written Torah was revealed at Sinai.[49] If the Torah was not given at one time, someone might claim that written Torah could still be revealed at a later date, i.e., that the extant text was not complete. "Nothing was left unrevealed. God's word was given in exhaustive fullness."[50] "Moses said unto them: You are not to suppose that another Moses will arise and bring us another Torah from heaven. I make known to you now: 'It is not in heaven' . . ."[51] Everything was given to Israel.

Such teachings were directed against the Christians and Gnostics who claimed that they had a later, fuller and more authentic Torah.[52] Even within the Torah where there seem to be communications by God after Sinai, the rabbis declared that these later revelations were mere repetitions of the first.[53] They also claimed that the prophetic pronouncements were also included at Sinai for the same reason.[54]

There was no more written Torah to be expected from God.[55]

Yet not all the Torah was written. While the written Torah would be taken over by gentiles, the oral Torah was given to Israel alone and was a demonstration of God's exclusive relationship with the Jewish people, according to the rabbis.[56] The oral tradition was regarded as unique to Judaism. The written Torah was adopted by the Christians who claimed that they were now the true Israel. That the oral Torah was given at the same time only to Israel demonstrated that the Jewish people living by it were God's true children.[57]

> Rabbi Yehudah says: This is to proclaim the excellence of the Israelites, for when they all stood before Mt. Sinai to receive the Torah they interpreted the divine word as soon as they heard it, for it is said: "He compassed it and he understood it and he kept it as the apple of his eye" (Deuteronomy 32:10). (Meaning) as soon as the word came out, they interpreted it. (*Mekhilta*, II, 267).

The study of Torah and the oral tradition begin almost simultaneously with the giving of the Torah. Rabbi Yeudah the Prince, the codifier of the first official Jewish legal code, the *Mishnah*, demonstrates that what he had done is simply to collect what had gone before. The oral tradition is legitimate because of its antiquity.

Rabbi Yehudah's statement was surely a defense of the oral tradition either against the attacks of Jews who did not want to accept the authority of the rabbis or various Christian groups which denigrated Judaism by pointing to differences between the written Torah and the rabbinic commentary on it. According to Rabbi Yehudah the very glory of Israel was to be found in the oral tradition of which the rabbis claim to be heirs.

> Rabbi Yudan said: the world was created for the sake of the merit of the Torah. Rabbi Y'hoshua bar Nehemiah said: For the merit of the tribes of Israel. (*Genesis Rabbah* 12:2).

According to Marmorstein these statements, especially the one regarding Israel, were examples of polemics against Christian teaching that Israel had not contributed to the betterment of the world and was a useless nation.[58] Apologetic in tone, they were answers to the writings of the Church Fathers who derided the Jewish people as rejected by God.

Rabbi Yudan taught that God participated in Israel's suffering, promising relief and redemption.[59] The Torah, containing the covenant between God and Israel, would not be in the world except for Israel who accepted it. Rabbi Y'hoshua, living around the same time as Rabbi Yudan, was even more explicit. It was the merit of the tribes of Israel for which the world was created.[60]

Conclusion

In its operational sense the covenant functioned as a means to make agreements that establish or reestablish communities. Covenant terminology provided the language that bound entities in shared experience, since all participants adopted that language as the foundation of the community.

However, covenant also identifies the specific community distinguishing and defining it sharply to set it apart. Rather than functioning as a process it has a model, usually rooted in the past, to which it measured itself and others to legitimize its own claims for existence. The language of such a "covenantal" community was not concerned with agreement-making, but rather a polemical tool to cast aside others who made similar claims. Since there is often confusion (sometimes purposeful) between the operational and polemical function of covenantal language, one must be careful in analyzing the purpose of the language; biblical language may be used to establish new communities or to attack others.

NOTES

1. Julius Guttman, *Philosophies of Judaism* (Philadelphia: The Jewish Publication Society, 1964), p. 31.

2. A. Hartom, *"Brit,"* Encyclopedia Mikra'it, II (1954), p. 348.

3. George E. Mendenhall, "Covenant," *The Interpreter's Dictionary of the Bible,* (New York: Abington Press, 1962), I, p. 716. See also W. Brueggemann, "Amos 14 4-13 and Israel's Covenant Worship," *Vetus Testamentum,* XV, No. 1, January, 1965, pp. 1-15. G. M. Tucker, "Covenant Forms and Contract Forms," *Vetus Testamentum,* XV, No. 4, October, 1965, pp. 487-503. He cites oaths (*'ala*) as essential to covenant in contrast to contract where they were not essential, for in the case of a contract a court could be convened which was not the case with covenants except in a symbolic sense.

4. Nelson Glueck, *Hesed in the Bible,* Translated by A. Gottschalk (Cincinnati: Hebrew Union College Press, 1967), p. 54ff.

5. Moshe Weinfeld, *Deuteronomy and the Deuteronomistic School* (Oxford: The Clarendon Press, 1972), p. 91, Note 1.

6. Martin Buber, *Kingship of God,* Translated by R. Scheimann (New York and Evanston: Harper Torchbooks, 1973), p. 121-130.

7. Delbert R. Hillers, *Covenant: the History of a Biblical Idea* (Baltimore: The Johns Hopkins Press, 1969), p. 168.

8. Louis Ginzberg, *The Legends of the Jews* (Philadelphia: The Jewish Publication Society, 1968) V, p. 267ff. *Sifra-Torat Kohanim* 2:3; *Avot* 3:11; *K'ritut* 9:11; *Talmud Yerushalmi Peah* VIII 21a; *Talmud Bavli Berakhot* 48b; *Shabbat* 132a-b, 137b.

9. *Sifra-Torat Kohanim, Ahare* 2:1; *K'doshim* 3:5.

10. E.g., *Numbers Rabbah, Naso,* XIV, 10.

11. See also *Toseftah Hala* 1:1; *Talmud Yerushalmi Peah* V, 21; *Talmud Bavli Pesahim* 38b; *Gitin* 60b; *Sotah* 37b; *Berachot* 59a. Used in the biblical sense (usually in connection with *halakhah*): *Talmud Bavli Rosh Hashanah* 17a; *Gitin* 66b; *Sifra Ahare* 8:10; *B'hukotai* 1 2:5. (Used in reference to biblical quotation); *Sifra, Nedavah,* 14:6.

12. *Talmud Bavli Pesahim* 68b, in a parallel text, quotes Rabbi Eliezer in place of Rabbi

Eleazar. There is some indication for parallel usage already in biblical literature in Daniel 9:11. Also, II Kings 28:8, 11 and 23:2, the "Book of Torah" and "Book of Covenant" are used in parallel. See K. Baltzer, *The Covenant Formulary in Old Testament, Jewish and Early Christian Writings*, Translated by D. Green (Philadelphia: Fortress Press, 1971) especially p. 59, Note 115 for other examples.

13. *Toseftah Hulin* 1:6; *Talmud Bavli Pesahim* 38b.

14. E.g., *Talmud Bavli Moed Katan* 18a; *Sanhedrin* 102a.

15. Solomon Schechter, *Documents of Jewish Sectaries* (New York: Ktav Publishing House, Inc., 1970). See especially W. D. Davies, *Torah in the Messianic Age and/or Age to Come* (Philadelphia: SBL, 1952), p. 89f, Note 8.

16. Klaus Baltzer, *The Covenant Formulary in Old Testament, Jewish and Early Christian Writings*, pp. 97-172. See also Boaz Cohen, "Letter and Spirit in Jewish and Roman Law", Moshe Davis, Editor, *Mordecai M. Kaplan Jubilee Volume* (New York: Jewish Theological Seminary of America, 1953), p. 111ff on the use of this term in Jewish-Christian polemic. See also Walter Selb, "*Diatheke* im Neuen Testament", *Journal of Jewish Studies*, XXV, No. 1, February, 1974, pp. 183-196 for a detailed exposition of that term and its significance in the New Testament. The writer is indebted to Ilse Schoenholz for translating this article.

17. Delbert R. Hillers, *Covenant: The History of a Biblical Idea*, p. 181.

18. See *Leviticus Rabbah* 19 for the use of *diatheke* in context. Natan ben Yehiel, *Arukh Hashalem*, Edited by A. Kohut (New York: Pardes Publishing House, Inc.), III, p. 55, gives other references for its usage as well as the usual Greek meaning of this term. See also Reuven Yaron, *Gifts in Contemplation of Death in Jewish and Roman Law* (Oxford: Oxford University Press, 1960), p. 19.

19. Erwin Hatch, *Essays in Biblical Greek* (Oxford: Clarendon Press, 1889), p. 47. He refers to its usage by Aristophanes AV 439.

20. *Talmud Bavli Shabbat* 33a.

21. E. H. Dodd, *The Bible and the Greeks* (London: Hodder and Stoughton, 1954), p. 25.

22. *Ibid.*, p. 26.

23. *Ibid.*, p. 32.

24. Isaac Heinemann, *Darkhay Ha'agadah* (Jerusalem: Magnes Press, 1954), p. 115f.

25. Josephus, *The Antiquities of the Jews* 20:264.

26. Heinemann, p. 116.

27. E.g., *Tosefta Hulin* 7:8; *Parah* 4:5; *Talmud Bavli Shabbat* 135a.

28. W. Bacher, *Erkhay Midrash* Translated by A.Z. Rabinowitz (Jerusalem: Karmiel, 1923), I, p. 133f. The Language of Covenant.

29. Abraham J. Heschel, *Torah Min Hashamayim B'aspaklaria Shel Hadorot* (London: Soncino Press, 1962), I, p. 88. See citations in Note 8.

30. Solomon Gandz, "Oral Tradition in the Bible", *Jewish Studies in Memory of George A. Kohut* Edited by S. W. Baron and A. Marx (New York: The Alexander Kohut Memorial Foundation, 1935), p. 253.

31. *Ibid.*

32. *Ibid.*, p. 253f.

33. *Ibid.*, p. 254.

34. *Ibid.*, p. 259f.

35. *Ibid.*, p. 260.

36. *Ibid.*, p. 261.

37. Efraim Urbach, *Hazal: Pirke Emunot V'de'ot* (Jerusalem: Magnes Press, 1978), p. 17. He cites *Sifre*, (Edited by L. Finkelstein), *D'varim* 28, p. 122, in regard to people who were idol worshippers, yet accepted the Torah or rejected idol worship but did not accept the Torah.

38. R. Travers Herford, "The Problem of the 'Minim' Further Considered," *Jewish Studies in Memory of George A. Kohut*, p. 361f.

39. Jacob Neusner, *From Politics to Piety* (Englewood Cliffs: Prentice-Hall, Inc., 1973), p. 137.

40. Eugene Milhaly, "A Rabbinic Defense of the Election of Israel," *Hebrew Union*

College Annual, XXXV (1964), p. 108f. See p. 105, Note 2 for parallels.

41. *Ibid.*, p. 117f.

42. *Ibid.*, p. 120f. This is essentially the Gnostic challenge to Israel.

43. *Ibid.*, pp. 122-124.

44. *Ibid.*, p. 129f.

45. Alexander Guttmann, "The Significance of Miracles for Talmudic Judaism," *Hebrew Union College Annual*, XX (1947), p. 385f. See especially his citation of sources in Note 29.

46. *Ibid.*, p. 386. Guttmann proposes that Rabbi Eliezer was suspected of Christian leanings because he seemed to be friendly towards Christians. See Note 32.

47. Bernard J. Bamberger, *Proselytism in the Talmudic Period* (Cincinnati: Hebrew Union College Press, 1939), p. 31f.

48. Bernard J. Bamberger, "Revelations of Torah After Sinai," *Hebrew Union College Annual*, XVI (1941), p. 112. See his citations in New Testament and Patristic literature in Note 59.

49. Bamberger, "Revelations of Torah After Sinai," p. 111.

50. *Ibid.*

51. *Deuteronomy Rabbah* 8:6 on Deuteronomy 30:12. Cited by Bamberger, "Revelations of Torah After Sinai," p. 111. See also *Talmud Bavli Bava M'tziah* 59b.

52. Bamberger, "Revelations of Torah After Sinai," p. 112.

53. *Talmud Bavli Sotah* 37b; *Hagigah* 6a; *Pesahim* 115b.

54. *Exodus Rabbah* 28:6.

55. Bamberger, "Revelations of Torah After Sinai," p. 113.

56. Moore, III, p. 74. He cites *Midrash Tanhumah, Ki Tissah* 17.

57. H. Graetz, *History of the Jews* (Philadelphia: Jewish Publication Society, 1893), II, p. 608.

58. Marmorstein, *Merits*, p. 27.

59. *Encyclopedia Judaica*, XVI, p. 867.

60. On the significance of merits, see above, Part I, "Merit".

PART III: RABBINIC POLITICAL THOUGHT - TORAH AS COVENANT

CHAPTER 1: MUTUALITY

The intimate relationship between God and Israel was perceived by the rabbis as bound by a mutual agreement. The content of this agreement is incorporated in the Torah. Both parties to the agreement are dependent on each other for the full realization of their existence.

> Rabbi Shimon ben Eleazar said: When the Israelites do God's will, his name is exalted in the world ...When they do not do his will, his name is profaned in the world, as it says, "And they profaned my holy name." (Ezekiel 36:20).[1]

> Rabbi Azariah in the name of Rabbi Yehudah ben Shimon said: When the Israelites do God's will, they add to the power of God on high. When the Israelites do not do God's will, they, as it were, weaken the great power of God on high.[2]

> "The tribes of Israel together." When they act as one band[3] and not when they are separate bands as it is said, "It is he who builds his upper chamber in heaven and has set his vault upon the earth" (Amos 9:6). Rabbi Shimon bar Yohai cites a parable of a man who brings two ships and binds them together with ropes and cords and builds a palace on them; while the ships are lashed together the palace stands; when they drift apart they cannot stand.[4] So it is with Israel: when they do God's will his chamber (is secure) in heaven. When they do not do God's will, "He has set his vault upon the earth" (i.e., his palace is not secure in heaven). Similarly, you say, "And you are my witnesses says the Lord, and I am God" (Isaiah 43:12). When you are my witnesses I am God, and when you are not my witnesses I am not God.[5]

> "You are my witnesses, says the Lord, and I am God" (Isaiah 43:12). That is, when you are my

74

witnesses, I am God and when you are not my witnesses, I am not your God. . .⁶

When the Israelites do God's will, they make his
left hand as his right hand. . .but when they do not
do his will, they make his right hand as his left. . .If
they do God's will, he sleeps not. . . but if they do
not do his will, if one may say so, he sleeps. . .If
they do his will, wrath is not by him. . .but if they
do not do his will, if one may say so, wrath is by
him. . .If they do his will, he fights for them. . .If
they do not do his will, he fights against them. . .
not only that but they make the merciful one cruel.⁷

"Doing God's will" refers to observing the Torah. These statements declare that Israel can effectuate God's behavior towards her
by her actions of maintaining the covenant. Marmorstein⁸ attributes
the last statement to Rabbi Akiba who constantly emphasized the
close relationship between God and Israel. God's compassion is
dependent upon Israel's obedience. Divine justice is executed as a
consequence of Israel's failure to obey.

"You forgot God who formed you" (Deuteronomy
32:18). Each time that I sought to do you good,
you weakened the power on high. You stood by the
sea and said, "This is my God and I will praise
him" (Exodus 15:2). And then you returned and
said, "let us make a captain, let us go back to
Egypt" (Numbers 14:4). You stood at Mt. Sinai
and said, "All that the Lord has spoken to us we
will do and we will obey: (Exodus 24:7), and I
sought to do you good. But you turned and said to
the calf, "This is your God, O Israel" (Exodus
32:4). Lo, whenever I seek to do you good, you
weaken the power which is on high.⁹

The relationship between God and Israel is here characterized as
interdependent. Each influences the other. The acts of one have consequences for the acts of the other. Each impinges on the other's
existence determining the other's existence. God's name and fame in
the world can either be exemplified and made special (holy) or
debased and profaned. His power can be increased or decreased.
These statements are examples of how Israel's behavior towards the
Torah can effect God.

Israel's observance or lack of it will result in rewards or punishments, i.e., God will determine if he should act on her behalf or not.
In doing God's will, i.e., maintaining the covenant, Israel proclaims
the legitimacy of its authority to the entire world. Israel demon-

strates that God's authority has manifested itself over Israel. The purpose of broadcasting this message universally is to fulfill the ideal that mankind will recognize that only God's authority has validity.

Profaning the name is regarded as an act of rebellion, since it demonstrates the lack of God's influence over Israel. If God cannot even rule over Israel, if his rule can so easily be ignored, then he is impotent in the world, an authority with little or no power to effectuate its rule.

By maintaining the covenant, Israel may influence the world to follow suit. Dedication and self-sacrifice to an idea, whether political or religious, which was to play such an important role in the history of Western Civilization, had one of its roots the Jewish concept of sanctification of the name.

> "And let those that hate you flee before you" (Numbers 10:35). Are there then any who hate Him Who Spoke and the World Was? But it means that he who hates Israel is as if he hated God...He who helps Israel is as if he helped God...Whenever Israel is enslaved, the *Shekhina* is enslaved with them as it says: "In all their afflications he was afflicted" (Isaiah 64:9).[10] And if you say this verse shows only that God was afflicted when the community of Israel was afflicted, how do we know that he is afflicted when an individual Israelite is afflicted? Because it says: "I will be with him (singular) in distress" (Psalms 91:15). Rabbi Akiba said: If it were not written in scripture it would be impossible to say it. Israel says to God: You have redeemed yourself...Whithersoever, Israel was exiled the *Shekhina* went with them...and when they return the *Shekhina* will return with them....[11]

Shekhina refers to the immanence of God, i.e., his intimate relationship with Israel. This entire statement conforms to Rabbi Akiba's almost mystical view of the spouse-like quality of God's concern for Israel. God, in redeeming Israel, redeems himself, according to this passage. Redemption, in this context, means the keeping of one's promise. By maintaining his faithfulness to his agreement with Israel, i.e., by redeeming Israel, he is redeemed.[12]

Cosmic Significance of the Covenant

> Rabbi Eleazer said: if it were not for the Torah, heaven and earth would not be established, as it is said: "Without my covenant day and night, the

76

laws of heaven and earth I would not place" (Jeremiah 33:25).[13]

Resh Lakish said: Why is it written, "And there was morning and there was evening *the* sixth day" (Genesis 1:13)? What is the purpose of the additional *the*? This teaches that the Holy One Blessed be He, stipulated with the works of creation and said to them, "If Israel accepts the Torah, you shall be established, if not, I will turn you back unto emptiness and formlessness."[14]

Rabbi Eleazar and Rabbi Yohanan: one says: You wrought righteousness for my word, in that you accepted my Torah, for had you not accepted my Torah, I should have caused the world to revert to void and desolation. Rabbi Huna said in the name of Rabbi Aha: When the earth and all the inhabitants there of are dissolved" (Psalms 75:4), means that the world would long have gone into dissolution had not Israel stood before Mt. Sinai. Who then set the world firmly upon its foundation? I, myself, establish the pillars of it; by the merit of "I", I have established its pillars forever. The other rabbi says: By the righteousness by which you wrought into yourselves in that you accepted my Torah, for were it not for this (act) I should have caused you to disappear from the nations.[15]

The receiving of the Torah took on cosmic significance; the very existence of the world depended on it. The Torah not only was a plan for moral order but the order of nature as well.[16] The creation of the world was understood to be connected to the giving of the Torah. Creation without Torah had no purpose; Torah gave structure, order, i.e., predictability and reliability to creation. But the Torah did not have significance unless it was accepted. Israel, in receiving the Torah, took on cosmic importance. Israel became the catalyst for the Torah coming into the world insuring the existence of the cosmos.

The rabbis thought of the Torah as God's plan for the creation of the world.[17] The Torah had to be accepted, in their view, to prevent a return to primeval chaos and confusion. The world was created on condition that it would eventually accept the Torah; the entire existence of the world depended on the agreement between creator and created. Without such an explicit acceptance of the agreement the created order of the world would not continue. Nature, then, was regarded as subservient to Torah. As Torah was continually revealed to man, his fear of nature decreased as his control over it increased.

Agreements, in order to be sustained, require trust. When all parties to the agreement understood its consequences, they would be able to live without uncertainty, since all conditions of the agreement as stated in the Torah were regarded as revealed rather than hidden. The rabbis taught that the fabric of society and creation were based upon trust, which increased as each party to the agreement realized that it was being observed. They maintained the belief that God would not break his agreement since it functioned as his connection to creation and the very reason for its creation and continued existence.

It would be far too simplistic to regard these statements as mere nationalistic hyperbole, a result of historic circumstances: a defeated and despised nation found its reason for existence tied to the existence of the world. Perhaps we can attribute part of the thrust of these statements to chauvinistic motives. However, what we see here is an interweaving of the particularism of Israel with the universalistic connotation of creation, a theme often found in rabbinic literature. Underlying the combination of these two tendencies was the understanding that the universe had no meaning without its particular application. Israel was part of the world. The whole was dependent on each of its parts. The Torah was the agent of the organization of the whole into its various parts, i.e., it differentiated, it celebrated the individuality of each separate part.

Individual and Community

Inherent in the idea of agreement is the individuality of each party.

Rabbi Yishmael says: Generalities were proclaimed
at Sinai, and particularities in the tent of meeting.
Rabbi Akiba says: Both generalities and particularities were proclaimed at Sinai, repeated in the tent
of meeting, and for the third time on the plains of
Moab. Consequently, there is not a single commandment written in the Torah in connection with
which 48 covenants were not made. Rabbi Shimon
ben Yehudah of K'far Acco said in the name of
Rabbi Shimon: There is not a single commandment written in the Torah in connection with which
48 x 603550 (number of people) covenants were not
made. Rabbi said of the words of Rabbi Shimon
ben Yehudah of K'far Acco who said in the name of
Rabbi Shimon: There is no single commandment
in the Torah that 48 x 603550 commandments were
not made by 603550 (people). What is the issue

between them? Rabbi Mesharsheya said: The point between them is that of personal responsiblity and responsibility for others.[18]

"And all the people saw the thunderings and the lightenings" (Exodus 20:15). The thunderings of thunderings upon thunderings and the lightenings of lightenings upon lightenings. How many thunderings were there and how many lightenings were there? It is simply this, they were heard by each man according to his capacity, as it is said, "The voice of the Lord was heard according to the strength" (Psalms 29:4).[19]

How did the voice go out? Rabbi Tanhuma said: The word of the Lord went forth in two aspects, slaying the heathen who would not accept it, but giving life to Israel who accepted the Torah. This is what Moses said to them at the end of forty years, "For who is there of all flesh that has heard the voice of the living God speaking out of the midst of the fire as we have, and lived" (Deuteronomy 5:23). Only you have heard his voice and lived, but the heathen heard it and died. Come and see how the voice went forth, coming to each Israelite with the force proportioned to his individual strength; to the old according to their strength, and to the young according to theirs; to the children and the babes and to the women, according to their strength, and even to Moses, according to his strength as it is said: "Moses spoke, and God answered him by a voice" (Exodus 19:19), with a voice which he could endure. Similarly it says: "The voice of the Lord is with power" (Psalms 29:4). Not with his power, but with power, that is with the power of each individual, even to pregnant women according to their strength. Thus to each person that was, according to his strength.[20]

Every single commandment had been given to each person and was binding on everyone because of the individual's experience of receiving the Torah. Each person perceived the event in a unique manner depending on his own ability to comprehend it. The collection of individuals became a community through the shared experience of the event. Ultimately, the covenant was the responsibility of each individual. However, because he was a member of the community he was liable for the failure of others to meet their obligations.

The community, as a corporate entity, was liable for the acts of its individual members. Communal responsibility towards the covenant is the source of its integrity and identity.

The Sinai event as interpreted by the rabbis created a community from disparate individuals who became responsible for one another because they agreed to accept the covenant.

> Rabbi Yehudah (the Prince) says: This proclaims the excellence of Israel, for when they all stood before Mt. Sinai to receive the Torah, they all made up their minds alike to accept the reign of God joyfully. Furthermore, they pledged themselves to one another concerning not only overt acts. The Holy one Blessed be He, revealed himself to them in order to make a covenant with them even in regard to secret acts, for it is said: "The secret things belong to the Lord our God, and the things that are revealed..." (Deuteronomy 29:28). They said to him, concerning overt acts, we are ready to make a covenant with you, but we will not make a covenant with you in regard to secret acts, lest one of us commits a sin secretly, and the entire community be held responsible for it.[21]

The concern for the terms of the covenant are here elucidated to prevent misunderstanding. An assumption that the people had the power to take exception to the terms of the covenant is emphasized here. The community could not bear the might of God's justice if it was liable for the secret sins of individuals. Since the acceptance of the Torah was both an individual as well as a communal matter, it would seem logical that every category of action and thought would be included. By excluding the secret acts of individuals the community could be relieved of what it could not control.

Struggle and Control

The individuality of covenant partners inevitably led to conflict and struggle. Assimilation of the ego into the divine is dichotomous with a covenant concept. Loss of individuality would mean that there could be no relationship. There would be no one with whom to relate. Basic to Jewish theology was the belief in divine uniqueness. Each person created in the divine image was also unique. The relationship between unique persons was the crux of the covenant concept. Just as the individual had no meaning if he stood alone, for then he would have no one with whom to compare himself, so God could not gain recognition outside the context of a world of individuals.

"Moses went up unto God" (Exodus 19:3). It is written: "You have ascended on high, you have fled captivity captive" (Psalms 68:19). What is the meaning of "You have ascended"? You have been exalted because you did wrestle with angels on high. No creature on high has prevailed as Moses did. Rabbi Berekhiah said: The length of the tablets was six handbreadths; two were, could we speak thus, in the hand of him that called the world into being. Two handbreadths were in the hands of Moses, and two handbreadths separated the two pairs of hands. Another explanation, "You have ascended on high, you have fled captivity captive," it is customary for one who enters the city to take away something unnoticed and prized by the inhabitants, but Moses ascended on high and took away the Torah on which all had their eyes; hence, "You have ascended on high, you have fled captivity, captive." Lest you think that because he captured it, he took it gratis, the psalmist adds: "You have received gifts among men," that is, it was given to him for a prize. Lest you think that he actually paid him money, the psalmist assures that it was a gift; it was given to him as a gift. At that moment the angels wished to attack Moses (because the angels had asked God to give the Torah to them, see *Talmud Bavli Shabbat* 88b). The Holy One Blessed be He made the features of Moses resemble those of Abraham and said to the angels, Are you not ashamed to touch this man to whom you descended from heaven and in whose house you ate? God said to Moses, It is only for the sake of Abraham that the Torah is given to you, as it is said, you have received gifts among men.[22]

Based on a legend that the angels did not want God to give the Torah to Israel, arguing that Israel would not keep it, this statement declared that Moses won the Torah for Israel by contending with the angels and wresting it from them. That he was able to keep it was the prize or gift that he received for winning it.

The Torah was given then because Israel deserved it, winning it in combat. In this legend, the angels represent God's justice. They wanted to prevent the Torah from coming into the world, just as they tried to prevent the very creation of the world. They represented that aspect of God which is parental: since the children do not deserve the gift, it would be foolhardy to give it to them.

The legend reflects an evident conflict going on within the authority figure: whether to take the risk and give the people the opportunity for responsibility or not. Meanwhile, the people wrest responsibility from authority through force which seems to settle the issue for the authority. By winning they prove themselves capable of and willing to accept responsibility. Unlike the story of Prometheus in Greek mythology where punishment is the consequence of audacity, here reward is given for wresting the Torah from its divine source. A parallel *midrash* (*Midrash on Psalms* 8:2, Buber edition, page 73f) adds that the reason God gave the angels for giving the Torah to man is that man had freedom of choice. To make a covenant with angels would not make any sense, for the angels had no choice but to keep God's word.

> There were three occasions when Moses spoke to God and God said: You have taught me. (Two are given here). Moses said before him, "Master of the world, how should the Israelites know that they did wrong? Were they not brought up in Egypt and were not all the Egyptians adulterers, and then when you gave the law you did not give it to them, and they were not really standing at Sinai, for it says, "And the people stood afar off," so you gave the law not to them but to me as it says: "And the Lord said unto Moses, come up unto the Lord" (Exodus 24:1). And when you gave the ten words you did not give them to the Israelites for you did not say, I am the Lord your (plural) God, but I am the Lord your (singular) God, you did speak to me; perhaps I have sinned. Then God said: You have spoken well, you have taught me, henceforth I will say, "I am the Lord your (plural) God". Then again when God said: "He visits the iniquities of the fathers upon the children," Moses said: Lord of the world, many wicked fathers beget righteous sons, should these bear the iniquities of their fathers? Terah was worshipper of images; Abraham, his son, was righteous. Ahaz was a sinner; Hezekiah was righteous. Amon was a sinner, Josiah was righteous. Is it fitting that the righteous should be punished for the sins of their fathers? Then God said: You have taught me. I cancel my word and confirm your word, as it is said, "The father shall not be put to death for the children, nor the children for the fathers." (Deuteronomy 24:16). And I will write it in your name as it is said, "According

to that which is written in the book of the Law of
Moses" (II Kings 14:6).[23]

Moses, pleading before God after the golden calf incident, argued
that the Israelites were conditioned by their Egyptian masters who
were adulterers. He also claimed that because God did not speak
directly to Israel, but spoke to Moses as an intermediary, they did
not realize that they were bound to the covenant. Authority must
relate directly to the people and not through intermediaries.

He also claimed that the Torah was not just since it contained the
concept of vicarious justice (the sins of the fathers will be visited on
the sons). The theme of the righteous arguing with God is biblical
(Abraham, regarding Sodom and Gomorrah, Genesis 18:22-32) and
continues in rabbinic literature.

> "The God of Israel said. the Rock of Israel spoke to
> me: Rule over men shall be the righteous, even he
> that rules in the fear of God" (II Samuel 23:3).
> What do they mean? Rabbi Abbahu said: They
> mean, I, God, rule over man. Who rules over me?
> The righteous, for I ordain a decree (of punishment)
> and he annuls it.[24]

God is limited by the righteous, who by observing the commandments, have power over him. The just life and the acts of compassion
of the righteous person may ameliorate God's severe decree. He may
contend with God and be victorious.

> Rabbi Yehudah bar Nahman said in the name of
> Resh Lakish: The Holy One Blessed be He says, In
> the hour that I conquer I suffer loss, but in the hour
> when I am conquered, I gain. I conquered at the
> generation of the flood but I lost, for I destroyed all
> those masses: so it was with the generation of the
> Tower of Babel and with the men of Sodom, but
> when the golden calf was made, Moses conquered
> me, and I gained all those masses; so I acquit all
> my creatures so that I may not suffer loss.[25]

God did not wish to conquer and destroy. He would rather be
conquered by the righteous.[26] A world of conflict and struggle was
accepted by the rabbis, if individual identity was to be maintained.
However, the content of this struggle should be directed over the
meaning of the covenant. The righteous demand that God keep his
word and rule compassionately. Contention occurs between intimate
partners who share an experience (revelation) and a relationship (the
covenant).

Partnership

"The covenant and the love" (Deuteronomy 7:12).
Rabbi Shimon ben Halafta said: The matter is like
the king who married a lady who brought him two
precious ornaments. And the king also added two
precious ornaments (to match them). But when his
wife abandoned her two ornaments, the king abandoned his. After a time she arose and purifed herself and brought back her two ornaments, and then
the king brought back his two. The king said, the
four together shall be made into a crown and shall
be put upon the queen's head. So you may find that
Abraham gave his descendants two precious ornaments, as it is said: "'For I know him that he will
command his children after him, and they keep the
way of the Lord to do righteousness and justice"
(Genesis 18:19). So when the Holy One Blessed be
He set up two ornaments to match the other two,
namely love and compassion as it is said: "And the
Lord your God will keep the covenant and the
love" (Deuteronomy 7:12; 13:18);...when the
Israelites abandoned their two, as it is said, "He
turned justice into gall and righteousness into hem-
lock" (Amos 6:12). So God also took his two, as it
is said, "I have taken away my peace from this people, even love and compassion" (Jeremiah 16:5).
Then Israel arose and purified herself and brought
its two back, and God restored his two likewise...
(Isaiah 1:27; 54:10). But when Israel brings its two,
God gives his two and God says: The four together
shall be made into a crown and shall be placed
upon Israel's as it is said, "I will betroth you unto
me in justice and in righteousness and in love and
in compassion" (Hosea 2:19).[27]

The Hebrew term, *hesed*, refers to covenant love, the love relationship between people who make agreements because of their mutual
feelings. The word, *rahamim*, refers to parental love (here translated
as compassion), since its root comes from the word, *rehem*, which
means womb. The verse quoted from Deuteronomy 7:12 places *hesed*
together with covenant in parallel which we would expect. The other
verses quoted include *hesed* and *rahamim*, so that to the rabbis,
rahamim was parallel to covenant. Perhaps the ancient biblical differentiation betwen these two words for love, *hesed* and *rahamim*, was no
longer significant for the rabbis. The usage of the two words was

regarded as synonymous for love. However, the rabbis regarded the giving of the covenant as an act of love and Israel's response was to be just and righteous, i.e., to act with responsibility.

The Jewish people were engaged in polemical warfare and a barrage of propaganda from Gnostics, Christians and pagans, all of whom regarded Israel's claim as God's chosen to be a false one as proven by the destruction of the Temple and the triumph of Rome over Jerusalem. This statement constitutes part of that polemic: it declares that just as God and Israel might have rejected each other, the opportunity for reconciliation was open. Indeed God would again honor his covenant with Israel upon Israel's return to it. It emphasizes that her defeat was temporary, and that the covenant is eternal.

> "My love, my undefiled" (Song of Songs 5:2). (the *midrash* makes a pun on the word for undefiled which in Hebrew is *tammati*.) Rabbi Yannai said: *teumati*, my twin, as if God said, I am not greater than she, and she is not greater than I. Rabbi Y'hoshua of Sikhnin said in the name of Rabbi Levi: As with twins, if one has a headache, the other feels it too, so God says of Israel, "I am with him in his distress" (Psalms 91:15).[28]

This statement emphasizes the equal covenant relationship and the mutuality of concern between God and Israel, using the metaphor of God and Israel as twins.

> Rabbi Tobiah ben Rabbi Yitzhak expounded: "I am the Lord your God." It was on this condition that I brought you out of the land of Egypt, viz, that you acknowledge me as your God. Another explanation of "I am the Lord your God": It can be compared to a princess, who having been taken captive by robbers was delivered by a king who subsequently wants to marry her. But prior to his proposal she says, What dowry do you give me? He replied, even if I have no other claim on you that I rescued you from the robbers that is sufficient.[29]

The literal Hebrew phrase for, "you acknowledge me as your God", is "that you should receive my divinity on yourselves,"[30] a bit awkward in translation. The exodus from Egypt had as its purpose the acceptance of God's role as a marriage partner. The rescue was to be Israel's dowry. The marriage was to be an exclusive relationship.

> Rabbi Akiba said: I will speak of the beauty and praise of God before all the nations. They ask Israel and say, what is your beloved more than another

> beloved that you do so charge us? (Song of Songs
> 5:9). That you die for him and that you are slain
> for him as it says, "Therefore do the maidens love
> you?" (Song of Songs 1:3). And they love you unto
> death, as it is written, "And for your sake are we
> slain all the day" (Psalms 44:23). Behold, they say,
> you are beautiful, you are mighty, come and mingle
> with us. But the Israelites replied, Do you know
> him? We will tell you a portion of his praise: "My
> beloved is clear-skinned ruddy" (Song of Songs
> 5:10). When they hear Israel thus, they say to the
> Israelites, We will go with you, as it is said,
> "Whither have your beloved gone, O you, fairest
> among women? Whither has your beloved turned
> him that we may seek him with you." (Song of
> Songs 6:1). But the Israelites say, You have no part
> of him, "For my beloved is mine, and I am his:
> (Song of Songs 2:16).[31]

Rabbi Akiba, who was to suffer martyrdom after leading a rebellion against Emperor Hadrian, interpreted the Song of Songs to be a love poem describing the relationship between God and Israel which insured its inclusion in the biblical canon. Rabbi Akiba has taken various verses from the Song of Songs and the Book of Psalms and formed a tapestry picturing the very special quality of the relationship between God and Israel. This love is that of spouses and is exclusive.

The love described is so intense that Israel is even slain for it. This statement is no mere theodicy; rather it is the type of political tract writing that gives a reason for Israel's suffering.

The covenant bound the nation together to defend itself against the claims and the might of the nations of the world. Like the *polis* for the Greeks and the *imperium* for the Romans, the covenant was not limited to a specific place. The covenant relationship established the basis of authority, the content of knowledge and the purpose of the community. God was the authority, but he offered the opportunity for partnership to those who fully participate in the relationship. Knowledge of the covenant was the key to full participation.

> "The Lord is my strength and my song" (Exodus
> 15:2). You are the subject of song which came into
> the world but yet (mean) more to me (that is to
> Israel)... He has proclaimed me of special distinction, and I have proclaimed him of special distinction...All the nations of the world tell the praise of
> He Who Spoke and the World Came into Being but
> my praise is (more) pleasant before him...Israel

says: "Hear, O Israel, the Lord our God, the Lord
is one." And the Holy Spirit calls from heaven and
says: "Who is like unto you, O Israel, a people
unique (one) upon the earth" (I Chronicles 17:21).
Israel says: "Who is like unto you the Lord among
gods" (Exodus 15:11). And the Holy Spirit calls
from heaven and says: "Happy are you, O Israel,
who is like you?" (Deuteronomy 33:29). The Israelites say: "Who is like the Lord who answers us
whenever we call upon him" (Deuteronomy 4:7).
And the Holy Spirit cries out and says: "What
great nation is there that has statutes and ordi-
nances so righteous" (Deuteronomy 4:8). Israel
says: "You are the glory of their strength" (Psalms
89:18). And the Holy Spirit cries out and says,
"Israel, in you I will be glorified" (Isaiah 49:30).[32]

The juxtaposition of various biblical citations is used to demonstrate intimacy. God and Israel are like two lovers. God is the only
one for Israel and Israel is the only one for God. As lovers they are
significant only for each other. Each one proclaims that the other is
incomparable. The glory of each is found in the relationship with the
other.

The name, "Holy Spirit," reflects this intimacy. God reveals himself, i.e., he shows himself to Israel. Even though the nations of the
world praise God, Israel's praise is special. It is the Torah that binds
them.

> Rabbi Tanhuma: Israel's only happiness consists in
> the fact that they choose the Holy One Blessed be
> He, to be their God, and the Holy One Blessed be
> He, chooses them to be his special treasure.[33]

This statement is seemingly pietistic in tone, yet emphasizes once
again the mutual relationship between God and Israel.

Choseness

> Rabbi Y'hoshua ben Hanina said: At first he went
> to the sons of Esau; he asked them, Will you
> receive the Torah? They said to him: Master of the
> World, what is written in it? He said to them, You
> shall not kill. They said to him: Our trust is depen-
> dent upon the sword, as it is said, "By your sword
> you shall live" (Genesis 27:4). We are unable to
> receive the Torah. After this, he went to the Amoni-
> tes and Moabites. He said to them: Will you

receive the Torah? They said to him, Master of the
World, what is written in it? He said: You shall not
commit adultery or lustful acts. They said to him:
They did not come into being except through lust
as it is written, "The two daughters of Lot (sup-
posed ancestors of Amon and Moab) conceived
through their father" (Genesis 19:36); we are
unable to receive the Torah. After that he went to
the Ishmaelites. He said to them: Will you receive
the Torah? They said to him: Master of the World,
what is written in it? He said to them: You shall not
steal. They said to him: They cannot live except
through stealing and theft, as it is written, "He will
be a wild man, his hand will be in everything"
(Genesis 16:12). We are unable to receive the
Torah. After that he went to Israel. They said: "We
will do and obey." As it is written, "The Lord from
Sinai comes and shines forth from Seir, he illumni-
nates from Mt. Paran and from myriads of Kadesh
from his right hand, a fiery law" (Deuteronomy
33:2). Israel said: The Holy one Blessed be He,
Master of the Universe, "Make haste, my beloved,
and be like a gazelle or a young hart upon the
mountains of spices" (Song of Songs 8:14). "Make
haste, my beloved," flee from the evil scent and
come to a good scent on the mountains of spices.
"Lift up their ten-stringed instruments" (Psalms
92:4), unless it is to receive the commandments and
the ten words. The instrument (*naval* from Psalms
92:4 can also be construed to mean, disgrace):
unless it is to become disgraced during the days of
religious persecution. Rabbi Shimon ben Levi said:
With joy: And the rabbis said: Not enforced labor,
and since the Holy One Blessed be He, saw the will
of Israel seeking to receive the Torah in love and
affection, fear, reverence, awe and trembling he
opened and said: "I am the Lord your God."[34]

This *midrash* begins with Hadrian's challenge to Rabbi Y'hoshua
ben Haninah that God is not concerned with the last five commandments which (according to Hadrian) were given to the nations of the
world, because God's name is not connected with them. After reply-
ing that Hadrian's argument had no validity, his students said that
his answer was not good enough for them. ("Master, you thrust off
that one with a broken reed of an answer! What answer will you give
us?") This statement is an answer to them.

The days of religious persecution[35] refer to the Hadrianic persecutions, 135 to 137 C.E. or the Jewish rebellion in the diaspora at the end of Trajan's reign. According to Braude, evil scent refers to the evil sins of heathen nations.[36] The instrument quoted from Psalms 92:4 is a play on words in Hebrew: *naval,* the instrument, can also mean disgrace. Forced labor was a consequence of the defeat of Bar Kokhba's rebellion in 137 C.E. or of the Jewish rebellion in the diaspora against Trajan.[37]

Unlike the nations of the world, Israel did not question the content of the Torah before accepting it. Israel's glory lies in her willling submission by accepting the Torah. This act of trust resulted in the intimate relationship between God and Israel (as characterized by the quotation from the Song of Songs).

Rabbi Y'hoshua's statement ends in a thinly-veiled plea to God to lift the disgrace of religious persecution from his people (the quote from Psalms 92:4), because Israel submitted herself to God's authority he must reciprocate by redeeming her from national disgrace. We cannot ascertain if the debate with Hadrian is legendary or not (perhaps it could have taken place during his trip to Rome). He certainly would have been an old man, even at the beginning of Hadrian's reign. However, the thrust of the debate and the subsequent explanation to his students is a legitimization of Israel's covenant with God because of her willingness to accept it unconditionally. Rabbi Shimon ben Levi's statement emphasizes the willingness of Israel to submit herself to God's authority. Not only is the relationship exclusive (Israel as opposed to the nations of the world), but it has an eternal quality as well. God chooses Israel and is willing to wait for the appropriate time when Israel is ready to reciprocate.

> "Fortunate are the pure in the way who walk in the Torah of the Lord." This is the generation of the wilderness. Rabbi Hezekiah Bar Hiya said: The Holy One Blessed be He waited, for no other generation was able to receive the Torah like that generation, and he waited for them. As it is said: "He will wait for the upright" (Proverbs 2:7).[38]

No other nation but Israel was fit to receive the Torah; no generation of Israel was fit to receive it except the generation of the wilderness, and that is why God waited for it instead of giving it to someone else before or afterward. A pietistic statement, its tone is apologetic, defending God's choice of Israel.

> "In the third month of the exodus of the children from Egypt." Why was the Torah not given as they left Egypt? It was not so. He said to Moses: "As you take out the people from Egypt you shall serve God on this mountain." (Exodus 3:12). Rabbi

> Yehudah bar Shalom said: It is a parable of a prince
> who was sick. His father said, I will wait for him for
> three months until his soul returns from the sick-
> ness, and after that I will take him to the house of
> the teacher to study Torah. When Israel left Egypt,
> they were blemished from the servitude. The Holy
> One Blessed be He said, I will wait for them until
> they are healed, and after that I will give them the
> Torah.[39]

Israel had to be in a certain state of mind before she could accept
the Torah. The people had to perceive itself as free, i.e., recovered
from the scourge of slavery. The image of a parent with a sick child is
used here as a demonstration of God's love. The parent cannot send
his child to school to learn his responsibilities (Torah) until the child
is strong enough and has full control of his senses, i.e., until he is no
longer distracted by his illness. The compassion of a ruler for his
people is connected to the type of agreement he is to make with it. It
cannot be asked to accept responsibility until the ruler nurtures it
back to health. Just as a parent serves his sick child until he is well,
not demanding him to fulfill his normal obligations to the family, so
a ruler cannot place such demands upon the people until it is suffi-
ciently recovered from the horrible experience of oppression.[40]

> God says: I testify by heaven and earth that I sit
> and wait for Israel, more than a father for his son,
> or than a mother for a daughter, that they would
> repent so that my words would be fulfilled.[41]

God is concerned and involved with Israel's actions. If Israel does
not keep her promises, the Torah cannot be fulfilled.

Repentance must be understood in its literal sense: turning.
Authority waits for the people to turn to him so that its relationship
may be consummated.

This *midrash* emphasizes that both sides are necessary for a relationship to be effective.

Sanctification of God's Name: An Act of Reciprocity

Because God chooses Israel through an exclusive relationship,
Israel reciprocates by sanctifying God's name.[42] Sanctification of self
is a sanctification of God. Holiness is attained by observing the commandments which make Israel unique among nations. The sanctifying act is a confirmation by Israel of this exclusive relationship.

> "And the Lord spoke to Moses, saying, speak unto
> all the congregation of Israel and say to them, holy
> shall you be for I the Lord your God, am holy."
> Why was this section of the law to be said before all

the congregation? Because the majority of the most important commandments of the law are contained in it. "Be holy for I am holy." That is, if you sanctify yourselves, I reckon it as if you sanctified me, and if you do not sanctify yourselves, I regard it as if you did not sanctify me. It does not mean to say, if you did not sanctify me I am not sanctified, and if you do not do so I am not sanctified, for it says, "I am holy." I abide in my holiness whether you sanctify me or not.[43]

God is independent of Israel. Yet God can be sanctified only through Israel. The world will not realize God's sanctity unless Israel acts on it. Holiness or sanctity is a manifestation of the kingdom of heaven. To sanctify it would be an act of legitimizing God's authority.

It says in Leviticus (11:45), "For I am the Lord your God who brought you up out of the land of Egypt to be your God. You shall be holy for I am holy . . ." That means, I brought you out of Egypt on the condition that you should receive the yoke of the commandments. He who acknowledges the yoke of the commandments acknowledges that I have brought Israel out of Egypt, and he who denies the yoke of the commandments denies that I brought Israel out of Egypt. "To be your God . . ." "against your will." You shall be holy even as I am separate you be separate. On the condition that I brought you out of Egypt, namely on the condition that you should surrender yourselves to the sanctification of my name to be your God (Leviticus 22:33).[44]

Mutuality is concretized through the sanctification of God's name. The act of surrender is a demonstration of allegiance to the Torah. God is Israel's ruler since his act of taking her out of Egypt is conditioned on her acceptance of his sovereignty. In order to free herself from the pharoah Israel agrees to be acquired by God. From that time on God is regarded as her only ruler even if she attempts to reject him ("against your will"). Israel's unique and mutual relationship with God is to lead to the rule of God in this world which cannot occur unless " . . . his kingship is received by mankind, for there is no king without a people."[45] God had " . . . concluded this covenant of mutuality with Israel . . . "[46] for the purpose of realizing his kingdom over the entire world.

Binding Quality of the Torah

The Torah must be mutually and eternally binding if the relationship between God and Israel is to exist.

> "To enter into the covenant of the Lord your God, which the Lord your God is concluding with you this day, with its sanctions" (Deuteronomy 29:11). Three times did the Holy One Blessed be He cut a covenant as they went out of Egypt. Once as they stood before Mt. Sinai, once in Horeb, and once here. Why did the Holy One Blessed be He cut a covenant with them here? He did so because the covenant that he made with them at Sinai, they had nullified by saying, "These are the gods. . ."[47] Therefore, he returned and made another covenant with them in Horeb and set before them a curse for those who would go back on his words.[48]

The assumption of this *midrash* is that the people had the ability to nullify agreements even when made with God. Hence making an agreement with penalties (the curse), would discourage people from going back on their agreements.

That God had to go through the process of making the covenant three times demonstrates that ability and the need to specify the consequences of failure to keep one's word. The character of any agreement depends on trust between the parties and full knowledge of the consequences of compliance or non-compliance. No matter how much power an authority has people tend to try to extricate themselves from an agreement if they find it no longer convenient, or no longer want the burden of the responsibility for that agreement, are in a mood of rebellion, or simply decide to change their minds.

> "Before me" (Exodus 20:3). Why is it said? In order not to give Israel an excuse for saying: Only those who came out from Egypt were commanded not to worship idols. Therefore, it is said, "Before me" - just as I am living and enduring forever, so also you and your son and your son's sons to the end of generations shall not worship idols.[49]

Although previous generations have covenanted with God the present generation might not feel compelled to give allegiance to his authority. Tacit consent, a solution of later contract theorists, i.e., by virtue of living in society the inhabitants consent to the government even though it was established by previous generations, solves the problem in a passive sense. To live in a society is to consent to its legitimacy; remaining in the society is regarded as a passive acceptance of the contract. Tacit consent makes sense in the context of Greek philosophy, or Roman jurisprudence where *polis* or *imperium* dissolves, when consent dissolves.

According to Jewish thought it is not the form of the state or society that is fundamental but the covenant relationship between persons and authority. Since the authority (God) is always present, the very legitimacy of the relationship abides with the existence of that authority, just as the very existence of the state forms the legitimacy of the social contract. The descendants, by virtue of the instruction of their fathers, by receiving the tradition and observing it, constantly renew the relationship. In political terms, the worship of idols would be understood as a rejection of divine authority leading to anarchy since a shared belief system would no longer unite the people; each would follow his own god.

Each generation is held accountable for the observance of the covenant.

> "When you have brought forth the people from
> Egypt, you will serve God upon this mountain."
> When you ask me by what merit I will bring them
> out of Egypt, know it is for the merit of the Torah
> which they will receive on this mountain from my
> hands that they will go forth from here.[50]

The exodus from Egypt is a consequence of the merit of the Torah. Without the giving of the Torah the exodus would have made no sense in rabbinic thought. The exodus was a fulfillment of one promise (to the patriarchs) which led to another promise (the covenant). The chain of promise and agreement solidified the relationship between God and Israel.

> Rabbi Y'hoshua ben Korkha: Why does the section
> "Hear, O Israel" (Deuteronomy 6:4-9) proceed,
> "And it shall come to pass if you shall harken..."
> (Deuteronomy 11:13-21)? So that a man shall first
> receive upon himself the yoke of the kingdom of
> heaven and afterwards receive upon himself the
> yoke of the commandments.[51]

Rabbi Y'hoshua ben Korkha explains the order of the biblical passages that are found in the daily Jewish liturgy, called the *k'ri'at shema*, the recitation of the declaration of God's oneness. Not merely a ritual, this declaration is a sort of oath of allegiance that is repeated twice daily. It functions as an acceptance of God's sovereignty and covenant that is parallel to the acceptance of the Torah by Israel at Sinai.

Three concepts interweave with each other in this statement: the kingdom of heaven, commandment and the giving of the Torah. The kingdom of heaven becomes a reality when the commandments are accepted. The authority for the commandments is the kingdom of heaven. When the declaration is made the "yoke of the kingdom of heaven and the yoke of the commandments: are received by the person, and he binds himself to the Torah.

The order of the statements is crucial. Perhaps Rabbi Y'hoshua ben Korkha assumed that one could accept God's kingship without accepting the commandments.[52] There were many semi-proselytes at the time who, while sympathetic with the Jewish belief in one God, would not observe the specific rituals of Judaism, and therefore, did not formally convert to Judaism. There seems to have been a recognition of these types of people who, for the most part, were respected by the rabbis.[53]

The acceptance of the commandments made the Jewish people unique. By receiving the two yokes of government and commandments (or law), the individual confirmed his membership in the Jewish community. The giving of the Torah was an historic event which the individual affirmed and reenacted for himself when he made the declaration.

> "And all of the people answered together..."
> (Exodus 19:8). They did not give this answer with
> hypocrisy. Nor did they get it one from the other,
> but all of them made up their mind alike, and said:
> "All that the Lord has spoken, we will do..."
> (Exodus 19:8).[54]

In accepting the Torah each individual received it without consultation with anyone else; there was no vote, group pressure or influence used to mediate the event. The covenant then was made directly with God. Each person decided for himself. That they all did so at the same time as individuals, bound them into a community. Before the event there was no community with which God could covenant.

Taken out of the theological context and placed in a political setting, mutuality refers to the reciprocal relationship between authority and people. Usually, political vocabulary demands the ruler-ruled dichotomy. While that might be relevant in the present context, it leaves out the possibility stressed by the rabbis of the ruled to become rulers over themselves. Every relationship has its benefits and costs. People enter a relationship hoping that the benefits will more than offset the costs. In the reciprocal relationship there are no hidden costs. The obligations of membership are explicit. The authority is clear concerning its intention and expectations. Compassion is emphasized in order to promote trust. It is clearly expected that punishment would be the consequence of disloyalty and rebellion. There is no need to fear the unknown whim of the authority. Fear of the unknown is not a tool to be used to insure compliance. In that sense the covenant relationship is open and explicit, i.e., it is revealed.

There are two ways of understanding reciprocity: rights, claims and penalties that parties to the agreement accept and/or trust, love and mutual expectation of the fulfillment of obligations resulting in security without losing the sense of individuality. The rabbis used the covenant theme to enhance the viability of the community during dangerous times. We have seen that they were not adverse to utilize it as a basis of polemic. But as the leaders of the people they pointed to the opportunity inherent in the covenant relationship, i.e., the establishment of the kingdom of heaven on earth which was the crux of the reciprocal relationship. The closer the relationship the stronger the authority the individual maintained over himself. This might seem paradoxical, for we usually expect the authority to maintain a distance from the governed in order to protect and enhance its power. In a sort of economy of power, the more power the authority has the less power there is for the governed. Or, if the relationship of the authority with the governed is a close one, we might expect the authority to be either weak or so overwhelming that it engulfs the governed (e.g., "big brother" in George Orwell's *1984*). In rabbinic political thought neither of these tendencies obtain. Since the relationship is mutual and reciprocal when the authority is close and clearly recognizable not only is its power increased but the power of the individual and community that accepts its rule is increased as well. Power is limited only by the failure of either party to maintain the agreement. The kingdom of heaven comes into being when the relationship becomes completely reciprocal; everyone would possess authority, and power of one over against another would become meaningless.

Against Mutuality

Although the predominant rabbinic view towards the relationship to authority and the concept of covenant is expressed in a sense of mutuality, there is contrary view as well. The latter projects God as a transcendent, independent authority who forcefully imposes his will in a threatening manner. According to this view, although a beneficent ruler, God imposes his will on his creation. Man is viewed as God's slave who is to serve his merciful master.

> Why is the exodus from Egypt mentioned in connection with every single commandment? (This) can be compared to a king, the son of whose friend was taken as a prisoner. The king ransomed him, not as a son but as a slave so that if he should make a decree and (the son) would not accept it upon himself, the latter could say, you are my slave. So

when he entered the state, the king said: Put on my
sandals for me, take my clothes to the bathhouse.
When the son protested, the king took out the bill
of sale and said, You are my slave. So when God
redeemed the children of Abraham, his friend, he
redeemed them not as his children but as slaves so
that if he imposed upon them decrees and they did
not accept them upon themselves, he could say, you
are my slaves. When they went out into the desert,
he began to decree upon them some light and some
heavy (commandments), e.g., Sabbath and incest
commands, and fringes and phylacteries. Israel
began to protest. Then God said, You are my
slaves, on this condition I redeemed you, that I
should decree and you should fulfill.[55] God's ways
are not like those of flesh and blood, for man
acquired slaves so that they may look after and sustain him, but God acquires slaves that he may look
after and sustain them.[56]

The text uses the legal expression, al tannai, on condition. The
redemption from Egypt was a fulfillment of the promise made to
Abraham and also on condition that Israel accept the covenant. The
very relationship with Abraham was based on its continuation into
the future.

The last part of this statement is a remarkable contrast between
God and a human king. The acquisition of slaves by God gives him
the opportunity to sustain them. The imposition of the covenant, as
viewed here, has a benevolent purpose (as contrast to the Gnostic
view that it was malevolent). The promise of redemption is fulfilled
in the exodus from Egypt and the giving of the Torah which partially
is a reaffirmation of promises made to Abraham. Specific commandments are manifestions of these two events; by observing them God
is able to fulfill his promises. God's compassion is demonstrated by
his concern for the people as they become his acquisition. God's justice will be executed by forcing the people to fulfill the covenant. The
imposition of authority is accepted in this statement. In return for
redemption Israel had accepted God's authority. The people cannot
refuse the Torah after they had become free. Inclusive in the agreement to be redeemed was the agreement to accept God's authority.

"To the end that he may establish you this day as
his people and be your God, and he promised you
and as he swore to your fathers, Abraham, Isaac
and Jacob" (Deuteronomy 29:12). Perhaps you
will say, what is the reason for all this trouble? It is
not because I need you, but what I did for you,

because I had previously promised to your fathers
(i.e., Abraham, Isaac and Jacob), so I cannot
change it with you and your children forever.
Therefore, it says, "To the end that he may establish you this day as his people and be your God, as
he promised you and as he swore to your fathers
. . ." And he will be for you a God as he spoke to
you and as it was promised to your fathers. . ." To
the end that he may establish you this day as his
people and be your God. . ." That I will not go
back on what I promised to your fathers. And not
only for yourselves but also for future generations
to come at that time, for it says, "For those who are
here today and those who are not here"
(Deuteronomy 29:14).[57]

Emphasizing God's transcendence, this statement explains God's
relationship with Israel, not in terms of his dependence on Israel or
because he needs Israel. Rather he is fulfilling a promise previously
made with the patriarchs to sustain their descendants. He has no
choice but to keep the covenant for every generation. Israel seems to
have a passive role here. Perhaps this passage is concerned with the
character of God, that he does not need the people except to be recipients of his promise. As the statement continues it is concerned with
the reliability of the promise. God seems to be reassuring the people
that the covenant is not temporary. Even though God's promise was
made in the past, it is applicable for every generation. If we but
remember the Christian attack on Judaism, that God had punished
Israel for her sins and had revoked his promise which was demonstrated by the loss of land and hegemony as well as the exile of the
people literally to the four corners of the earth, we can understand
this *midrash* in its historical context. Just as Israel suffered temporary
oppression at the hands of the Egyptians even though they had been
innocent, God redeemed them because of his promise: the present
condition of Israel is temporary as well. Since God is transcendent
and independent even of Israel, he has the power to keep his promise
to every generation.

"And they stood under the mountain" (Exodus
19:17). Rabbi Abdimi bar Hama bar Hasa said:
This teaches that the Holy One Blessed be he over-
turned the mountain upon them like an inverted
cask and said to them, If you accept the Torah, it is
well, if not, there shall be your graves. Rabbi Aha
bar Jacob said: This furnished a great protest
against the Torah. Said Rabba: But even so, the
generation accepted it in the days of Ahasuerus, for

> it is written, "The Jews confirmed and accept..."
> (Esther 9:27), they confirmed what they had
> accepted before.[58]

This statement was made in Babylonia sometime in the fourth century when all three rabbis lived. Commenting on Exodus 19:17, Rabbi Abdimi bar Hama interpreted the covenant as a forceful imposition of the Torah on Israel. According to David Daube, this statement was a consequence of Constantius II's persecution of the Jews in Palestine.[59] Examining this statement from the point of view of comparative jurisprudence, Daube explains that a covenant made under duress is still binding although outrageous. The victim of such a covenant in private law can attempt to make a claim and perhaps be given relief in the courts if he cannot keep the covenant.

Rabbi Aha bar Jacob is fearful that to view the covenant in this manner may present an excuse for its abandonment. Rabba answers that the covenant was later voluntarily reaffirmed in the Book of Esther. We may note that a passage which follows this statement (in *Talmud Bavli Avodah Zarah* 2b) quotes Rabbi Y'hoshua ben Levi (third century Palestinian *amorah*) as follows: "The Holy One, Blessed be He, does not rule despotically over his creatures."[60] This might mean that it is not the nature of God to impose agreements.

The point of these statements is that Israel is a passive recipient of the covenant and does not seem to have much choice. The imposition of authority and the master-slave relationship sets God as an independent sovereign, i.e., his rule exists as an end unto itself. The ruler, by virtue of his office, is set apart and transcends the community lest his authority be compromised.

NOTES

1. *Mekhilta*, II, p. 28.
2. *Lamentations Rabbah* 1:35 on 1:6.
3. Play on the word, *agudah*, a bin or vault. The idea of this *midrash* is to contrast Israel when it is united with those times that it is disunited.
4. C.G. Montefiore and H. Loewe, *A Rabbinic Anthology* (Philadelphia: Jewish Publication Society of America, 1960), p. 382, Note 64, on the image of a palace built on two ships.
5. *Sifre*, 346, 144a on Deuteronomy 33:5.
6. *Midrash on Psalms* 123:1. *Pesikta D'rav Kahanah* 12:6, quotes that *midrash* in the name of Rabbi Shimon bar Yokhai.
7. *Mekhilta*, II, 41. Mutuality
8. Marmorstein, *Doctrine*, II, p. 130.
9. *Sifre, Ha'azinu*, 319, 136bf.
10. Scriptural proof is given that this holds true in terms of the community and the individual.
11. *Sifre, B'ha'alotekha*, 84, 22b; see also *Mekhilta*, I, 114.
12. Heschel, I, pp. 68-70 cites a number of rabbinic statements in the genre of mutual dependence.
13. *Talmud Bavli Pesahim* 68b.

14. *Talmud Bavli Shabbat* 88a; *Avodah Zarah* 3a.

15. *Ruth Rabbah*, Proem 1.

16. The statement uses the phrase, *tohu vavohu* (Genesis 1:2) to indicate the primordial state of chaos.

17. *Genesis Rabbah* 1:1.

18. *Talmud Bavli Sota* 37b; *Hagigah* 6a; *Zevahim* 115b.

19. *Mekhilta*, II, 297.

20. *Exodus Rabbah* 5:9. The voice refers to that of God at the giving of the Torah.

21. *Mekhilta* 1, II, 230 (translation revised by present author). In terms of the period that this statement was made, perhaps as late as the third century (since the name of God used here is the Holy One, Blessed be He, and the author is Rabbi Yehudah, the Prince, who lived at that time), one could imagine the concern with secret mystic groups, apocalyptic sects, crypto-Christians and Gnostics who could not be detected. Rabbi Yehudah, responsible for the community and concerned for the observance of the Torah, realized that secret acts could be harmful to the community but was probably at a loss to know how to deal with them.

22. *Exodus Rabbah* 28:1.

23. *Numbers Rabbah* 19:20

24. *Talmud Bavli Moed Katan* 16b.

25. *Pesikta Rabbati*, 40, 166b. See also David Daube, "*Kerdaino* as a Missionary Term," *Harvard Theological Review*, XL, No. 2 (April, 1957) p. 116f.

26. A famous example of God being conquered by the rabbis is found in *Talmud Bavli Bava Metziah* 59a-b.

27. *Deuteronomy Rabbah* 3:9.

28. *Song of Songs Rabbah* 5:3.

29. *Exodus Rabbah* 29:3.

30. *Sh't'kabel elhoti alekha.*

31. *Mekhilta*, II, 26.

32. *Ibid.*, 23.

33. *Numbers Rabbah* 44:22.

34. *Pesikta Rabbati: Aseret Hadibrot* 21:99a-b. See also *Exodus Rabbah* 27:8.

35. *Y'may sh'mad.*

36. *Pesikta Rabbati*, Translated by W. G. Braude (New Haven: Yale University Press, 1968), p. 418.

37. The text uses the term, *angaria.*

38. *Midrash on Psalms* 119:1.

39. *Midrash Tanhuma, Yitro*, 10.

40. It is important to point out that slavery is likened to sickness. It is neither the normal condition of people nor is it healthy. It is the responsibility of the ruler to insure the freedom of his people.

41. *Tanna D'bay Eliyahu*, 163.

42. See above, Part I, "The Sanctification of the Name and the Profanation of the Name."

43. *Sifra*, 86b.

44. *Sifra*, 57a, 99b.

45. Heschel, I, 82. He cites *Midrash on Psalms* 25:9.

46. Eliezer Berkovits, "Conversion 'According to Halachah' - What Is It?" *Judaism* XXIII, No. 4 (Fall, 1974), p. 478.

47. Reference to the golden calf incident.

48. *Midrash Tanhuma, N'tzavim*, 3 (on Deuteronomy 29:11).

49. *Mekhilta*, II, 241. See also *Exodus Rabbah* 28:6.

50. *Exodus Rabbah* 3:5.

51. *Mishnah B'rakhot* 2:2.

52. Max Radin, *The Jews Among the Greeks and Romans* (Philadelphia: Jewish Publication Society of America, 1915), p. 320. He discusses the separation of *ol mitzvot* from *ol malkhut.*

53. Cohen, "The Talmudic Age," p. 185f.

54. *Mekhilta*, II, 207. See also *Talmud Bavli Sota* 37b; *Hagigah* 6a; *Zevahim* 115b.

55. *Sifre, Sh'lah*, 115, 35a.

56. *Sifre, Ekev*, 38, 77a.

57. *Midrash Tanhuma, N'tzavim*, 3 on Deuteronomy 29:11.

58. *Talmud Bavli Shabbat* 88a; *Avodah Zarah* 2b. See also *Sifre, D'varim*, end of 40 for a parallel concept stated in the name of Rabbi Shimon bar Yohai.

59. David Daube, "Covenanting Under Duress," *The Irish Jurist*, II (New Series), Part 2 (Winter, 1967), p. 357.

60. See also parallels: *Pesikta* (Edited by Buber), 200a; *Midrash Tanhuma* (Edited by Buber), 283b. The word used here is *tirania*, which, according to Jastrow, *A Dictionary of the Targum, The Talmud Babli and Yerushalmi and the Midrashic Literature*, I, 534, is derived from the Greek, *tyrannia*, meaning sovereignty, absolute rule, usurpation, i.e., tyranny.

CHAPTER 2: THE CHARACTER OF POLITICAL AUTHORITY

God's rule is different from that of human kings. The author of laws and regulations observes his own legal system. He is not beyond the law. While a human king was not beyond the law (at least according to Juvenal) he often broke his own decrees. The rabbis, in contrasting ᴀ human king to God, emphasized that while "...a human king issues a decree and if he chooses he obeys it, otherwise others obey it,...the Holy One Blessed be He issues a decree (and) is the first to obey it."[1]

God's Direct Rule

God intervenes directly on Israel's behalf.

"You have seen" (Exodus 19:4). What I tell you is not received by tradition. I do not have to send documents to you. I do not have to present witnesses to you, but you yourselves have seen what I have done to the Egyptians. Notice how many offenses of idolatry, sensuous practices and murder they have in the past been guilty before me, and I punished them only on your account.[2]

An appeal to experience is made in this statement. The logic of a defeated people at the hand of the Romans implies that Israel is rejected by God. However, the people's own historical experience that God punished Egyptian oppressors on Israel's account should encourage them that he would also punish her Roman oppressors. Because Israel is loyal to God, he will exact punishment from those who oppress her.

God's compassion for Israel is manifest in the contrast between her behavior and that of the idolatrous Romans. The political overtones are hardly disguised in a recollection of distant historical events. The people are to realize that God still maintains the covenant, and that Israel is still a viable nation.

All who hear (of their own accord) draw near to God; God draws near to him.[3]

The act of drawing near emphasizes trust in authority which makes itself accessible to people. Instead of obstruction to shield authority we have the opposite tendency here.

"And you shall be unto me" (Exodus 19:5). As it were, I shall not appoint or delegate anyone else to rule over you, but I (myself) shall rule over you. And so it says, "Behold he that keeps Israel does not slumber nor sleep" (Psalms 121:4).[4]

101

The concept of the kingdom of heaven interweaves with God's com-passion for Israel. Since God is omnipotent, needing no rest like a human ruler, his protection is much more preferable than that of a human ruler. His rule is direct, i.e., no intermediaries are necessary. He does not need administrators, provincial governors, or a bureaucracy. The people can have a direct relationship with their ruler. In contrast to the Roman empire with its many officials, cor-rupt and rapacious bureaucracy, this statement must have been seen as a comfort to the people. The *Talmud* recounts many delegations of rabbis sent to Rome to negotiate with the emperor in order to ame-liorate the oppression of the people in Judea by provincial governors.

The kingdom of heaven was not regarded as some type of eschato-logical phenomenon to come at the end of days, but rather a political possibility. Seen in this context, the statement is in stark contrast to Roman practice. It served as a polemic against Rome and as propa-ganda to rally the people under the banner of God.

The rabbis may have been impressed by the contrast between the lower echelons of the Roman government with which they dealt and their meetings with the emperor. In most bureaucracies there is a tendency for the lower levels to be harsher, for there is a fear that if some rule or regulation is not followed to the letter, terrible conse-quences from the supervisory level might result. The lower levels of government do not have the authority to interpret policies freely or to change them: the source of the policy can be more flexible since it initiated it. Their experience might have led the rabbis to consider the initiator of policies as the only person who not only had the power to change a specific ruling or policy but who was more under-standing as well. They could then extrapolate such experiences onto the relationship between God and Israel. Without intermediaries God would be most flexible in setting his policies. After all, he was answerable to none. The kingdom of heaven was ideal because God could understand each situation; hard and fast rules need not be made if the people trusted the compassionate ruler. Immediately we understand Plato's unhappiness with the rule of law. If the philos-pher-king was fit to rule then he should not be hampered by laws but should be given the power to do so. By virtue of his innate abilities and his training he had the confidence of the governed. The rabbis could conceive only of God's rule as deserving of such trust and con-fidence.

> "And Moses reported the words of the people unto
> the Lord" (Exodus 19:8). God wished at the
> moment to give them the Torah and to speak with
> them, but Moses was still standing, and God said:
> What can I do because of Moses? Rabbi Levi said:
> It can be compared with a king who wished to pass

acts without consulting the lieutenant governor. When he said to him: Do this thing, the reply was: It has already been done. The king tried once again: Go and call this counselor so that he may come with you. When he was gone the king carried out his wish. When God desired to give the ten commandments, Moses was standing at his side. God thought: When I reveal the heavens to them and say, " I am the Lord your God," they will ask: Who is speaking, God or Moses? Let Moses therefore descend and then I will proclaim, "I am the Lord your God." Hence, when God said to Moses: "Go to the people and sanctify them today and tomorrow and let them wash their garments," he said: I have already sanctified them. For it says, "For you did charge us saying, Set bounds about the mountain and sanctify it." And God said unto him: "Go get down and you shall come up, you and Aaron with you." And as Moses descended, God revealed himself, for immediately after it says, "For Moses went down unto the people," we are told that God spoke.[5]

The king wishes to speak directly to his people but cannot do so because his next in command to whom that task is usually delegated is present. A humorous image, the king does not know what to do with his loyal servant in order to get rid of him. He attempts to send him on errands to find that his minister has been only too efficient and had already anticipated and completed all assignments. Finally, the king succeeds in sending the minister away so that he could speak directly to the people. Moses, having been such a good servant, cannot be thrust out unceremoniously; he must be treated with tact. Using a ruse by ostensibly sending him on some task, the king now has the opportunity he sought.

Rabbi Hananiah ben Antigonos said: Come and consider the expressions chosen by the Torah. "To Molech"[6] (Leviticus 18:21), that is, anything at all that you declare as ruling over you, even if it be a chip of wood or a piece of potsherd. Rabbi Yehudah (the Prince) said: "Other gods" -gods who are later than that which was the last in the order of creation. And who was it that was last of the things that were created? - The one that calls them "gods."[7]

Rabbi Hananiah ben Antigonos was of a priestly family, and many of his teachings were concerned with Temple ritual. One might imagine that he would be concerned with any rival of Temple ritual, even though the Temple had been destroyed by the time he made this statement (during the second century). To be sure, to worship any-thing but God would horrify any of the rabbis. However, in the con-text of Rabbi Hananiah's other statements, it has a special poign-ancy. With none of the drama of the Temple ritual of sacrifice available to the people, they might attempt to find substitutes in pagan cults. Nothing must rule over Israel except God himself, even though the Temple no longer existed. With Roman temples and vari-ous other pagan cults available it was necessary to identify them as specifically forbidden to the people of Israel.

Rabbi Yehudah's statement can be understood in terms of placing the objects of worship in a definition of time. The sun, moon, stars, trees, etc., all were created before man according to the Genesis story. The very purpose of creation was to respond to God. Idolatry perverts this purpose, since man, an object of creation, rather than worship the subject of creation which transcends him, tries to become a subject himself by creating gods. Man and creation have universal connotations whereas idolatry, which is the worship by each man of his own creation, separates man from the rest of the universe. The stimulus for these statements is God's command in the Torah to establish God's kingdom. Creation itself must not be wor-shipped, for this would pervert allegiance to God. Man can either be ruled by his own creations or directly by the God who created him.

> "Shall not the judge of all the earth do right" (Gen-esis 18:25). Rabbi Yehudah ben Shimon said: So said Abraham to God thus: for a king of flesh and blood an appeal lies from the dux to the eparch and from the eparch to the commander-in-chief. But as no appeal lies from you, should not the judge of the whole world do right? When you did desire to judge your world you did deliver it into the hands of two, Remus and Romulus, so that if one sought to do anything, the other would restrain him, but seeing that none shall restrain you, should not the judge of the whole world do right?[8]

The phraseology of this statement is legal and political. The word used for appeal is the legal one for an appeal of a court decision.[9] The various offices mentioned are of the chain of command of the Roman military government. To appeal a decision of the local court Jewish leaders would often go directly to Rome by-passing the Roman mili-tary hierarchy. Contrasting their experience with God's rule where all judgments are direct, what appeal could be possible? Since there cannot be any appeal, for there is only one judge, God must be just. There can be no alternative if he is not just. The rabbis perceived

Remus and Romulus as restraining each other. But God cannot be restrained.

God's Compassionate Rule

> Rabbi Abba ben Kahana said: As it is written in
> the section of Hannah, "The Lord will judge the
> gathering of earth" (I Samuel 2:10). When does
> God judge the creatures and find merit in them?
> On Rosh Hashanah he judges his creatures and
> finds merit in them, for he desires to find merit in
> his creatures and not to find them liable as it says:
> "As I live, I desire not the death of the wicked"
> (Ezekiel 33:11). God desires to justify his creatures
> as it says: "It pleased the Lord to justify him"
> (Isaiah 42:21, a playful mistranslation of this
> verse); he wants to justify his creatures.[10]

The use of legal terminology, "find merit," "to find liable," "to justify," in this *midrash* implies an agreement between God and mankind which is held responsible to keep it. The statement points to the possibility of change and reconciliation despite previous acts of rebellion against the agreement.

The character of authority that is described is that of a compassionate ruler. Despite the power of the creator of the universe, he is willing to temper justice with compassion when judging man for his deeds.

The Legitimacy of God's Authority Dependent on Proving Itself

> Why were not the ten commandments at the begin-
> ning of the Torah? They gave a parable. It can be
> compared to a king who entered the state. He said
> to them: I will rule over you. They said to him: You
> have not done anything good for us that you should
> rule over us. What did he do? He built a wall for
> them. He brought water for them. He fought their
> wars. He said to them: I will rule over you. They
> said: Yes, yes. So with God - he took Israel out of
> Egypt. He split the sea for them. He brought man-
> nah for them. He brought forth a well for them. He
> sent out quail for them. He fought Amalek for
> them. He said to them: I will rule over you. They
> said: Yes, yes.[11]

Here we see a convergence of several concepts that are concretized in the concept of the giving of the Torah: the exodus from Egypt, miracles, the kingdom of heaven, and Israel. The exodus and the miracles are manifestations of the kingdom of heaven; God has the power, ability and will to fulfill his promises. They find significance in the giving of the Torah, here expressed in the words, "I will rule over you. They said: Yes, yes." The exodus and the miracles were not ends in themselves; they were consummated in the giving of the Torah. God must prove himself to the people before they are willing to accept him.

As an explicit understanding of the nature of authority, the rabbis taught that power, ability and will are not enough to effectuate the covenant relationship. The text emphasizes that the authority has to prove itself before the people accept it. The relationship could not be consummated before such an acceptance.

Strategies in Dealing with Political Authority

The system of rhetoric, comprised of "...devices and strategies to help the client win his case, was not developed by the rabbis."[12] Its origin was Greek. However, the rabbis utilized it in pleading before their ultimate political authority, God.

> Rabbi Shimon said: What skilled craftsmen are the Israelites that they know how to appease and win the favor of the Creator? Rabbi Yudan said: Like those Cuthaeans who are clever at begging. One of them came to a woman and said to her, have you an onion? Give it to me. When she gave it to him, he said: Can one eat an onion without bread? When she gave it to him he said: Can one eat without drinking? So he got food and drink. Rabbi Aha said: Some women are clever at asking, some are not. A woman who is clever at asking comes to her neighbor. The door is open but she knocks and says: Peace be with you, neighbor. How fare you, how fares your husband, how are your children? May I come in? The other answers: Come in, what do you want? She rejoins: Do you have such and such an article, will you give it to me? She replied: Yes. The woman who is not clever at asking comes to her neighbor. The door is shut. She opens it and says: Have you such and such an article? The answer is no. Rabbi Haninah said: Some tenant farmers are clever at asking, some are not. The clever one observes that he is going downhill on his farm. He plucks up heart of grace. He combs his

hair, he whitens his clothes, and with a bright coun-
tenance and with the stick in hand and rings on his
fingers, he goes to his landlord who says: How is
the land, will you be able to eat of its fruits with
joy? How are the oxen, will you be able to enjoy
their fat? How are the goats, will you set yourself
with the kids? What do you want? The farmer says:
Have you ten dinari? Will you give them to me? If
you want twenty, take them. He who does not know
how to ask goes with unkempt hair, dirty clothes
and with a miserable face to his landlord, who says
to him: How is the land? He replied: Oh that it
produced what we have put into it. How are the
oxen? They are weak. What do you want? Can you
give me ten dinari? He replied: Bring me first what
you owe me. Rabbi Onias said: David was one of
the clever farmers. He first sang God's praises and
said: "The heavens tell of the glory of God"
(Psalms 19:1). God said: Perhaps he wants something: He said, "And the firmament shows his
handiwork." God said: Perhaps he wants something. He said: "Day upon day utter speech." Then
the Holy One Blessed be He said: "What do you
require?" Then David replied: "Who can understand his errors. The errors that I have done before
you pardon." God said: They are dismissed and
forgiven. Then David said: "Cleanse you me from
secret faults from the hidden sins that I have com-
mitted before you." God replied: These, too, are
dismissed and forgiven. Then he said: "From the
presumptuous sins keep back your servant; the pre-
meditated sins. Let them not have dominion over
me, then shall I be innocent." These are the big
iniquities — "and pure of transgression." For
David said to God: Master of the World, for you
are a great God and my trespasses are great. It
befits the great God to pardon the great trespasses
as it is written: "For the sake of my name, pardon
my iniquity, for it is great" (Psalms 28:11).[13]

The purpose of these statements, all of which are parallel, is to
construct a strategy to deal with authority. The concepts — ethics,
Torah, righteousness, prayer, repentance and atonement — are concretized in the instruction to the citizen regarding the proper
approach to authority. The date of the various statements ranges
from the third to the fourth centuries, and all are native to the land

of Israel. Whether they deal with some specific historical event or generally comment on the best way to deal with God is difficult to determine.

Authority is approachable. It is not so far removed that it has nothing to do with individuals and their problems. By making oneself presentable one could achieve one's objectives, i.e., getting the authority to assist a person in time of need. Perhaps it was the experience of these rabbis when dealing with Jewish authorities, that proper demeanor would aid in the success of a request.

> "Draw me, we will run after you" (Song of Songs 1:4). Rabbi Meir said: When Israel stood before Mt. Sinai to receive the Torah, the Holy One Blessed be He said to them: Shall I give you the Torah? Bring me good sureties that you will keep it, and then I will give it to you. They replied: Sovereign of the Universe, our ancestors will be our guarantors. He said to them: Your ancestors themselves require sureties. They are like the man who went to borrow from the king and the king said, Give me a surety and I will lend you. He went and brought him a surety, whereupon the king said, Your surety himself requires a surety. He went and brought a second surety. Said the king to him: Your surety requires a surety. When he brought to him a third surety, he said to him: Know for the sake of this man I lend you. So when Israel stood ready to receive the Torah, he said to them: I will give you my Torah but bring me good surety that you will keep it, and I will give it to you. They said: Our ancestors are our sureties. I can find fault with Abraham because he said . . . (the *midrash* proceeds to find faults with all of the ancestors). Then they said: Sovereign of the Universe, our prophets will be our sureties. He replied, I have faults to find with them. As it says, "And the shepherds transgressed against me" (Jeremiah 2:8). (The *midrash* proceeds to find problems with the prophets). Still bring me good sureties, and I will give it to you. They said to him: Our children shall be our sureties. To which God replied: Verily these are good sureties. For their sake I will give it to you.[14]

Rabbi Meir connects the word for pledge, *mashkan*, with the verse, *moshkeni* (draw me). He regards the Torah as being given on trust, like a loan, which can be recalled if payments are not kept. The fathers and the prophets are rejected as guarantors; proof texts are used to demonstrate that they are wanting. Finally, the children are accepted as a guarantee for they are not burdened by the disadvantages of the fathers and prophets whose accounts are overdrawn. The *midrash* goes on to state that for this reason a father is to teach his son Torah so that he will remain a good surety for the covenant. Another *midrash* (on Psalms 8:2, Buber edition, p. 73f) uses the same theme, pointing out that the reason the patriarchs are rejected as sureties is that they are already obligated to God. The children are accepted because they are not yet obligated. God asks the children while they are yet in their mothers' wombs if they would be willing to be guarantors for Israel, warning them of the consequences if the covenant is not maintained. After the children assented, God gave the ten commandments. This charming legend explains how the future insures the present. It emphasizes the hope for the continuation of Israel. Even if the past and the present do not live up to the covenant, it is hoped that the future will insure the security of the present relationship between God and Israel. The hope of the future is an effective strategy before God.

NOTES

1. Lieberman, *Greek in Jewish Palestine,* p. 37ff. He cites *Talmud Yerushalmi Rosh Hashanah* 1:3, 57a in the name of Rabbi Eleazar ben Pedat. See also, David Daube, "Princeps Legibus Salutus," in *Studi in Memoria di Paolo Koschaker* (Milan: Multa Paucis, 1954), pp. 463-465 on this statement and its relation to Roman law.

2. *Mekhilta,* II, 201.

3. *Sifre, B'ha'alotecha,* 78, 20b.

4. *Mekhilta,* II, 204.

5. *Exodus Rabbah* 28:3.

6. A play on words; *Molekh* was the god frequently an object of Israelite idolatry. *Molekh* comes from the same word root as the word, to rule (*m l kh*).

7. *Mekhilta,* II, 240f.

8. *Genesis Rabbah* 49:19.

9. *Ankeliton-appellatio.* M. Jastrow, *A Dictionary of the Targum, the Talmud Babli and Yerushalmi, and the Midrashic Literature* (New York: Pardes Publishing House, Inc., 1950) I, p. 88.

10. *Pesikta Rabbati,* 40, 166b (on Leviticus 23:24). See also *Midrash Tanhuma, Yitro,* 10.

11. *Mekhilta,* II, p.229f. See also *Exodus Rabbah* 29:3.

12. Boaz Cohen, "Letter and Spirit in Jewish and Roman Law," *Mordecai Kaplan Jubilee Volume.* Edited by M. Davis (New York: Jewish Theological Seminary of America, 1953), I, p. 132.

13. *Leviticus Rabbah* 5:8.

14. *Songs of Songs Rabbah* 1:4, 1; parallel version found in *Midrash Tanhuma, Vayigash,* 2, 67b.

CHAPTER 3: LEADERSHIP

The Legitimacy of the Leader in Relation to God

Rabbi Menahem in the name of Rabbi Tanhuma
bar Hiyya and Rabbi Mani in the name of Rabbi
Yose bar Zevida supported Rabbi Ze'eira's interpretation of Exodus 20:7 (that one is not to take
upon himself God's authority as voiced in the Torah
if he is not worthy of such authority) by citing
another verse: "He that philanders with a woman
lacks understanding" (Proverbs 6:32), that is,
whenever a man takes on Torah's authority merely
to use it, he is no more than a philanderer who uses
a woman's body (but does not truly possess her). . . .
According to Rabbi Abbahu, God said: I am called
holy and (when you take on Torah's authority) you
too, may be called holy (but take care). Unless you
have all those attributes of mine which I revealed to
Moses (Exodus 34:6-7), you may not take on such
authority.[1]

Human authority must be modeled on the authortity of God.
Power is corruptible when, instead of serving the community, it is
used for self-aggrandizement. Yose bar Zevida[2] and Mani[3] were
heads of academies, while Tanhuma bar Hiyya was a wealthy man.
All of these rabbis, because of their positions, appreciated the use of
power. Rule, even by the authority of the Torah, may become an
opportunity for self-aggrandizement. Rabbi Abbahu[4] had constant
contact with the Roman government and was concerned lest Jewish
government become like that of the Romans. The attainment of holiness is to bring recognition of the kingdom of heaven. Specifically, it
refers to the imitation of God.[5] This statement compares human rule
and divine rule. To be a legitimate ruler one must be holy like God.[6]
Holiness is attained by adhering to the Torah. This commitment to
attempt to conform with some transcendent force might seem strange
at first. However, this phenomenon is pervasive in human thought;
only the transcendent force changes: nature or history, even the
"objectivity" of modern science as a standard to which the human
endeavor is to strive, gives direction and discipline to human
thought. It seems that humanity attempts to transcend itself. In
examining political thought one must try to discover the vision or
ideal that it used as the measuring rod by the specific thinker. He
might even have a concept of human potential that transcends the
present situation as he perceives it. He understands his world and
explains political phenomenon in terms of that vision; problems are

caused by the failure to conform to that vision or transcendent force.

The rabbis regarded themselves as partners with God in their interpretation of the Torah and its application to the community. According to the *midrash* God studied the Torah and uttered various traditions in the name of their rabbinic authors.[7] Because they shared the act of study with God, their right to interpret the Torah was regarded as legitimate.

The Leader Wrestles With God

Rabbi Nehemiah said: It is said in regard to *haverim*, so long as a man is a *haver*, he is not bound to the community (he need not concern himself with its affairs), and he is not punished for its sins, but when he is appointed to a post and receives the *tallit* (of investiture), then he must not say, I am concerned only with my own good, I am not bound to the community. On the contrary, all the burdens of the community are upon him. If he sees a man doing wrong to his neighbor and does not stop him, he will be punished.[8] The Holy Spirit cries out to him, My son, you have become a surety for your neighbor (Proverbs 6:1). You are responsible for him, or have struck a bargain with a foreigner (play on words — *zar*, foreigner; *zera* — arena). God says to him: You have entered the arena, and he who enters the arena must be either conquered or conquerer. The Holy One Blessed be He says to him: You and I stand in the arena, either you conquer or I conquer you.[9]

Rabbi Nehemiah, one of the few of Rabbi Akiba's students to survive the Hadrianic persecutions and the subsequent Bar Kokhba rebellion, was instrumental in reconstructing Jewish life at Usha after the rebellion failed.[10] His concern and experience with the risks of communal life not only in regard to dealing with external uncertainty, *i.e.*, the Roman provincial military authority, but the problems of reconstructing life for a defeated people is certainly demonstrated in this statement. A *haver* was a member of a group of students and teachers, individuals whose life was dedicated to the study of the Torah and the observance of its commandments. The *tallit* was the outer garment worn with the ritual fringes (see Numbers 15:37-41), a reminder of the commandments to the wearer. A special *tallit* was a sign of authority.

Rabbi Nehemiah differentiated between a private person and a public official. By gaining a position of authority he was responsible for the entire community — their sins became his sins. To enter the arena of political life with all of its risks, one had to bear responsibility for the actions of each person and actively work to see that people did not wrong each other.

The metaphor of the arena, where gladiators often fought to the death, is an appropriate one for the political life of a Jewish official in the land of Israel during the latter part of the second century. That the official fought with God in order to survive is not as odd as it might first appear. In a struggle there is a trust between the contenders, i.e., known ground rules of the contest. The political official took the risks of office and contended with the ultimate authority, God, to fight temptations placed before him, fulfill his responsibilities and use his power legitimately.

The verse quoted from Proverbs points to his responsibility. He is like a surety,[11] guaranteeing the destiny of the community. As a leader he must encourage the community to fulfill the covenant.

The Leader Unites His Destiny With That of the Community

> Moses saw that there was no continuation for Israel, so he united his life with their life, and he broke the tablets and said to God: They have sinned and I have sinned, for I have broken the tablets. If you will pardon them, pardon me too, but if you will not pardon them, then pardon not me, blot me out of your book.[12]

Atonement is concretized in Moses' act. He sought reconciliation with God for Israel by throwing his lot with the people. Moses' authority, so directly identified with the destiny of the people, was used to appeal to God's compassion because it was similar to God's authority relationship to Israel.

> Rabbi Yose bar Yermiah: How can we compare the prophets to women? Just as a woman is not embarrassed to make claims for the needs of her household from her husband, so the prophets were not embarrassed to make claims for the needs of their household of Israel before the Holy One Blessed be He.[13]

Israel has a right to make claims before God because it has accepted the Torah. People have the legitimate right to make claims against the authority with which it has made agreements. The statement says that when Israel makes such claims God will answer her, for the prophets represent those claims before God.

Rabbinic Claims of Authority in Relation to the Community

The rabbis had to be accepted by the community in order to be effective leaders. Their claim to authority was based on their exclusive knowledge of the Torah which they were willing to impart.[14] Their program emphasized ". . .loyalty to a way of life based on literature."[15] The criterion for this loyalty was adherence to the Torah. The rabbis had always claimed that their interpretations were authentic. Their sanction was from Sinai, transmitted from one generation to the next. The chain of tradition recounted in *Mishnah Avot* 1:1 was the basis of their claim that the Torah had passed from Moses ultimately to them. Only the rabbis could claim that their traditions emanated directly from Sinai.

In the ancient world antiquity was a determining factor of authenticity and was probably the motivating factor behind the declarations that all of the Torah both oral and written were from Sinai.[16] The task the rabbis set for themselves was to determine through interpretation of the Bible, God's purpose.[17] The people were taught exactly what God required of them by those who possessed that special knowledge. They firmly believed that the foundation of creation was dependent on the correct observance of the Torah according to their interpretation.[18] This all-consuming sense of mission as well as the enthusiastic manner in which the rabbis went about their task impressed the people and encouraged acceptance of rabbinic leadership. In sum, the rabbis based their claim to authenticity on the chain of tradition as they understood it. That chain did not include kings and priests. Since the priests had lost their influence with the loss of the Temple ritual, and kings no longer ruled, there was really no one within the community who could effectively oppose their claim. The chain of tradition was also very attractive to the people because it was not exclusive. It was open to anyone who studied Torah. Tales of the humble beginnings of Hillel and Akiba were popular and emphasized that ability and character were the criteria for leadership.

The goal of the rabbis was to organize in such a way as to become recognized as the legitimate Jewish government in the land of Israel.[19] They attempted to gain support from the people to attain this goal in place of any other government whether it be Jewish or pagan. While temporarily the Romans had power, God would eventually support the rabbis because they had knowledge of the Torah.[20]

In contending for influence with the exilarch in Babylonia, they argued that redemption would be the result of knowledge of the Torah rather than subservience to the house of David (the exilarch).[21] Throughout this conflict of claims, "Political argument was phrased in theological language. . . Political theory obviously was subsumed under the eschatological and messianic issue: How is Israel to be saved?"[22] By the fourth century the rabbis were triumphant, for the exilarchs became rabbis themselves.[23] By the end of the fifth century the rabbis and exilarchs were so tied to each other that there was a unity of purpose. The exilarchate survived as a separate institution but was rabbinical in its program and influence.[24] Although the rabbis never achieved political independence, their program succeeded through the support of the exilarch.

The school became the most significant institution of post-biblical Judaism.[25] The rabbis had exclusive control over the schools which became the training ground for rabbinic political aspirations.[26] Knowledge of the Torah as taught by the rabbis became the source of authority. The rabbis, like Plato, understood the role of education as a means of molding the community. However, in contrast to Plato, their education was not to lead to differentiation between rulers and ruled. The universality of education was to effectuate the biblical vision of a "kingdom of priests."

Rabbis as Priests and Prophets

Another explanation of "God spoke all these words saying." Rabbi Yitzhak said: The prophets received from Sinai the messages they were to prophesize to subsequent generations, for Moses told Israel: "But with him that stands here with us this day before the Lord our God, and also with him that is not with us this day" (Deuteronomy 29:14). It does not say that is not standing with us this day, but just with us this day. These are the souls that will one day be created and because there is not yet any substance in them, the word, standing, is not used with them. Although they did not yet exist, still each one received his share (of the Torah). (The *midrash* then proceeds with examples of the various prophets.)[27]

Rabbi Yitzhak, of the school of Rabbi Yishmael, interpreted the biblical passage narrowly to include only the prophets, who by receiving the Torah from Sinai, had legitimate claims to present God's word to later generations. Apparently, there was a question as to the authority of the prophets to make divine pronouncements. Later in this same *midrash*, it is stated that the rabbis of every generation received their wisdom from Sinai. In at least one other interpretation[28] this verse refers to all future generations; it is not limited merely to the prophets.

Marmorstein describes the school of Rabbi Yishmael as more rationalistic that the school of Rabbi Akiba, using allegories and metaphors to prevent anthropomorphism and to ameliorate what to Rabbi Yishmael's school were irrational verses in the Bible. The prophets, who had divine communication, could have been at Sinai, which would seem more plausible than each and every individual of future generations.

The main point of the *midrash* is that legitimacy for the prophets and the rabbis stemmed from the giving of the Torah, or God's revelation at Sinai. As each prophet received his share of Torah, he was able, like the people at Sinai, to be a witness to the covenant, the observance of which was the basic theme of prophetic admonition.

> Rabbi Abdimi from Haifa said: Since the day when the Temple was destroyed prophecy has been taken from the prophets and given to the wise.[29] Is then a wise man not also a prophet? What he meant was this: Although it has been taken from the prophets, it has not been taken from the wise. Amemar said: A wise man is even superior to a prophet as it says, "And a prophet has a heart of wisdom" (Psalms 90:12). Who is compared with whom? Is not the smaller compared with the greater? Abaye said: The proof (that prophecy has not been taken from the wise) is that a great man[30] makes a statement, and the same is then reported in the name of another great man. . . .[31]

The rabbis (the wise) as interpreters of God's word were, in a sense, God's spokesmen and were not adverse to confronting God like their prophetic predecessors.[32] Their confidence in the knowledge of God's word led to a wide latitude in their interpretations of the written Torah.[33] According to Herford, the rabbis functioned as a continuation and application of the prophetic tradition.[34] Where the prophets failed in spreading God's word, the rabbis succeeded through their schools which educated the people in the ways of Torah on a massive scale.[35] Whereas the prophets represented God, the rabbis represented God's word, the Torah, through their thorough knowledge of it. All Israel was to become " . . . a kingdom of priests and a holy nation" (Exodus 19:6). According to Louis Ginzberg, if it were not for Israel's apostasy before the golden calf there would not have been any need for a specific tribe of priests. All of Israel would have become a universal priesthood.[36]

The rabbis took this injunction (Exodus 19:6) seriously. The Pharisees consciously adopted all the priestly laws of purity and were careful to use only properly tithed products to attain this parity with the priests in the Temple. While achieving this parity the Pharisees also contended for power with the priests.[37] Yet as long as the Temple stood, the priests still maintained their special status since the rabbis could not perform sacrifices in the Temple. After the destruction the priests lost this special function, and the rabbis, by virtue of adopting priestly laws of purity, attained the same status.[38]

Rabbi Yohanan ben Zakkai taught that the Temple was not an end in itself. The Temple was a means to serve God through sacrifice.[39] Now that there was no longer a Temple he taught that what counted were Torah and piety rather than power and national political independence (which the Temple symbolized). When the Pharisees were involved in national politics (at times they even had control during the pre-Herodian period) their purpose was to maintain the laws of the Torah so that all Jews could live the life of the priest and fulfill the command to be members of the kingdom of priests. The Temple in Jerusalem could be in every person's home. After 70 C.E. the rabbis essentially collaborated with the Romans in order to gain internal autonomy to insure the fulfillment of the Torah.[40]

Priestly ritual purity was to be universally observed in order to expiate sin everywhere — in the home and in the market place. Sacrifice was interpreted in terms of acts of compassion and prayer which could expiate the sin (replacing the sin offerings which could no longer be brought).[41] Following the concepts of the prophets before them (e.g., Isaiah 58:6) they taught that the proper ritual of atonement was to free the oppressed, feed the hungry, take care of the poor and clothe the naked.[42]

The rabbis interpreted the Torah applying it to their situation and transmitted their traditions to the community. They exercised leadership and influence primarily as teachers and preachers. While their political authority was formalized through ordination, it was dependent on the acceptance and recognition of the people. The rabbi, as teacher, was a powerful force who insured the survival of the community. Usually, the teacher's role is an external influence on the polity, obliquely effecting those in power. Here we have a different phenomenon of political leadership. The rabbi, by virtue of his teaching, was recognized as the political leader. His knowledge was truly political since he used it as a means of control and discipline. The teacher extended his own knowledge and shared it with his students who, in turn, became teachers themselves. The rabbi was the teacher par excellence for he had internalized his own knowledge. He was recognized as the communal authority, for he represented embodiment of the Torah. His students became teachers by internalizing the traditions and myths of the community, i.e., the oral tradition. Continuity insuring the security and integrity of the polity was a consequence of the instruction and indoctrination of communal values. When the teacher was influential (and therefore, powerful) and was involved in the decision-making process, he could be a successful authority figure while training students to succeed him.

NOTES

1. *Pesikta Rabbati* 111a, Translated by W. G. Braude, I, p. 457f. *Sh'rarah* is translated as authority.
2. *Encyclopedia Judaica,* XVI, p. 150.
3. *Ibid.,* XI, p. 74.
4. *Ibid.,* I, p. 35. Rabbi Abbahu, who lived in Caesaria, the center of Roman rule and Palestinian Christianity, was learned in mathematics, rhetoric, and Greek. He was held in high esteem by Roman authorities who regarded him as the spokesman for the Jewish people.
5. See above, Part I, "Holiness."
6. The phraseology used in the text is *t'kabel alekha* "to accept upon yourself," which is the same as that used for accepting the covenant. To accept rule is to accept a covenant with God which legitimizes authority.
7. *Talmud Bavli Hagigah* 15b. Statement of Rabbah bar Shilo.
8. For his neglect.
9. *Exodus Rabbah* 27:8. See also *Exodus Rabbah* 28:1; *Numbers Rabbah* 19:20.
10. *Encyclopedia Judaica,* XII, p. 937.
11. The word for surety is *arev.*
12. *Exodus Rabbah* 46:1.
13. *Pesikta D'rav Kahanah* 12:1.
14. Alexander Guttman, "Foundation of Rabbinic Judaism," *Hebrew Union College Annual,* XXIII, Part 1, (1950-1951), p. 455.
15. Moses Hadas, "The First Encounter of Judaism with Europeanism," *The Menorah Treasury.* Edited by L. Schwartz (Philadelphia: Jewish Publication Society of America, 1964), p. 47.
16. Baron, *A History,* p. 161. See *Talmud Bavli B'rakhot* 5a. Statement of Rabbi Shimon ben Lakish; *Sanhedrin* 21b; *Genesis Rabbah* 8:2, 57.
17. George F. Moore, "The Idea of Torah in Judaism," *The Menorah Treasury,* p. 18.
18. Jacob Neusner, *A History of the Jews in Babylonia* (Leiden: E.J. Brill, 1968), III, p. 47. See also Lauterbach, *Rabbinic Essays,* p.235. He attributes the change in forms from the *midrash* to the *Mishnah* as an aim to " . . . assert their authority and to show that they were absolutely necessary for the interpretation of the religious teachings . . ." Which were no longer tied to the biblical text. Their teachings were no longer tied to the written Torah in the change of form. Only the rabbis knew the oral Torah. The authority of the rabbis was all that was necessary.
19. Neusner, *A History of the Jews in Babylonia,* III, p. 46.
20. *Ibid.* Neusner does not give any sources to support this view.
21. Neusner, *There We Sat Down,* p. 78. The rabbis regarded themselves as the embodiment of oral revelation for " . . . all his actions constituted paradigms that were not merely correct, but actually heavenly."
22. *Ibid.,* p. 60.
23. *Ibid.,* p. 66f. Leadership
24. Neusner, *A History of the Jews of Babylonia,* V, p. 258.
25. Ginzberg, *Students, Saints and Scholars,* p. 5.
26. Neusner, *There We Sat Down,* p. 126. This was largely due to the efforts of the rabbis.
27. *Exodus Rabbah* 28:6.
28. *Talmud Bavli Shavuot* 39a.
29. *Hakhamim.*
30. *Gavra Rabbah.*.
31. *Talmud Bavli Bava M'tziah* 12a.
32. *Talmud Bavli Bava M'tziah* 58b f.
33. J. Newman, *Halachic Sources from the Beginning to the Ninth Century* (Leiden: E.J. Brill, 1969), p. 5. See in regard to statement in *Talmud Bavli Gitin* 36a concerning Hillel's *prosbul.*

34. Herford, *The Pharisees,* p. 137f.

35. Ginzberg, *Students, Scholars and Saints,* p. 2.

36. Ginzberg, *The Legends of the Jews,* III, p. 187. The entire nation was bound to the Torah. The priests separated their rulings from the actual written Torah, yet tied their authority to the Torah. If they had identified their rulings with the Torah, anyone opposing them could also make the same claims. Rather, they limited the Torah's scope. See Herford, *The Pharisees,* p. 61.

37. Weber, *Ancient Judaism,* p. 385. He understands the motive for the maintenance of the priestly laws of purity on the part of the Pharisees as a reaction against Hellenism. See also, Lauterbach, *Rabbinic Essays,* p. 105f. He attributes a Greek influence, i.e., that the people should rule (*demos*) rather than the priests.

38. Weber, p. 391.

39. Neusner, *From Politics to Piety,* p. 146.

40. *Ibid.*

41. *Ibid.,* p. 152.

42. *Ibid.,* p. 153.

CHAPTER 4: THE CONSEQUENCES OF ACCEPTING THE REVEALED TORAH

The agreement between God and Israel was significant only in terms of its actualization in speech or action. On each occasion when the Torah was observed the agreement was sustained. When the Torah was not observed the agreement was broken. The consequences as set down in the Torah were realized in the form of rewards and punishments. The goal of the rabbis was to insure that the agreement was maintained as they understood it. By consciously studying the content of the covenant they could discover God's will to insure its implementation.[1] Israel, they taught, would be redeemed through the observance of the agreement.

To accomplish this task the rabbis attempted a universal education; their purpose was to make every Jew a rabbi.[2] If this goal could be attained the Jewish people could transcend historical forces.[3] While the goal of a universal rabbinate might seem similar to the universal ministry of some later Protestant groups, its tone was quite different: the former was primarily an intellectual enterprise, while the latter tended to be an emotional experience.

The rabbis believed in the final victory and triumph of Israel and had faith that the people would live forever by receiving the Torah.[4] By observing the commandments eternal life could be acquired.[5] Rabbi Nehemiah taught that receiving the Torah frees one from government; Rabbi Yehudah taught that receiving the Torah frees one from the angel of death.[6]

> Why was the Torah given in the wilderness? It was done to teach you that if man does not search himself as a wilderness, he would not merit the words of the Torah. Just as the wilderness has no limit, so the words of the Torah have no limit. As it is said: "It is longer than the earth in measure and wider than the sea" (Job 11:9). Just as they have no end, so the giving of reward has no limit, as it is said: "How abundant is your goodness which you await for those who fear you" (Psalms 31:20).[7]

Through the use of the metaphor of wilderness, the giving of the Torah is described. It has no limit in space or time, that is, it is eternally applicable in every place and in every situation. The giving of the Torah is significant because of its unlimited consequences in terms of reward. The very integrity of the Jewish people was at stake. If the people were to survive, it had to be assured that the covenant was worth maintaining. Unlimited reward was its appealing aspect. The Torah's scope reminded the people that the covenant was still binding. However, if the agreement was not kept, Israel would be punished.

> Rabbi Yohanan said: Sixty myriads of ministering angels ascended with the Holy One Blessed be He at Sinai with a crown in the hand of each, with which to crown every individual of Israel. Rabbi Aba ben Kahana said in the name of Rabbi Yohanan: One hundred and twenty myriads descended, one to adorn each Israelite and another to crown him.[8]

> Rabbi Simai interpreted at the hour that the Israelites gave precedence to "...we will do..." to "...we will harken..." (Exodus 24:7), six hundred thousand ministering angels came and set two crowns on each Israelite, one for "we will do" and the other for "we will harken". Then as soon as Israel sinned one million two hundred thousand destroying angels descended and removed them. As it is said: "And the children of Israel stripped themselves of their ornaments from Mt. Horeb" (Exodus 33:6).[9]

The concept emphasized here is "measure for measure", that the reward for receiving the Torah was removed when the Israelites rejected the Torah, i.e., they returned to their previous status that they held prior to receiving the Torah. They lost their crowns — their nobility, when they rejected the Torah.

> The following have no portion in the world to come ...he who maintains that the Torah was not divinely revealed (literally, "the Torah is not from heaven")[10]

Justice will be realized in the world to come for those who reject the divine source of the Torah. Statements that include "the world to come" as an aspect of God's justice emphasize the ultimate liability of each person. Once the agreement is made liability is in force for every party. The implication is that if punishment is not manifest in this world it will be forthcoming in a most terrible form in the world to come.

God had to reveal his will in order to make the agreement with Israel. To deny that such an act had ever occurred would mean that the Torah, in which such a claim was made, was not in force.

The Revelation of the Oral Torah

> Rabbi Yohanan said: God makes a covenant[11] with

Israel only for the sake of that which is transmitted orally,[12] as it says: "For by the mouth of these words, I have made a covenant with you and with Israel" (Exodus 34:27).[13]

By attributing their teachings and interpretations to Torah, i.e., to divine revelation rather than to themselves the rabbis considered their authority as having emanated from the Torah.[14] By interpreting the covenant they continued to reveal God's word.

"These are the laws, judgments and teachings"[15] (Leviticus 26:46). "The laws" — these are the interpretations. "The judgments" — these are the decisions. "The teachings" (*torot*) — teaches that two Torahs were given to Israel, one written and one oral. Rabbi Akiba said, were there two Torahs (given) to Israel? Were not many Torahs given to Israel, "This is the Torah of the holocaust sacrifice"; "this is the Torah of the sin offering"; "this is the Torah of the peace sacrifice"; "this is the Torah if a man dies in a tent." "That which the Lord gave between him and the children of Israel" — Moses merited to be the messenger between Israel and their father in heaven. "On Mt. Sinai at the hand of Moses" — to teach that the Torah was given, its laws, details and interpretations by the hand of Moses from Sinai.[16]

Urbach points out that the rabbis regarded their studies as given at Sinai and viewed the prophets askance — if it were not for Israel's sins, the prophets would not have been needed.[17] The revelation not only included the Torah and its interpretation but the very authority for continual interpretaion. The interpretations of the rabbis had at least an equal status with the written Torah. They declared that the written Torah was dependent on the oral one.[18] Urbach demonstrates that the rabbis believed the oral Torah, which they regarded as the essence of the covenant, more beloved by God than the written one.[19]

In *Avot d'Rabbi Natan*, chapter 15, there is a discussion between Hillel and Shammai regarding the two Torahs. In a homily about the alphabet it is stated that the identification of each letter is possible because of traditions that are handed down from one generation to the next. To Shammai this concept is so evident that the discussion seems preposterous. Hillel, while agreeing, exhibits more patience making the point that the written Torah has no meaning without the tradition of interpretation.[20] The rabbis were aware of the tension between past and present, between the given and the application of the given, between that which is revealed and its meaning. By stating that their interpretations were revealed they were not merely giving themselves divine authority to prove the legitimacy of their traditions. They declared that revelation is not complete without a response. Their exposition of the Torah was the response, an aspect of revelation. Just as God revealed his will to the rabbis, the rabbis revealed their will to God. *Mishnah Ta'anit* 4:8 explains, "The day of espousals" (Song of Songs 3:11), as the giving of the Torah, i.e., revelation was an act of marriage between God and Israel. Israel's revelation is the oral tradition. The rabbis made explicit through their interpretations what was implicit during the act of revelation.[21] They discovered God's will through their relationship with the text. They understood the revelation as the result of the interaction between God and man.[22]

The tradition (oral Torah) was a continuous interpretation and application of revelation in their view.[23] This connection with the sources provided the continuity that maintained the Jewish community. The source of truth for the rabbis was established through revelation rather than through reason alone.[24] It was given once, and the task then became one of transmission.[25] Truth is not approached through system and form, but through a direct relationship to the text, i.e., commentary.[26]

This mutual interdependence exemplified by revelation and commentary, between authority and community, marked the rabbinic concept of government and rule. Everyone who participated in revelation by studying and applying the text to life participated in God's rule. God did not govern from some transcendent place handing down edicts to be obeyed. Rather, the reality of government came from the active response towards the revealed word.

Revelation, in a political context, could be translated as accessibility and the assumption that decisions are not made arbitrarily.[27] The will of the authority is not only knowable, but it is the duty of the governed continually to discover, decipher and relate to it. The obligation to respond completes the act of governing. As the governed progressively know more of the will of the authority it becomes its own authority. Each person is ultimately to govern himself by relating to the agreement that binds him to authority. The shared experience of relating to the agreement binds him to others who participate in the same type of endeavor.

The Availability of the Torah to the Entire World

God is willing to make an agreement with whomsoever chooses to accept his sovereignty.

> Why was the Torah not given in the land of Israel?
> In order that the nations of the world should not
> have the excuse, saying: Because it was given in

Israel's land, therefore, we have not accepted it. Another reason: To avoid causing dissension among the tribes, or else one might have said: In my territory the Torah was given, and the other might have said: In my territory the Torah was given. Therefore, the Torah was given in the desert, publicly and openly in a place belonging to no one. To three things the Torah is likened, to the desert, to fire and to water. This is to tell you that just as these three things are free to all that come into the world, so also are the words of the Torah, free to all that come into the world.[28]

Claims against God and Israel stemming from the place where the Torah was given could not be presented either by the nations of the world or by the various tribes (against each other) because the wilderness was regarded as a public domain. The second part of the statement is directed towards would-be converts. Proseyltism was encouraged before the decrees of Christian Roman emperors prevented it. If Rome tried to conquer the world by force, Israel tried to convert the world to the covenant.

Communal Myth and Revelation

The community maintained memories of the past which could explain its present situation. These memories evoked the covenant of distant generations, a history of agreements, that the community carried within its consciousness as it stood before Mt. Sinai.

"And the Lord called unto him out of the mountain saying" (Exodus 19:3): for the sake of the patriarchs who are refered to as the mountain, for it says: "Hear all you mountains the Lord's controversy" (Micah 6:2). And Moses went up unto God, he went up in a cloud and descended in a cloud, the merit of the fathers ascended and descended with him.[29]

The mountain is the symbol for the patriarchs. For their merit the Torah is given to Israel. The question this statement seems to ask is, why did Moses have to ascend the mountain to receive the covenant? God could have spoken to Moses anywhere. When the people, attuned to the symbolic significance of the mountain, see Moses ascend the mountain they are reminded of the patriarchs, i.e., the previous covenants that God had made with them upon which their present claims depend.

The image of the merit of the fathers ascending and descending with Moses is suggestive of Jacob's dream of the ladder with angels ascending and descending upon it (Genesis 28:10-15), and the subsequent covenant made between God and Jacob. Unlike the covenant with the patriarchs before him, the covenant of Jacob included a promise of safety and well-being which would be appropriate to the situation of Israel in the wilderness, seeking assurance for the future.

The Torah's pre-mundane existence was also an aspect of the communal myth.

> Rabbi Eliezer ben Yose Haglili said: The Torah was written nine hundred and seventy-four generations before the world was created and rested in the bosom of the Holy One Blessed be He. And he chanted the song[30] with the ministering angels as it is said, "Then I was by him, as a nursling, it was daily all delight, playing before him"; and it says: "playing in his habitable earth and my delights are with the sons of men" (Proverbs 8:30f).[31]

The Torah existed a thousand generations before revelation, according to rabbinic legend. Yet, until it was revealed to the world ("... my delights are with the sons of men") it had no significance. It was created for the world and not for heaven.

Moses lived in the twenty-sixth generation after creation, hence, the Torah was written nine hundred and seventy-four generations before creation. Prior to revelation the world, without the guide of the Torah, was "... sustained by the grace of God."[32] A millenium of grace existed before the covenant. During this period God proved himself by sustaining the world, and especially a particular people during national trauma (slavery in Egypt). He demonstrated his power not only through creation but through a particular people by freeing it from slavery.

The people were prepared to enter into a covenant with God, for it recognized his might. That the Torah was revealed to man demonstrated God's willingness to enter into history. It marked the end of the period of grace. From that time, the world was to be sustained by the trust inherent in the act of making agreements. Political relationships, i.e., those between authority and the individual and community were to be based on mutual obligation. Both the governor and governed were to have a stake in this relationship, without which neither could exist.

Political crises usually evoke a re-examination not only of the structure of the polity but of its myths, purposes and direction as well. The political thinker may return to the origins of society and re-interpret its beginnings in order to find new purpose for the existence of the community. Must political thought was a consequence of crises that were provoked by historical circumstances. War, revolution, the introduction of new groups into the society, the strengthening or weakening of existing social classes due to changing economic conditions will provoke a profound disorientation to the polity. Under such conditions the old answers and solutions no longer seem appropriate.

One strategy in dealing with such crises is to forge new paths to establish new purposes. Political tradition is abandoned as new forms and ideas are presented (sometimes merely a superficial cover for the "old"). Another strategy is to interpret recent events in the light of ancient traditions. This strategy is especially relevant when the condition of the community during and after the crisis is so weak that it is necessary to establish continuity and security and to demonstrate that the old ways are still relevant even though the situation might seem to have changed. Old prophecies and ancient predictions might be revived to explain that what seems new has already been foretold by previous sources. It was the latter strategy that was used by the rabbis. The crisis was certainly a profound one. The entire structure of the community had been destroyed. Yet the rabbis were able to successfully respond by reinterpreting the communal myth to give purpose and meaning to the new political reality. Using the ancient biblical covenant as a theme they were confronted by the problem that many groups claimed to be the inheritors of that same covenant. By changing covenant terminology and using it as a polemic they claimed that their interpretations originated at the same time as the biblical covenant and exclusively given to their group as an inheritance. By virtue of their traditions of interpretation they were the true Israel.

Through their activity as teachers they could transmit their tradition and embellish it. By making it universally available to all Jews they could encourage the people to share their authority. Education became the means to survival. Yet there was a cost howbeit offset by the benefits. Everyone who had an ascribed role lost power; priests and claimants to the Davidic dynasty whose influence and power had been almost exclusive lost most of their authority. While given status in the form of certain liturgical privileges for the priests and the offices of patriarch and exilarch to Davidic descendants, their role was pre-empted by the rabbis. All Jews had to perform the priestly function through prayer and acts of compassion. David was given rabbinic characteristics in their interpretations of the biblical text. There was a constant danger of messianic pretenders. The messiah was transformed from the Davidic warrior-king to a rabbi in an attempt to diffuse the disastrous tendency to rebel against Rome. While some rabbis encouraged rebellions, after a number of defeats, their successors realized that to maintain the Jewish people accommodation with the Romans, however bitter that might be, was their only realistic choice. Their all-consuming study of Torah was the rabbi's response to the national crisis. Their oral tradition attained near sanctity. It provided the needed direction for the future while insuring a continuity with the past.

The present study has been an attempt to examine some of the political ramifications of the oral tradition. While political thought is usually an examination of structure and finds authority embedded in it, it seems incredible, at least to the present writer, that a society could exist without such structure and that authority need not be clothed in a specific form in order to be effective. Surely form and structure give us some picture of the polity. Yet they are not the only factors that determine its viability or give it meaning and direction. If a group has no purpose and direction it cannot endure for long no matter how elaborate its structure. Rousseau's understanding of the "general will" is certainly a realization that the values of individuality must be considered in the structure of the polity. Machiavelli realizes that the relationship between the ruler and the ruled is more significant than structure.

The rabbis taught that authority to be acceptable not only had to prove that it had the power and will to be effective but that it was willing to constantly be directly accessible to the community. Those in authority had to be willing to share their power by encouraging the study of rabbinic traditions. Since anyone could become a rabbi and study was encouraged, structure was meaningless, for every rabbi was an authority. The control over the curriculum and careful indoctrination by the rabbis of the community was the method to prevent anarchy. Although there were schisms, those who remained in the community were socialized by the knowledge they received. Enough flexibility was possible so that a certain amount of dissent was practically institutionalized: both majority and minority opinions were recorded in discussions of Jewish law, and a wide latitude of interpretation was granted in the lore. The basis of the community was to be found in the shared experiences and values which held it together. Each person could participate in the study of the ancient knowledge. Finally, the promise of the kingdom of heaven apparently had great meaning for the community. This goal was carefully articulated giving it a cosmic direction. The Jew could save not only his own world, but the entire universe by accepting divine rule and its revealed word. Political knowledge in rabbinic epistemology meant that the connection with the past gave continuity to existence. The promise of the future gave a purpose for existence. The universal availability of power and authority became not only the means to effectuate future goals but was a factor in sharing communal responsibility. Even divine authority related mutually and reciprocally with the community. The destiny of each was intertwined with the other.

NOTES

1. Neusner, *There We Sat Down*, p. 97.
2. *Ibid.*, p. 78.
3. *Ibid.*, p. 79.
4. Marmorstein, *Doctrine*, II.
5. *Ibid.*
6. *Sifre, Devarim*, 323 on Deuteronomy 32:32.
7. *Pesikta D'Rav Kahanah*, 12:20.
8. *Lamentations Rabbah* 2:21.
9. *Talmud Bavli Shabbat* 88a.
10. *Mishnah Sanhedrin* 10:1
11. *Lo karet hakadosh baruch hu.*
12. *D'varim sh'ba'al peh.*
13. *Talmud Bavli Gitin* 60b; see also *Shavuot* 39a.
14. Herford, *The Pharisees*, p. 66.
15. *Torot* (plural of Torah).
16. *Sifra, B'hukotai*, 8:12 (my translation).
17. Urbach, *Hazal: Pirke Emunot V'deot*, p. 266f.
18. *Ibid.*, See his citations.
19. *Ibid.*, p. 271.
20. See Daube, "Rabbinic Methods of Interpretation and Hellenistic Rhetoric," p. 244, Note 17.
21. Herford, *The Pharisees*, p. 85. See *Talmud Yerushalmi Peah* 2,5.
22. Samuel S. Cohon, "Authority in Judaism," *Hebrew Union College Annual* II (1936), p. 597.
23. Gershon G. Scholem, *The Messianic Idea in Judaism* (New York: Schocken Books, 1972), p. 50.
24. Cohon, "Authority in Judaism," p. 596.
25. Scholem, *The Messianic Idea in Judaism*, p. 289.
26. *Ibid.* Even though the *Mishnah* is organized it is based on *midrash*. Later the *Gemarrah* returns to the commentary form.
27. Herford, *The Pharisees*, p. 141f.
28. *Mekhilta*, II, 236. See also *Pesikta Rabbati, Aseret Hadibrot*, 21, 99a f; *Exodus Rabbah* 27:8.
29. *Exodus Rabbah* 28:2.
30. Ezekiel 3:12.
31. *Avot D'Rabbi Natan*, chapter 31. Ginzberg, *The Legends of the Jews*, V, p. 3, Note 5, on other sources for this legend.
32. *B'hasdo, Talmud Bavli Pesahim* 118a. See Ginzberg, *Legends of the Jews*, VI, p. 30, Note 177.

CONCLUSION

Plato and Aristotle taught that man could find complete fulfillment only through the communal life of the *polis*. In ancient Israel, man could fulfill himself through the covenant whether it be through communal or individual living. Both Judaism and Christianity taught that creative survival was possible even without a *polis*, in changing conditions throughout history. The Greek was confined to his *polis*; the Jew and the Christian could find fulfillment outside the community, alone in the world.

The epitome of the rabbinic contribution to political thought is found in the idea that government is a commentary on the original purpose of society. Each person is to transcend himself by becoming his own authority. All those who share this purpose and experience the original intent share this goal. The social framework is to allow for maximum interaction without the imposition of the will of one on another. The task of government is accomplished through learning so that each person can internalize this goal, i.e., political relationships must be reciprocal.

From this epitome we can extract a number of political themes. Participation is emphasized by the rabbis but contrasts with the concept of participation of Athenian democracy. We may learn from Plato's criticism of democracy that it tended towards interest politics and lobbying casting one force against another. Decision-making consisted in juggling those forces and interests to come to some sort of synthesis by giving weight to the strongest influence. The interest of a specific group seemed to take precedence over the concern of the *polis* as a whole. Plato's correction of this system of government which he experienced and detested was to institutionalize authority in the person of the philosopher-king who ruled because of his innate ability and education. His experiment in Syracuse failed. It was difficult to establish such a polity and to guarantee that its leader would share his vision of reality. The ideal was never realized.

Participation allows for the wide distribution of political responsibility. The more people involved in making the decisions the less the tendency to cast blame on others. If the citizen shares in the decisions of the polity he has a personal stake in its policy. In Athens, interest and factions destroyed the vision; there was no vision to share by those who participated. Instead each had his own vision which he independently pursued with apparent disregard for the vision of others.

The rabbis must have understood that participation was necessary in order to insure the inclusion of separate views to prevent destructive sectarianism and schismatic breaks. The Jewish community was too weak, too widely scattered and too few in number, especially in the land of Israel, to withstand groups breaking away and starting their own religions. Yet there had to be some way to prevent factionalism. Participation, they taught, was available to all who were politically socialized, i.e., to all those who internalized the goal of the society and participated in studying and interpreting the rabbinic traditions.

We may attribute the contrasting rabbinic and Greek solutions to differing psychologies. Categorization was a direct outcome of Greek space-oriented psychology. The process of time, they thought, led to death; time could not enhance chances for survival. The polity could only survive if it found the proper structure that was harmonious with eternal nature. In that polity each had to find his proper place. Taken to its logical conclusion, if each found his own sphere the only way to relate to others was to be included in someone else's sphere by being subsumed through conquest or total assimilation and loss of self. With this psychology of space we should not be surprised that interest politics was the outcome, and the very solution to its destructive tendency was limited to the search for better structures. Even Pericles could rally his polity only by emphasizing the common external threat, i.e., the fear of conquest.

Rabbinic psychology emphasized time, rejecting space which could result in idolatry, i.e., the worship of objects of creation rather than their author. In time-oriented psychology relationships are real, for the significance of the individual can only be attained through his relationship with others. If someone is isolated and ignored his existence has no meaning. One of the most terrible punishments in Jewish law was excommunication (*herem*) when a person was ostracized either temporarily or permanently by the community. On the other hand, the most important activity of the Jewish community was the give and take of study (*shakla v'tarya* in Talmudic terminology) where the presence of each is immediate. The covenant is the model for relationships when all time, past and future, coalesce into the present. Words, which initiate relationships, are to lead to trust when they are fulfilled and the relationship is thereby consummated. Trust was the basis of the polity rather than structure.

What distinguished Christian and Jewish thought was the type of relationship emphasized. Grace was predominant in Christian thought because it explained why God would relate to an imperfect humanity. It was his nature to be gracious by entering history to save mankind which was otherwise doomed. Extrapolated into political thought it led to the concept of the paternal authority figure who would take responsibility for society. Augustine despaired that such a human authority could ever be found outside of the heavenly kingdom (and so did the rabbis). Politics was disparaged for it corrupted the participant. If one enters the political life he could not come out clean or unsullied. The very process was immoral and tainted. Politics was not the profession for saints. Political thought was then engaged in discovering either the proper regime which could corrupt the leader in the least possible way, or insuring the protection of the citizen from the encroachment by the regime on his rights. Even Machiavelli knew his limits. If the government is corrupt or a person's rights are abused then there is no reason for him to remain in the polity.

The rabbinic solution was to choose reciprocity in preference to grace which meant that the authority was completely dependent on his constituency. It could throw him out at any time through sheer whim. The authority, realizing that his relationship was contingent on recognition and acceptance (an outcome of rabbinic time-oriented psychology), had to serve the polity and constantly prove that he was fit to rule. Even God was challenged. The check on corruptibility of power was the withdrawal of acceptance. Everyone knew the rules. If promises were broken the consequences were cruel indeed: the dissolution of the polity and the utter insignificance of the authority. He no longer had anyone to rule. Because of the terrible responsibility of the authority, he wanted everyone to share his burden. In that way he was not fully responsible when things went wrong. But the reverse was also true: as each individual shared the authority and fulfilled his promise then surely the kingdom of heaven could be realized.

Redemption was understood as the fulfillment of the covenant agreement. According to Jewish thought, redemption is to be public, historical, and "...within the community."[1] It occurs within the visible world. The Christian concept of redemption provides no help for this world which is unredeemable.[2] Mankind must suffer government and politics, for salvation comes only through the church as, according to Augustine, "...a community of the mysteriously redeemed within an unredeemed world."[3]

According to the rabbis right action led to redemption. When everyone would keep his agreement, government by men over men would no longer be necessary. The rabbis wanted every person to become a rabbi, i.e., participate in revelation, to be one's own authority.[4] There was to be, in other words, self-rule by each individual in God's kingdom. "And the Lord will be king over all the earth; on that day the Lord will be one and his name one" (Zachariah 14:9).

NOTES

1. Scholem, *The Messianic Idea in Judaism*, p. 1.
2. *Ibid.*
3. *Ibid.*
4. Jacob L. Talmon, *The Unique and the Universal* (London: Secker and Warburg, 1965), p. 78.

THE POLITICAL CONCEPTS IN
LITURGICAL SOURCES

The main section of the daily Jewish prayerbook may be regarded as a source for the political-theological views of a people who attributes sovereignty to God. The commands of the sovereign are accepted on the basis of attribution, for a role must be first accepted; only then are its communications regarded as emanating from the divine source.

The study of liturgy as a source for political thought contributes to the understanding of how the body politic is formed, since liturgy is a dramatic reenactment of the relationship between God and people, or, in political terms, between the ruler and ruled. Liturgy contains the expression of national hope and reasserts the sense of purpose. Sovereignty, authority and legitimacy are all themes of liturgy; one must translate the terminology from the theological to the political. Liturgy attempts to renew and inspire the person who experiences it. Public liturgy binds all participants because it offers a shared experience. Instead of depending on some historic or pseudo-historic (e.g., Locke) explanation of the formation of society, its reenactment may be followed step by step through the examination of liturgy.

The study of liturgy also provides an opportunity to examine the internal coherence of a community since it is the official declaration of its attitudes toward authority. That the section of the prayerbook here studied has been left virtually unchanged over eighteen centuries helps us understand how the community was able to maintain its continuity. The attempt is being made to examine the original sources on their own in the historical context in which they were composed. However, it is important to emphaszie that the unchanging aspect of the liturgy may have been the original intent of the rabbis who composed it in order to foster internal coherence of the Jewish community over time and space. The Jewish liturgy as a socializing force has special significance since those who used it were dispersed throughout the world without a national center. Since there was no explicit or external manifestation of Jewish government or a national center, government, through liturgy, was completely internalized. The community shared its allegiance and recognition of divine government as dramatized by the prayerbook. In this sense, the recitation of daily prayers was a substitution for the loss of the explicitness of government. Instead of a flag to salute or the trappings of power surrounding the political leader that could be visualized, the salute was internalized throught the recitation of the *Shema* ("Hear, Israel. . ."), the trappings of power were internalized by rit-

131

ualized genuflection found in the *Amidah* (the standing, silent prayer).

It will be demonstrated that:

1. sovereignty creates a government in order to attain recognition;
2. agreements between the ruler and the ruled are reciprocal;
3. the legitimacy of government is dependent on recognition;
4. the liturgical experience is the reenactment of the formation of the body politic.

For this study the core of the daily, traditional liturgy has been selected (*matbe'ah*). This core requires a quorum of the constituency in order to be completely recited.

The Nature of Sovereignty and its Authorization

The *barkhu* marks the beginning of public worship. It is a declaration that the community formally recognizes the sovereign's presence. The creative nature of the sovereign is then elucidated. All existence (emphasized through the merism, light and dark) is attributed to him; his creative acts are continual. Man, one of the results of his creative acts, recognizes that he has been created by him. The creature, through attribution, is authorizing that this is the sovereign's purpose and activity. At the same time he is ruling out other causes for his existence. He places himself in God's realm since there is no other alternative if he wants to continue to exist. One source for the sovereign's legitimacy is the power to create.

God creates the world in order to attain significance. The entire world owes its existence to God. The world, and especially mankind, is created so that it will respond to God. God has a need to create.

The political significance of the creation concept lies in its universal scope and in its vision of the inherent individuality of man, while at the same time recognizing that each person is related to the next because all share the same parent. The source of this universality transcends man rather than being created by him.

Usually the sovereign is examined from its point of view, isolated from the governed. Here it is understood from the vantage of the governed. The sovereign creates his own constituency in order to be authorized to rule.

Even though the sovereign creates and possesses his own constituency, he must receive authorization in order to be accepted. After stating that the holy beings (*k'doshim*), i.e., the heavenly servants, angels, etc. were created by the sovereign, they must still accept upon themselves the government of heaven (*malchut shamayim*). The ruler creates his constituency in order to receive authorization to rule them. Authorization comes in the form of attribution of roles which is one of the main purposes of prayer.

The relationship is based on the maintenance of the individuality of each aspect created by the sovereign, even the heavenly beings. The sovereign must remain separate in order to attain recognition, for if all the objects are symbiotically joined and assimilated into the creator, he really has not created anything, nor can he be recognized.

Government rules a group, a community, a constituency, not an individual. Only by agreeing to be so constituted (*zeh mizeh*, "...this one from that one...") can government become possible. First, they agree to be constituted, and then they authorize the sovereign to rule over them ("...and they give jurisdiction this one to that one..."), i.e., they give authorization to each individual in the community to accept the sovereign who is then, in turn, accepted by the community.

The realization of the "kingdom of heaven" is dependent on universal recognition. Yet this concept is not necessarily apocalyptical — it can be realized in this world.[1] Israel acknowledges God's rule through its study and observance of the Torah by each generation. The first of the ten commandments is interpreted as an expression of God's sovereignty through which the rest of the commandments gain significance, i.e., a commandment presupposes an authority initiating it and insuring compliance.[2] The manifestation of the "kingdom of heaven" is found in the acquiescence to the Torah by the majority of Israel and later of mankind.[3]

God did not become king until he created mankind which made it possible for someone to choose him.[4] Hence, the creation of angels or beasts was not satisfying to God because they could not choose.[5] The *midrash, Exodus Rabbah* 23:1 has God telling the angels: "If my people decline to proclaim me as king upon earth, my kingdom ceases also in heaven."[6] The sovereign is exclusively ("himself alone") authorized to create ("makes might acts"), revise (*m'hadesh*), defend his constituency ("master of wars"), establish a system of justice ("he sows justice"), to have all victory attributed to him alone ("causes salvation to sprout forth"), to heal ("creates cures"), which are all positive acts ("with his goodness"). He performs these acts to reciprocate ("his mutual love") the recognition he receives. Since we are analyzing the morning prayer, the light is specified; just as God creates light every day, so may he create light over Zion. This switch in nuance using the same word marks the flow to the next theme, communication.

Zion, the symbol of the political aspirations of the Jewish people, is as certain to be renewed as the light every day because the Jewish people recognizes and authorizes his rule. In response, the sovereign reciprocates ("love") by recognizing his constituency. The grammar changes from third person to a dialogue between first (Israel) and second (God) persons. The constituency declares that it has descended from those who had initiated the relationship ("our fathers"), the inheritors of the ancient promise. The sovereign is a loving parent ("our father") ("compassionate father who has compassion"): teaching the child to understand, discern, listen, i.e., to be open to communication in order to relate to others, especially the sovereign. He also wishes to study and to teach, to maintain and establish the content of the communication with the same love that the parent gives the child. The child aspires to become a parent and thus, in turn, receive recognition in his own right. In political terms, the governed in authorizing, wants to be authorized in order to govern itself. Just as the goal of the parent is to facilitate the maturity, growth and eventual parenthood of the child, so that the parent can ultimately share the experience of parenthood with his child, so the sovereign wants to facilitate the maturity and growth of the constituency so that it, too, can be able to rule itself and thus share the experience of government. The sovereign not only authorizes government, but authorizes his constituency to share the responsibilities of government.

However, this process can only take place if the constituency is fully socialized in the language of the communication ("enlighten our eyes in your Torah"). By sharing the same values, language, method and content of communication, there will be no fear from inimical sources of power that subjugate the consituency ("and we will not be ashamed forever"). All the members of the constituency will be unified ("and he will bring us in peace from the four corners of the earth"), and previous promises made by the sovereign will have been fulfilled ("because you are a God who makes acts of salvation"). The promise is maintained because of the exclusive recognition by the constituency ("and you chose us") of the sovereign.

The sovereign makes his will known through communication which, when accepted, becomes an agreement that binds sovereign and constituency. Prayer as communication functions to maintain the relationship between the two. The *shema* ("Hear, Israel, the Lord your God, the Lord is one") repeated by the constituency, is an acceptance of the legitimacy and and authority of government.[7] It reenacts the Sinai covenant when the community was established through its reception of the sovereign's communication (see Exodus 24:7).

The concept of tacit consent is not utilized. The constituency actively consents when it recites the *shema*, aware of the presence of the sovereign (*k'vod malkhuto*). The sovereign is declared to be one, i.e., there is no alternative. Allegiance is pledged, and the content of the communication is accepted, ("the yoke of the commandments"). Complete allegiance is required which must not only be internalized ("on your heart") but must be inherent all through the social process, in the family (*v'shinantem l'vanekha*), with the peer group ("when you go on the road") and even within the isolated individual ("when you lie down and when you rise up"). It must also be manifest externally (wearing of *tefillin* and the *m'zuzah* on the door) so that all will see to whom one owes his allegiance.

Although written in an agricultural vocabulary, we can understand the consequences of the agreement, that the cosmos will sustain the constituency if it maintains its allegiance. The ability of the sovereign to keep promises has already been established — not only has he created the world but renews it daily. The negative consequences are also set forth — if it breaks the promise then the cosmos will be brought against the constituency. Treason is defined as refusing to maintain the exclusive relationship with one sovereign; he who has caused the existence of the constituency will now destroy it ("and you will perish quickly from the good land").

The relationship is to be kept in mind constantly ("observe my words on your heart") and is concretized in the binding of physical strength ("on your hands") and intellect ("between your eyes") in allegiance to the sovereign. Instruction of children (insuring the future) maintenance of peer group allegiance (similar to the exchange of *r'shut*, jurisdiction, between the heavenly beings to accept the sovereign) and personal commitment are emphasized.

Since the sovereign is not physically manifest this emphasis is necessary. Unconditional allegiance is more pressing because the sovereign's coercive power is a matter of interpretation.

Knot symbols (*tzitzit*) on clothing are commanded as a reminder. One of the differences between animals and people is the wearing of clothing suggesting human willfulness to transcend nature. The knot symbol on clothing accentuates this difference, for just as man goes beyond his natural state, so he must go beyond his social and instinctual state to serve a transcendent sovereign. These knots are to remind the wearer of the requirements (*mitzvot*) of the sovereign so that he does not follow his instincts ("your heart") and societal demands ("your eyes"). The *tzitzit* can also be understood as a covenant sign (as suggested by Daniel Elazar) since the knot ties separate strands together, expressing the binding quality of the covenant for separate individuals. The knots are reminders of the covenant to which the individual is bound. By maintaining the allegiance the constituency becomes special (*k'doshim*) to the sovereign.

The sovereign claimed responsibility for the exodus. To deny this event was to deny the commandments; similarly to deny the commandments was to deny this event, so intertwined were the two.[8] The exodus was regarded as a manifestation of God's promise-keeping and his response to the people when they complained of their servitude (Genesis 15:13-14; Exodus 2:23-25). In turn, Israel is bound to God to keep her promise to observe the covenant she had accepted as a consequence of redemption. The basis of God's authority to rule was the very acts he had performed on Israel's behalf,[9] i.e., the exodus. In the preliminary service the exodus is reenacted through the chanting of the Song of the Sea.

The sovereign is dependable (*emet*) and reliable (*v'yatziv*) throughout time. He is eternal, and legitimacy, his power, his sovereignty and authority are lasting. His communications exist for all time which is capsulated in the present. The past ("our fathers") as well as the future ("our children") give significance to the present ("for us").

Just as he kept his promises in the past, redeeming ancestors, so he keeps his word and redeems us. It is this power of redemption that makes him unique ("there is no God like you").

This section of the prayerbook, called the *k'riat shema* (the recitation of the words, "Hear, Israel...") may be divided into three parts:

1. the legitimacy of the sovereign is established by describing him as creator and communicator;
2. the constituency witnesses the sovereign's authority by declaring its allegiance;
3. trust is inherent in the relationship because the sovereign has kept his word.

This section is a reflection of ancient pre-biblical and biblical covenant patterns.[10] The political thought found in this section can be epitomized as follows: the basis of legitimacy of the sovereign is recognition by the constituency which he has created as a separate, identifiable entity. This recognition is a result of a reciprocal relationship between members of the constituency and its authorization of the sovereign to rule.

The Specifics of Establishing Legitimacy

The *amidah* (standing devotion) grants recognition to the sovereign. A list of activities attributed to the sovereign describes his immanence-transcendence and the recognition and authorization granted by the constituency.

The transcendent sovereign limits his discretion by making and maintaining promises through gaining legitimacy through recognition. The more he limits himself, the more recognition he achieves and the greater his influence in the relationship with his constituency. The more direct the relationship, the greater is his reality.

The sovereign is approached formally (three steps forward and a bow) and directly (*atah* - "you"). The constituent describes himself as a descendant of the group to which promises have been made.

The concept of merit of the fathers (*zakhut avot*) is here emphasized to explain that even though God created the world for his own sake, and no amount of merits could possibly be a recompense for all that God has done, man can improve himself; merits emphasize that man's action can effect the world. Merits of the fathers[11] led to Israel's redemption from Egypt, the giving of the Torah and atonement for the sin of the golden calf according to the *midrash* and *Talmud*.[12] Indicative of this concept is that the past serves the present.[13] The concept of imputed merits, whether they be of the past (fathers) or the future (the children), answers the question why authority chooses to make covenant agreements with the people. Present agreement fulfills previous promises made as a recompense for the merits that the fathers had or the children will have as a result of living according to the Torah. The concept of merits also functions as a method by which the claims of the society were made vis-a-vis authority, a demand to fulfill previous agreements. Emphasizing the reciprocal quality of the relationship by calling for recognition of the constituency, it is comunication to the sovereign creating a new reality by reestablishing the relationship. As the *k'riat shema* establishes the sovereign, so the *amidah* establishes the constituency. In the former, the constituency accepts and receives the sovereign; in the latter, it gains recognition.

The claim of the past is reciprocal (*gomel hasadim* - "does reciprocal acts of loving-kindness") which allows for its fulfillment ("and he brings a redeemer") in the present ("their children's children," i.e., the present generation). This relationship is consummated intimately ("with love") which we have seen above also characterized the creative and communicative acts of the sovereign.

Since the sovereign has control over time ("makes alive the dead"), he can sustain all life ("sustains life") both now and even after death (*m'hayay maytim*). He can change conditions by supporting those who have failed ("lifts the fallen"), healing the sick and releasing captives; in sum, he will keep all his promises to those who have kept their promises to him.

In return for the sovereign's beneficent rule, the constituency responds legitimizing his rule through public acclamation so that the entire world can witness that this ruler has a constituency recognized throughout all time and space (*olam*). An earthly parallel to the angelic declaration of the sovereign's unique role as a ruler is made in the first person ("we will make holy" — "just as they make him holy in high places"). The constituency agrees to be constituted (the *mi khamokha* — "who is like you" — sung before the *amidah* recognizes that the sovereign, by redeeming his promises, has acquired a constituency). It also authorizes and accepts the sovereign's rule. The rest of the *amidah* specifies the sovereign's legitimacy after the climax of recognition that the sovereign will reign forever (*yimlokh*). His reign will last in the future since the constituency pledges to continue to recognize it ("every generation tells of his greatness").

The next three paragraphs elucidate the authority relationship between ruler and ruled. Knowledge is granted, emphasizing the ability to make decisions. The greater the knowledge and independence of the constituency, the more important is its act of recognition. The sovereign, as creator, is the source of all knowledge; his willingness to communicate and teach (*m'lamed*) demonstrates his desire to share his experience. In receiving that knowledge, the constituency learns to rule itself. The separate roles of ruler and ruled then become blurred; and constituency enters a reciprocal relationship which insures the existence of each.

The next paragraph specifies the type of knowledge that is communicated. Man has the ability to seek the direct communication ("your Torah") of the sovereign. Asking to be returned to the Torah, he seeks to share the original communication so that the ruler and the ruled might be brought closer (*v'karvaynu*). Reconciliation (*t'shuvah*) is required after the failure to maintain an exclusive relationship to the sovereign. Despite past failures and disloyalty, the constituent seeks to renew the relationship. The character of authority emphasized here is that of reconcilability.

The last paragraph of this section points to the willingness to forgive. Although the relationship has been broken by the constituent, the relationship can be restored because the sovereign is forgiving. The authority needs to be accepted in order to rule, and he is willing to be reconciled.

Once the relationship is restored, the constituent specifically authorizes the sovereign to act so that the very existence of the constituency can be ameliorated and guaranteed. The next section authorizes solutions to problems caused by previous disloyalty — its adverse condition of affliction and oppression. By serving other sovereigns, it has been abandoned to their servitude. Turning to the original relationship it seeks relief in order to exclusively serve the one sovereign. The other sovereigns have no real power, for intrinsic power is attributed to God alone; only he can keep his promises. The constituency demands reciprocation for its recognition, asking that his promises be fulfilled.

A sick person is ineffectual and enjoys only partial existence since part of his body is not functioning properly. The healing that is requested in the next paragraph can be attained through a complete recognition. Part of the body politic is sick ("our illnesses"). The sovereign is authorized to heal it. Within the request is the recognition of the ability of the sovereign to fulfill it.

The body politic has to be sustained. The next request is for adequate sustenance ("he satisfies us with your goodness"). The very authorization to sustain is a communication to the sovereign that his power to do so is recognized.

The restoration of the political entity by gathering the exiles to one's own land is an aspiration which emphasizes the self-consciousness and identity of the group. Freedom (*l'hayrutaynu*) is here understood as eschatological: end of time. All the people sharing the same aspiration and historic experience will be gathered together.

One of the sources for the lack of wholeness ("sadness and sighing") of the constituency (beside adverse conditions, sickness, the need for sustenance, and dispersal) is that it cannot rule itself. Hence, the sovereign is authorized to reinstitute a system of justice. The rule of the sovereign ("and rule over us") can only be complete when judges are directly appointed by the sovereign. If the sovereign is to rule exclusively (*l'vado* — "by himself") then those administering justice must be recipients of the communications of the sovereign and respond to them by insuring justice.

It must be noted that this prayer asks for the return of judges and counsellors and not a king. The judge precedes the king historically and its inclusion here might refer to the time when it seemed that God ruled directly over his people. At least one biblical source (I Samuel 8) regards kingship as superfluous at best since God is already ruling as king.

The authorization in the next paragraphs emphasizes political identity, i.e., the difference between this constituency and other people. Enemies, internal ("informers") and external ("your enemies") are identified as the sovereign's enemies as well. They are to be completely destroyed if God's justice is to be realized.

In contrast, those who maintain the agreement are to be rewarded since they trust the sovereign and have faith that he will fulfill his promises. The righteous and pious mentioned in this paragraph are to be emulated by the people. Their good deeds are affected by the study of Torah.

Jerusalem, recognized as the constituency's center, is to be restored to its former position of significance. This goal is to be accomplished through the restoration of the sovereign's presence. Jerusalem and the Davidic dynasty are symbols for the political unity and integrity of the Jewish people and the complete restoration of the people, having definite eschatological overtones. Every political entity has such a symbol system which characterizes cultural or ethnic aspirations. When these aspirations are finally and completely fulfilled, then all agreements will come to fruition. By maintaining these symbols, the constituency informs the sovereign of its desire for integrity. The constituency declares that just as it has heeded and accepted the sovereign's communication, thereby maintaining the agreement, so the sovereign must heed and accept its communication ("listen to our voice") with compassion (*rahamim*).

The act of prayer is the communication of the constituency to the sovereign. It has a myth and eschaton that are unified through symbols of national aspiration. The communal myth is based on the original communication and the way it was liturgically celebrated. Since the break of communication the method of liturgy changed (from the sacrificial service at Jerusalem to the act of prayer in synagogues). Return to the ancient form represents its fruition in the future ("may it be your will always"). The presence (*sh'chinato*) of the sovereign at the national center can then be recognized and its legitimacy fully realized.

As a declaration of allegiance, the constituency thanks the sovereign (*modim*) for its very existence. In the congregational response, the sovereign is recognized as the creator who has the power to restore the body politic. The constituency indicates its dedication to the sovereign at all times (*tamid*) since all existence ("and all life") recognizes ("thanks you") his power.

The final theme, peace, in the sense of wholeness and integrity, is presented. The entire constituency ("over us and all Israel") declares its dedication to the reciprocal relationship. In return for the communication ("a living teaching") it completes the circle: just as the sovereign gives, the constituency receives; its response is to accept. The *amidah* specifies the sovereign's legitimacy as follows:

1. the constituency declares that it recognizes the promises made to its forebearers by requesting their fulfillment;

2. the sovereign's ability to fulfill promises is recognized and authorized by the constituency;

3. the act of prayer, a reenactment of previous communications, constitutes the maintenance of the agreement by the constituency by restoring the relationship, insuring its political identity and fulfilling its aspirations for self-rule in order to achieve integrity.

Liturgy is a source for political concepts and represents the mind of the constituency legitimizing the sovereign through authorization and maintaining the polity. Government fulfills the sovereign's need for recognition. That element in society which is authorized to rule enters into reciprocal agreements with the constituency in order to fulfill its purpose.

1. Sovereignty creates a government in order to attain recognition. The *k'riat shema* establishes the basis of sovereignty in creation and communication. He creates a universe so that he can attain a constituency to whom he can communicate his will. In response, the constituency recognizes him, thereby attaining significance and legitimacy. The *sh'ma* declaration is a direct witness of the sovereign's existence giving allegiance to the sovereign. The reciprocity of recog-

nition legitimized the relationship.

2. Agreements between ruler and the ruled are reciprocal. A trusting relationship between ruler and ruled is envisioned in the prayerbook and is accomplished when both sovereign and constituency observe the agreement. Blessings and success are attributed to the merits of previous generations and reliability of the sovereign. Dysfunction is attributed to disloyalty toward the sovereign and the breaking of the agreement.

3. The legitimacy of the government is dependent on recognition. For the purposes of this study, government refers to the relationship between ruler and ruled. The legitimacy of government is dependent on its recognition by both sovereign and constituency. Government functions through agreements which are ratified by both sides. The constituency attributes to the sovereign reliability — he keeps his promises. The *amidah* calls for the fulfillment of the agreements, thereby recognizing and accepting their legitimacy. The constituency bases its claim on ancestry; the original promises, made in the past, were meant to be fulfilled in the future. By declaring that it is the direct descendant of those ancient generations, it asks for the fulfillment of the agreements in the present.

The very request for the fulfillment of the agreements is a recognition of the sovereign's ability and power. When the constituency makes the request, it is authorizing its fulfillment. The governmental process begins with recognition of ability which is followed by its request and authorization.

4. The liturgical experience is the reenactment of the formation of the body politic. Liturgy is the communication of the constituency with the sovereign. It is a response either to natural experience or the sovereign's communication. The prayer book reenacts the creation of the constituency and its reception of the sovereign's communication, thereby educating and socializing the constituency which depends on the reciprocal relationship for its meaning and purpose. The reenactment involves a restoration of the relationship which had been broken by corporate and/or individual failure to maintain the agreement. In so doing, the liturgical experience emphasizes the constituency's political identity and its aspirations to achieve integrity.

NOTES

1. Kadushin, *The Theology of Seder Eliahu*, p. 58f.
2. Kadushin, *The Rabbinic Mind*, pp. 21, 130.
3. Schechter, *Aspects of Rabbinic Theology* (New York: Schocken Books, 1961), p. 64, Note 3.
4. *Ibid.*, p. 65.
5. *Ibid.*, p. 81f.
6. Translated by Schechter, p. 85.

7. *Mishnah B'rachot* 2:2.
8. Kadushin, *The Rabbinic Mind*, p. 358f.
9. See *Mekhilta*, 11, Ch. 5.
10. Weinfeld, *Deuteronomy and the Deuteronomic School*, esp. pp.59-116.
11. Marmorstein, *Doctrine* p. 10f.
12. *Exodus Rabbah* 1:36, *Genesis Rabbah* 28:1,2, *Talmud Bavli Shabbat* 42a, as cited by Schechter, p. 174.
13. *Ibid.*, p. 183f.

APPENDIX II

HISTORICAL CONTEXT OF RABBINIC THOUGHT

> ...political philosophy is first and foremost con-
> cerned with the immediate activity of politics, that
> the great political philosophers were themselves
> partners who were vitally concerned with urgent
> problems arising in their own historical contexts, or
> that they themselves were often political actors.[1]

The statements in rabbinic literature certainly reflect the conditions of the time. Most of the rabbis quoted in this work lived in the
second century in the land of Israel which at the time was part of the
Roman Empire. They were primarily concerned with reestablishing
Jewish authority over a dissipated community, the aftermath of the
unsuccessful rebellion against Rome. The devastating war, which
followed the rebellion to attain political independence, ended with
the destruction of the Second Temple in the year 70 C.E.

The rebellion itself was the occasion for internecine fighting
among various Jewish groups. Pro-Roman groups were represented
by the aristocracy and the higher echelons of the priesthood. The
rabbis themselves were not united. Some supported the Zealots in
their fight against Rome, while others, not happy with its rule, realized that it was not realistic to challenge the mighty Roman Empire.

The Jewish population at the time of the destruction of the Temple has been estimated at about eight million, approximately one-
tenth of the world population at that time.[2] There were significant
Jewish communities in Alexandria and Babylonia. In almost every
urban center in the Mediterranean Jewish congregations could be
found. Before the destruction of the Temple, Jews outside of the land
of Israel as well as within the land would make significant contributions to the Temple. These communities were also represented in
Jerusalem during the three annual pilgrimage festivals.

> Jews belonged...to the most virile groups in the
> empire. They consistently refused to surrender to
> the overwhelming force of Roman aggression or
> hostile public opinion. Long inured to resisting the
> forces of nature, deeply convinced that the inner
> dynamism of their ultimate historic destiny would
> help them overcome all difficulties, however stag-
> gering, they succeeded in coloring their pessimistic
> outlook on the immediate future with an optimistic
> hue of the ultimate good which must come from the

divine guidance of history generally and God's pledges to their people in particular.[3]

Rabbis and Rome

Before the destruction of the Temple the rabbis were engaged in an almost constant struggle for power with the Sadducees.[4] The rabbis, called the Pharisees[5] before 70 C.E., were popular with the people since they came from their own ranks. There is a wide difference of opinion regarding the program of the Pharisees. According to Herford, during Hasmonean times they were religiously rather than politically oriented, for when they lost political power they still had religous authority over the people.[6] After the death of Alexandra Salome (69 B.C.E.), they lost their control over the Sanhedrin (court) and removed themselves from governmental affairs since they mistrusted the intention of the reigning power.[7]

According to Urbach, until the last days of the Second Commonwealth, the rabbis did not perceive themselves as a separate group attempting to maintain political power. Rather, they regarded themselves as private individuals who had God's work to do. They were not even organized into distinct parties. We see the rise of separate rabbinic parties towards the end of the Second Temple with the king, priesthood and rabbinic schools (House of Hillel and House of Shammai) each representing separate interests. Each rabbinic school attracted different types of people. The House of Shammai was more aristocratic while the House of Hillel was open to anyone.[8]

Alon, however, understands the role of the rabbis quite differently. He states that Judea was completely negative to Rome at all times, a unique stance in the context of other Roman provinces, because the people could not accept Rome as a savior or the Roman emperor as a god. Hence, they constantly sought national, political and social freedom.[9] Even after 70 C.E. the attitudes towards Rome did not change.[10] The majority of the rabbis were people in the tradition of real-politics. They were conscious political actors trying to deal one way or another with the generally negative attitude towards Rome on the one hand and the realization of the might of its military power on the other.[11]

Alon does not agree with scholars who understand that the political interests of the Pharisees were limited only to their dedication to Torah and *mitzvot* (observance of the commandments). He points to the fact that most of their work was comprised of civil law and the laws of the community and state. The purpose of their activity cannot be attributed to purely religious motivations, although the basis of their beliefs was certainly Torah and religion.[12]

During the war (66-70 C.E.) the Pharisees were split over their attitudes towards Rome. Some supported the Zealots who led the war. Others were more accommodating, e.g., the statement of Hanina, the deputy priest (*Mishnah Avot* 3:2), who appreciated the security offered by the Roman government. These differing attitudes survived throughout the several centuries of Roman rule. For example, in the second century Rabbi Yehudah was pro-Roman while Rabbi Yose seemed neutral, and Rabbi Shimon bar Yohai was anti-Roman.[13] In the third century we still find differing attitudes.[14]

However, the main view held was one born of realistic considerations. For example, while Rabban Shimon ben Gamliel was against the Romans, he did not follow the Zealots because he felt that too much blood would be shed. He represented the classical Pharisaic method of nationalistic realism which did not end in 70 C.E. While the destruction of Jerusalem did not dampen their spirited quest for political freedom, they were willing to wait for the appropriate time when they would have a chance to succeed.[15]

Despairing after the defeat, some Pharisees held the view that the Roman government would last until the coming of the Messiah who would redeem the Jewish nation; Rome ruled by heavenly decree (see *Talmud Bavli Avodah Zarah* 18a). But they were in the minority.[16]

After the period of war and rebellion (66 to 135 C.E.), there was no need to substantially change Judaism since it already functioned as an integrated belief system.[17] The experience of the first exile of the Jewish people had proved that the tradition could continue on foreign soil and in the midst of strange civilizations. However, due to the loss of a political base and a religious center, the aggressive expansionism (through widespread proselytizing activity) had to be abandoned. Judaism from this time forth became more inwardly directed and as a result, consolidated and unified. The various sectarian tendencies virtually came to an end. It was Christianity that inherited from Judaism its expansionism and the resulting sectarian currents which threatened its unity.[18]

The explanation for national disaster was the classic prophetic answer. Israel had brought upon herself her own tragedies because of national sin. Following the lead of Rabban Yohanan ben Zakkai, who reestablished a Jewish court system and academy of learning after the destruction of the Temple, the Jewish community understood that just as its sins had brought God's punishments so good deeds would bring redemption.[19] Explanation of events in any other way would deter national reconstruction. To offer eschatological solutions might cause further turmoil and confusion, i.e., a flight from reality that would hamper the consideration of actual problems.

There was no consious effort to preserve history during Talmudic times, for it was too grievous a burden on which to dwell. Redemption, the rabbis taught, would come through inner reformation rather than through political and military actions.[20] Rabban Yohanan ben Zakkai's solution to the problem of national recovery was obedience to God's will (see *Talmud Bavli Ketubot* 66b). The ancient means of reconciliation between God and man, the Temple cult and sacrificial system had been destroyed. He declared that prayer, study and deeds of loving-kindness would be the main means of reconciliation.[21]

By the third century such means of reconciliation became the method of bringing the messiah in rabbinic circles (see *Talmud Bavli Shabbat* 139a and *Sanhedrin* 98a). Rav and Sh'muel Babylonian leaders carefully avoided eschatological promises that could only fire up the people to engage in proclaiming a messiah who would lead them to the same military defeat suffered in 135 C.E.[22]

The Bar Kokhba rebellion (132-135 C.E.) was messianic in tone and fervor. Rabbi Akiba had declared this military leader the messiah who would free the Jewish people from the Roman yoke. The rebellion ended tragically. The land and the people were cruelly decimated, and Hadrian enacted severe decrees that made Judaism an illicit faith and Jewish practice a crime of treason punishable by death.[23] Jewish leaders went underground in their attempt somehow to secure the future of the people.

Once the decrees were lifted, a rabbinic synod of the surviving leadership was convened in Usha (140 C.E.).[24] This synod, unlike the earlier one in Yavneh (which began after 70 C.E. and lasted until the Bar Kokhba rebellion), took pains to redact historical materials because they realized that there was a significant change in Israel as a consequence of the Bar Kokhba rebellion.[25] In order to rebuild the community and lay claim to the legitimacy of their authority, they attempted to demonstrate that their line of authority flowed directly from Moses, i.e., that the oral traditions were Mosaic in origin. In fact, the major theme of the rabbis of Usha was the history of the oral Torah from Sinai to Usha.[26]

This reconstruction of history demonstrates an awareness that a definite break had occurred as a result of the Bar Kokhba rebellion and its aftermath. Rabbis Meir and Yehudah bar Ilai recorded the histories of the supernatural, the messianic blessing, the Pharisaic contribution to the oral Torah and finally, the history of the cult.[27]

The constitution of Caracalla was issued in the year 212 C.E.[28] Among the provisions was the grant of Roman citizenship to everyone who was not a slave in the empire. Roman law was to be the only law recognized. The *Mishnah*, the first code of Jewish law, was edited by Rabbi Yehudah the Patriarch and his court around the same time. Perhaps the coincidence of these two events was not accidental. There had been a reluctance to issue a final edition of a code of Jewish law, but the situation of Jews spread throughout the world and the consequent decline of the influence of the Judean Jewish community as a center for Jewish legal authority probably stimulated the need for a uniform authoritative code. The new Roman constitution might well have been seen as a threat to Jewish law, unless its traditions were codified in an authorized manner.

After the edition of the *Mishnah* the economic and political situation in the land of Israel remained fairly static for the next two centuries. The patriarchate, recognized as the authority over the Jewish community by the Roman government, continued to function until the fifth century. Action against the Roman Empire was frowned upon by the rabbis, and the patriarchate during this time. Rebellion would only result in further devastation of the community.[29] While there was no religious persecution of Jews such as had existed under Hadrian during the third and fourth centuries, the reign of Constinatius (337-361) was a dark period for the Jewish population. They were prey to tax collectors who exploited them both as provincials and as Jews.[30]

Meanwhile, the academies in Babylonia were gaining prestige. Although challenged by the authority of the *Mishnah* and the radical change of government under the Sassanids which resulted in continuous religious struggle against Zoroastrianism, Babylonia soon became the dominant Jewish center.[31] Babylonian Jewish academies did not create the great collections of *midrash* literature (especially those of lore) like those in the land of Israel, but legal studies and interpretation of the oral tradition proceeded to the point at which Jewish communities throughout the world turned to Babylonia for legal authority.[32]

The Role of the Rabbis

The rabbis were scholars who were to be honored above one's own father. One was even to stand before them.[33] Despite the honor that was paid to the rabbi, he had difficulties dealing with the community. There was a great gulf between popular Judaism and that of the rabbis who were confronted by widespread ignorance on the one hand and the use of pagan imagery on the other. The rabbis preached and taught against its use. Yet even some rabbis were influenced by angelology and demonology. In areas where they had little or no control there was a greater degree of pagan influence.[34] Jewish use of pagan symbols reflected a syncretism of values.[35] Where successful, the rabbis were able to substitute the symbols of word and letter for pagan symbolism.[36]

They tried to assert their authority in opposition to the established and recognized head of the Jewish community in the land of Israel, the patriarch. However, the patriarch, realizing that his major task

147

was to insure the integrity of the community, acted as a buffer between the community and the Roman government.[37] He refused Roman help in imposing his authority and kept Rome out of the academies. The mechanism of Jewish government would have to be self-imposed if it was to have authority.[38] The greatest communal offender was the informer to the Roman government of activities in the court and the academy.

Yet the rabbis had a wide following outside the court and appointed their own judges. Often local academies would refuse to follow rulings of the patriarchal court resulting in conflict, sometimes leading to excommunication. After the destruction of the Temple, the rabbis regarded themselves as bearers of the oral tradition. This claim was based upon their superior knowledge of the Torah and its interpretation. Anyone who had such knowledge had the authority to make decisions and transmit that authority to others.[39] The rabbinate was not a clergy or a priesthood since anyone could become a rabbi who could fulfill the standards of knowledge. Rabbinical submission to the patriarch was an act of self-discipline on their part, in recognition of the precarious condition of the community.[40]

During the third and fourth centuries, lay courts, appointed by the patriarch whose members were of the upper classes and the wealthy, existed along side those of ordained rabbis. They competed with each other for recognition and power. While some rabbis recognized such courts as communal courts of arbitration, hence not requiring Torah learning, others rejected their validity.[41]

The community was basically egalitarian in nature. Privileges were granted the patriarch and the exilarch (in Babylonia) because they were recognized as members of the Davidic line, the memory of which acted as a symbol of the hope for independence, yet, they in fact had little power. Rabbinical courts and academies took on more and more power in the community.[42]

There were elective offices of membership in the city council, charity administrators and collectors. But the Roman administration imposed tax collection duties on elected officials. Hence people tried to avoid being elected. While the rabbis at first openly disparaged ambitious office seekers, they later realized that responsibilities for the community's welfare had to be fulfilled.[43]

> If someone says: Why should I concern myself with
> communal troubles, bother with men's controver-
> sies and listen to their voices? Peace be unto you,
> my soul, such a one is destroying the world.[44]

The rabbis counselled against removing oneself from the community and its responsibilities, despite the imposition of the unpleasant obligation of collecting rapacious Roman taxes.

Messianic Politics

The hope for the coming of the messiah[45] was comforting during Israel's bleakest hours. Yet there was an incipient danger in the messianic concept, for the spark of hope might become inflamed, the consequences of which could be devastating. The higher the hopes the graver the emotional and spiritual devastation brought by disappointment when the Messiah inevitably proved to be false. Messianic fervor also led to a false sense of power, might and miscalculation. The contagious fire and enthusiasm could not insure that ill-advised military plans would result in victory in battle over superior, professional armies.

There have been many persons claiming to be the messiah throughout Jewish history. They usually came at times that seemed hopeless and made promises to a people who were clutching at any straw to ameliorate their terrible condition. The promises were never fulfilled; the shock and disillusionment caused the Jewish people even greater pain. The rabbis realized the dangers of messianic concepts. They understood that dependency on messiahs was risky at best. Yet often, they, too, were carried away by messianic fever. It was Rabbi Akiba, the greatest sage of his generation, who declared Bar Kokhba to be the messiah.

Of all the various messianic theories, the most popular was that he was to come from the House of David. That God promised David an everlasting dynasty led to the belief that God's anointed would again deliver Israel from the hand of its enemies just as David had done. Telling legends and creating myths of the past were ways of keeping hopes alive. The rabbis mythologized the past; but in their legends about David they attempted to transform him by giving him rabbinic features.[46] The messiah of the future would be a rabbi, i.e., redemption would not come as a result of military victory but through the study and teaching of the Torah. This use of legend to change the image of David was a way of keeping the hope of the messiah alive, yet sublimating it into a program which would prevent acts of desperation.[47]

While neutralization of possible messianic pretension was a device to prevent dangerous uprisings that would disrupt the Jewish people, the hope of the messiah was retained in the liturgy. The prayers for the restoration of the land and redemption of the people wre recited thrice daily. The very thrust of messianism was kept alive unequivocally in the liturgy.[48] Yet, as opposed to political rhetoric, such prayers as intense as they might be, were an unactualized outlet.

According to rabbinic eschatology, the Romans were viewed as the fourth and last kingdom of oppression, following Greece, Babylonia and Egypt. The Roman Empire had only provisional, temporary hegemony over the Jewish people.[49] Even though the rabbis had such strong negative feelings towards Rome, they were sensitive to the real political situation and would not support any further rebellion against Rome.[50] While their attitude towards Rome seemed accommodating, they did not recognize the legitimacy of the empire. They were specifically negative towards Roman taxes, tax collectors and their corruption.[51]

In an effort to defuse messianism the rabbis emphasized that the Torah was from Sinai only. The danger of new divine revelations were reactions to Christian claims of later prophecy that abrogated the Torah as well as messianic pretenders who would threaten communal authority.[52]

Christian messianic claims were made on the basis of interpretation of the Old Testament. In reaction to the specific instances of such interpretations the rabbis shied away from allegorical interpretations and urged the use of the plain[53] meaning of the text. They also attributed messianic foreboding in the Old Testament (e.g., Psalms 110:1, see Matthew 22:43-45) as ". . . historical reflections of past events"[54] rather than indications of future promises. Thus, the rabbis largely succeeded in sublimating messianism while keeping hopes alive. The people were cautioned to bide their time until conditions would be more conducive to redemption.

Preservation and Survival

Significant for political thought is the ability of a people to preserve itself without a formal community structure that could impose its will upon individuals who live within its bounds. Especially during the period of the present study, to leave the community and assimilate into the pagan, Christian or Zoroastrian communities was relatively easy. There is no doubt that many took advantage of the opportunities that such conversion might have brought. But many, if not most, remained within the community, exhibiting a unity despite dispersion, a discipline of ritual observance despite the advantages of entering the dominant culture, yet developing and enhancing the tradition through intense study.

There was a Jewish government within both the Roman provincial administration in the land of Israel and the Persian Empire. Yet Jews in distant lands still looked to the rabbis as leaders. Even after these Jewish governments had utterly disappeared, the integrity of the Jewish people remained intact. The Jewish governments themselves were not strong enough to exert much force (people could always abandon their jurisdiction) and were constantly challenged by the rabbis.

The rabbinic courts dealt with every aspect of Jewish law; distant communities would turn to them for advice and counsel on all aspects of life and felt bound by their decisions. In many instances these courts had some coercive power granted by the governments in which they existed. However, that power was limited, and there was always a means of escape. The strategy for survival utilized by the rabbis of the *Talmud* was to encourage the study of Torah.[55] They consolidated the traditions thus offering a mode of behavior that would unify the people.

Also, there was the reward for those loyal to the tradition, i.e., the world to come and the fear of God's punishment for those who broke the covenant. But most important was the program of daily living which insured the specific identity of the individual within the communal context.[56] That a marriage to a learned man was preferred over marriage into a higher social class, wealth or family geneology, is a demonstration of the high esteem in which the community held the rabbi.[57]

The Jewish communities attained a basic unity through the belief that the Torah was authorized by God's direct revelation.[58] Jewish solidarity fostered self-help motivated by the need for mutual support in order to survive.[59] The underlying faith was based upon the special relationship that God had for this despised and defeated people.[60]

Rabbis and/or Philosophers

The permanence of Jewish settlements outside the land of Israel led to contact with the ubiquitous Hellenistic culture.[61] While some individuals assimilated into that culture, the Jewish community, for the most part, maintained its identity. The cohesion of Jews in each city was maintained by the synagogue. The links within the community were based on the common feelings of loyalty to the land of Israel, the Temple and the Sanhedrin.[62] Financial support from the diaspora helped maintain these institutions. Even after the destruction of the Temple the academies and courts continued to receive support and allegiance from diaspora communities.

But most significant was the unifying belief in the destiny of the Jewish people as God's chosen. The synagogue encouraged this belief by emphasizing study of the Torah and the indoctrination of the covenant through the celebration of holidays and observance of various rituals. The thrust of these factors was self-awareness and identity which acted to prevent Judaism from becoming absorbed in the sea of Hellenism.[63]

The rabbis did not engage in philosophic inquiry in the style of the Greeks. Primarily due to the fear of the allegorical method which could endanger the actualization of Jewish monotheism, the rabbis reject Hellenistic metaphysics and theology.[64] To regard the image and symbol as reality might compete with God who could not be symbolized and whose image it was forbidden to represent in any form.

In rabbinic literature there is no mention of Plato, Aristotle or the Stoics.[65] The only philosophers mentioned were Epicurus, who was regarded as the source of heresy, and Oenomause of Gadera, later regarded as the greatest non-Jewish philosopher.[66] The Epicurean teaching of the fundamental unconcern of the gods for mankind threatened the Jewish teaching of human accountability and thus was completely rejected.[67] Greek technical philosophical terminology is largely absent from the entire corpus of rabbinic literature.[68] Yet, the rabbis utilized non-Jewish legal terminology which was adapted for Jewish use.[69]

However, some scholars detect the influence of Plato and the Stoics on the rabbis. They cite the concept of pre-existence of the Torah as parallel to the Platonic concept of the idea.[70] Saul Lieberman seems to admit that the center of contact between the rabbis and the Stoics lay in ethical principles.[71] Yet the question of which was the source of these ideas has not been fully answered.

Cyrus Gordon cites numerous borrowings back and forth between ancient Jewish and Greek traditions and attributes a common source of both to the Minoans.[72] But he emphasizes that the differences between the cultures are profound. In Homer, the extreme humanization of the gods is a projection of human needs and weaknesses. The hearers of these stories were not strengthened in their belief in the cult. In contrast, in spite of the anthropomorphism of the Bible and rabbinic literature, God was distinct and divine, transcending mankind. The stories told strengthened belief in him.[73]

Gordon attributes the different consequences to the purpose of the literature and the significance to the audience. Homer's epics were widely read by scattered Greek settlements with varied cults.[74] The Bible was meant for the Jewish people who were united in their cult and ritual. The stories were meant to enhance that unity.[75]

Boman and Dodd contrast Greek and Jewish thinking. Greek thought was concerned with the primarily static quality of space.[76] Sight and visual perception were emphasized.[77] Jewish thought was concerned with the dynamic quality of time.[78] The most important sense perception was hearing; visual images might result in forbidden imagery.[79] While for the Jews, movement was the only reality, the Eleatic school of philosophy rejected the reality of change and motion and would only accept the existence of that which was unchanging and static.[80]

Although Heracitus saw the significance of change, and he stands alone among Greek thinkers,[81] he had to use a forced diction in order to even express his views, since customary Greek language made it difficult for him.[82]

Plato's thought follows the same pattern as the Eleatic school. The object of his thinking is the given,[83] existence, then, he regarded as at rest, higher existence, eternal and unchanging.[84]

But in Jewish thought, God makes himself known through speech. God's word, *davar*, the very manifestation of divinity in human experience.[85] Boman explains the art of the Dura Synagogue as significantly Jewish for there is no picture of God there despite all the pictures of biblical personalities.[86]

The monotheism inherent in Plato and Stoic philosophies is much different from that of the Jews. Plato's god is personal only metaphorically, while the god of the Stoics is a rational principle.[87] In Judaism, the one God is very personal and intimately relates to the life of the people and to the individual.[88]

The rabbis did learn from the Greeks. Rather than changing Jewish tradition to harmonize with Greek learning, however, they selected what was needed and transformed its character. That which was selected became Judaized.[89] What the rabbis did find useful were the Greek methods of exegesis.[90] Derived from Hellenistic rhetoric, the rabbinic methods of interpretation were applied to the Torah.[91]

Hillel was confronted with the dichotomy between ancient traditions which formed the basis of authority and a logical rational determination of law, which was the same problem already solved by Greek rhetoric.[92] By proving that ancient traditions were derivable by of means hermeneutical rules, he could then use those same rules to further the interpretation of the Torah. He gave a scriptural basis for these hermeneutical traditions and thereby provided a method for expanding the Torah grounded on the rules themselves without using the tradition as authority. Hence what was not in scripture could then be derived on the basis of reasoning methods.[93] The next part of this process was to raise in status the results of the hermeneutically based interpretations to the sanctity of the text itself so that it could be regarded as divinely revealed.[94]

The dichotomy between written and oral traditions was already known by the Greeks.[95] Also, the use of the tradition as a protection (or fence) around the written law to prevent any possible transgression was derived from Greek theory.[96] In the same sense, the conception that all law, written and oral, was given at Sinai, was ultimately derived from Greek and Roman philosophy.[97] Written and oral law had equal force derived from its divine source. From rhetoric came the concept later adapted by Rabbi Yishmael that the purpose of the law-giver was to present the fundamental concepts from which the detailed applications could later be derived.[98]

David Daube demonstrates that not only were all seven of Hillel's hermeneutical rules derived, at least in their final shape, from Greek rhetorical methods but even the sequence was maintained.[99] These rules were part of the Hellenistic world and were adopted by Philo, Hillel and Cicero.[100] Just as Cicero latinized them to fit his purposes, so the rabbis hebraized them to fit theirs.[101]

Henry Fishel points to the structure of some rabbinic literature as parallel to Greek literary forms.[102] He shows that the rabbis even adapted the form of the much hated Epicureans in some of the sources. They were able to make such adaptations even though their contents were antithetical to Judaism because tradition and law were indigenous and basic to the belief system; there was enough confidence to be able to adopt a useful technical system.[103] He explains how Rabbi Akiba successfully learned the methods of Epicurean philosophy which he completely assimilated and transformed for the purpose of ordering the Jewish oral tradition.[104] He took the methods and forms and rejected the content. However, with all the parallels to Greek philosophic forms that Fishel presents, it is intriguing to wonder why the rabbis did not systematize their non-legal thought.

We have examined some of the differences between Jewish and Greek thinking and what the rabbis adopted from Greek philosophy. According to some scholars, aspects of Greek philosophy seem to have been influenced by Jewish thought. Barker, for example, compares Plato's *Laws* to the prophets, Isaiah and Ezekiel. Specifically, he points to the concept of a God with a perfect mind, his providence and justice, i.e., he observes the law.[105] Plato advocates a state-enforced creed and prosecution of religious violators.[106] His emphasis on the state being bound by a commonly-held creed seems very close to the role of the biblical covenant.[107]

In the *Republic*, Plato teaches that reason binds men together fostering understanding and love.[108] To the rabbis it was Torah study and observance that bound the community. Both held that what ultimately binds the community are teaching and the minds of men rather than external force. We do not know if there was any link between Plato and the Jewish community or whether their ideas developed separately. Dodd, however, finds a Jewish influence on hermetic philosophy in particular,[109] and on higher pagan thought in general.[110]

A final word about the parallels, contrasts and comparisons between Jewish and Greek thought is in order. Despite their quite different methods of pursuing political questions, both projected the institutions of human government into heaven.[111] It seems fruitful then to examine that which is usually relegated to theology to discover these concepts of authority relationships, power, community leadership, and other pertinent political issues. The gods seemed to have failed the Greeks. In their search for an adequate system of government to establish some order in their *polis*, they had to turn to man. They celebrated man's potential rationality and applied it to statecraft. The gods were assigned to some distant sphere, away from man. On first glance, it seems that Aristotle's perfect god has to be abstract lest he become corrupt. But one wonders after reading the myths and cosmogonies if Aristotle was more concerned lest the gods corrupt man. Rationality would be the way out, the solution to the quest for order. If there could be order in the mind of man, then perhaps order could be achieved in the community.

For the rabbis, man's rationality was to be used in the service of God, like all the gifts granted by him. God did not fail man. Man had failed God; hence man needed him even more. The anthropomorphisms of the Bible are even more pronounced in rabbinic literature to emphasize God's intimacy with his creation.

Of all the ancient Jewish thinkers, Philo comes closest to being philosophical. He wrote in Greek, which he knew far better than Hebrew (there is even a question if he knew any Hebrew). His work tends to demonstrate how Judaism could fit into the philosophical mode of his day. He is an example of an acculturated Jew in the Hellenistic world hailing from the most acculturated Jewish community, Alexandria. Yet, he rejected Aristotle because the doctrine of the eternity of matter was a restriction of God's power. He also rejected Aristotle's inactive god.[112]

Philo also rejected Plato because of his doctrine of the pre-existence of matter which assumed the eternity of uncreated matter — a restriction of God's power.[113] He rejected as well the Stoic god as fate which limited God's power and his ability to act with freedom.[114] Philo's god is omnipotent and benevolent. He is desperately needed by mankind.

In the development of Jewish thought, God the creator, the all-powerful eternal and transcendent being, becomes the God of revelation.

> When the Holy One, Blessed be he, created the
> world he decreed and said: "The heavens are for
> the Lord and earth he gave to men" (Psalms
> 115:16). When he wanted to give the Torah he can-
> celled the first decree and said: the lower spheres
> will ascend to the upper spheres, and the upper
> spheres will descend to the lower spheres, and I will
> begin, as it is said: "The Lord descended on Mt.
> Sinai" (Exodus 19:20). And it is written: "And he
> said to Moses, ascend to the Lord" (Exodus 24:1).
> Moses made the lower spheres to the upper spheres
> and the upper spheres to the lower.[115]

This statement reflects the rabbis' concept of authority: the idea has no reality until it relates to the community.

In *Midrash Tanhumah* (*Tazria* 5) a legendary discussion between Rabbi Akiba and Tyranus Rufus is recorded.[116] The question was asked if the works of God or the works of man were preferable. Tyranus Rufus argued that certainly the works of God were better, while Rabbi Akiba declared that the works of man were better for they complete God's creation.[117] Rabbi Akiba, defending Jewish attitudes, understood that the world itself is precious because it was created by God's speech. Reflecting rabbinic thought Rabbi Akiba did not accept the concept that this world is inadequate compared to the higher, divine sphere, a reflection of Platonic forms and ideas.[118]

A comparison of Hesiod's *Theogony* and Plato and Aristotle demonstrates the change in the power the gods could wield. For Hesiod and his precursors, political decisions were made not on earth but in the heavenly pantheon. Human polity was a mere reflection of divine decision-making.

Socrates, following the Sophists before him, drove the gods out of the political process. Man's ability to use his own mind was then celebrated. Epitomized by the highest being, the philosopher-king, the *polis* was not a place for gods or barbarians. Human beings could determine their own fate and destiny. Pious statements to the contrary, the intelligentsia knew that political acts were in human hands. Aristotle drove his god higher and higher until his god reached the peak of the mountain, where after initiating creation, he no longer concerned himself with man. Relegated to an upper sphere because his perfection forbade him from dealing with an imperfect world, his god was theologized into oblivion.

Once the more ethereal mythological gods were abandoned, it was soon discovered that replacements were needed. While transcendent authority was still seen as the only way to achieve acquiescence from the populace, the identification of such authority was made using different criteria. If rationality was the quintessence of being human, then those who were or could become most rational were fit to rule. Only later it was determined that in order to achieve acquiescence those who were to be ruled should participate in choosing the ruler.

Emphasis was placed on the need for a ruler in order for a people or society to survive. Different theories of government contributed answers as to how and who was to rule. For example, the Roman emperors declared themselves divine, perhaps for a political end, to unify a far-flung empire of disparate barbarians.

The question was turned around by Jewish thinkers. The ruler has no significance without a people, just as a parent has no meaning without children, a teacher without students, etc. People then can make legitimate demands on their rulers, for without them rulers have no purpose. While it was realized that God was the transcendent authority, it was also emphasized that he had no reality without the people.

The Jewish Leader

The rabbis were leaders of their communities. They had influence without formally ruling over the community. For the most part individual rabbis exercised influence because of their scholarship and piety.[119] Living in scattered communities throughout the world, Jewish people voluntarily accepted the authority of the rabbis and their legal decisons.[120] Without hierarchies, chief rabbis, formal organizations (except for those in Babylonia and the land of Israel), individual rabbis still commanded respect and were influential. The rabbis could independently render decisions even without biblical support (during some periods) whose correctness was determined by his strength of character.[121] During some periods he did not even need supportive arguments, for it was felt that he would know the real purpose and intent of the biblical text which he was ultimately interpreting.[122]

Some rabbis were appointed as judges or administrators by the exilarch (the court-appointed head of the Babylonia Jewish community who had royal prerogatives as a descendant of the house of David). These rabbis also wielded political power.[123] Jacob Neusner claims that their religious power derived from the perception of the masses, who regarded them as having special theurgic abilities and the knowledge of using blessings and curses.[124] Their popular support often encouraged them to contend with the exilarch, his court and the priests for power.[125]

They used persuasion and sometimes were backed by the non-Jewish government over against the exilarchate[126] and patriarchate in the land of Israel. They successfully attempted to utilize the courts and schools they controlled to effect social change. The rabbis wanted to be independent and wield solid authority while not establishing a separate society or hierarchy. Over against the royal Davidic claims of the exilarch they declared that the entire Jewish community was chosen. No section or group could claim any special privileges because of genealogy.[127]

Political Realities

The rabbis, while attempting to maintain the viability of the community, had to deal with the actual political and economic problems faced by their communities. They were, for the most part, reluctant to be appointed to posts that might corrupt them.

Rabban Gamliel was told of two rabbis, Rabbi

> Eleazar Hismi and Rabbi Yohanan ben Gudga-
> dah[128] who were very clever and very poor. He
> determined to appoint them to a salary post. He
> sent for them, but they did not come. He sent
> again, and they came. He said to them: You
> thought I was going to offer you rule. It is service
> that I am giving you. And he quoted I Kings 12:7:
> "If you will be a servant to these people this day."[129]

This statement is an example of the political realities of the time
(after the Hadrianic persecutions during Roman rule, late second
century). It points to the difficulty of finding proper people for community posts because responsibilities probably included collection of
imposts, fines and taxes. Even though the two rabbis were destitute,
the corrupting tendencies of the office along with its unpopularity
were grounds for their reluctance.

That Rabban Gamliel, the patriarch of the community, was faced
with the problem of appointing people to insure the flow of monies to
the Roman authorities is demonstrated by his plea that they need not
perceive themselves as rulers who could be corrupted by the office,
but rather as servants of the people. By taking the unsavory post,
they would insure that the wrath of Roman rulers would be placated
by the flow of monies.

By the third century the taxation by the Romans in the land of
Israel became so rapacious that many people fled the area. The taxes
bled the economy so that there was a general impoverishment.[130]

> When Rabbi Haggai appointed and instituted offi-
> cers, he was wont to put a scroll of the law in their
> hands and say that all rules given to man are given
> from the Torah. While Rabbi Eliezer was a *parnas*
> (communal administrator), he one day went to his
> house and he said to the members of his household:
> How have you fared? They replied: A band of trav-
> ellers came here and ate and drank and prayed for
> you. He said: Then there will be no good reward.
> On a similar occasion the reply was: Another band
> of travellers ate and drank and cursed you. He
> said: the reward will be and good. When it was
> desired to make Rabbi Akiba a communal officer,
> he said: I will consult my wife. Those who followed
> him to her house heard her say: Take it on condi-
> tion that you are cursed and despised.[131]

The thrust of the concerns of some rabbis was different from most
politicians. Being pious people they were more concerned with God's
reward than with their own popularity. It they were popular (people
praying for them), then perhaps they were not acting righteously

according to the demands of the Torah. If they were despised and cursed, they were not giving in to the temptation to act so that they would be popular. Obviously, one in position of authority cannot please everyone; some would be unhappy with their decisions which had to be made. Authority had to expect derision and criticism if it was to carry out its responsibilities properly.

Rabbi Haggai tried to instill this dedication to Torah rather than concern with popularity. The installation ceremony of new officers included a placing of a Torah scroll in their hands to emphasize that the law was to follow the God-given covenant rather than placating popular will. The ritual was probably observed in order to evoke the giving of the Torah at Mt. Sinai. The new communal officer, by receiving the scroll, was affirming his allegiance to the Torah.

Schools of Thought

There was by no means unanimity of opinion on the part of the rabbis. Instead, there were deep intellectual and conceptual differences. The main exponents of schools of thought during the period between the two wars (i.e., between 70 and 132 C.E.) were Rabbi Akiba and Rabbi Yishmael. Each probably represented very old trends in rabbinic thought.

Rabbi Yishmael is usually represented as a rationalist and allegorist, while Rabbi Akiba is depicted as a mystic.[132] As leaders of schools they had students who represented their views which can be traced throughout the history of Jewish thought.[133] The rationalist trend taught *imitatio dei*, that one is to imitate God's ways.[134] God is a model to which man is to look in order to know how to act. Allegory is a method of depicting God's actions. The Akiban trend, on the other hand, seeks close contact with God. Problems of anthropomorphism are not a real concern. Their experience of God is real, mystical and direct.[135]

These differences in thought resulted in different attitudes toward interpretation. Rabbi Yishmael's purpose was to refine the written word on the assumption that the Torah was given in the language of mankind.[136] Rabbi Akiba accepted the text as God's inimitable word. There was no need to refine it. From apparent difficulties he derived yet another interpretation. For Akiba, God came to man, and man came to God. While the Torah was from heaven it was brought to man.[137]

Another consequence of these trends was their contrasting attitudes towards Rome. The rationalists seemed to seek safety during Roman persecution, hiding until the danger passed. The mystics, as epitomized by Rabbi Akiba's support of Bar Kokhba, tended to be activists in resisting Roman power. The character of their resistance was clearly messianic.[138]

Most appropriate to this study is their contrasting conceptions of revelation and Torah. Rabbi Akiba taught that the entire Torah was given at Sinai including the oral traditions.[139] For the Akiban school, the chronology of the tradition was not as central as the source of the tradition. All Torah, including the interpretation of future generations, had a common source in time and space which validated it as authentic tradition. All possibilities were revealed at Sinai. Interpretation was a process of discovering these possibilities. Revelation was an actual experience that was continual through study. One could still discover new aspects of the original revelation which might have gone previously ignored. Revelation was not merely divine inspiration or a revelation of God's will. Rather, according to the Akiban school, the Torah, in its entirety, came from heaven.[140] Revelation refers to the contact between God and man.

The school of Yishmael had a different understanding of revelation and Torah. What was actually revealed at Sinai were the Ten Commandments, an epitome of all the Torah (there are six hundred and thirteen letters in the Ten Commandments, each signifying the six hundred and thirteen commandments).[141]

The act of revelation was limited as well. Since the Torah was given in the language of mankind, esoteric or obscure interpretations were not necessary. With the rules of hermeneutics which Rabbi Yishmael had expanded (from Hillel's seven to thirteen) and human reason, the text could be explicated. Within the Pentateuch there are many statements by Moses who heard God's word and intent and then wrote most of the Torah himself. So the words of the Pentateuch were not actually all of God's own words.[142]

These differences are not confined to the rabbis. Plato and Aristotle also represent two different trends of thought. Platonism became the model for mystic speculation. Aristotelian study in the Middle Ages led to a reintroduction of rationalistic trends of thought.

The significance of these trends for rabbinic political thought is manifested in differing outlooks toward Torah. For the mystic, Akiban, trend a continual experience of revelation is possible. God and man can be in constant contact. For the rationalistic, Yishmaelian, trend, God is transcendent; after the primary revelation it is up to man to find his own accommodation to tradition.

NOTES

1. Neal Wood, review of *History of Political Philosophy* Edited by Leo Strauss and J. Cropsey, *Political Theory*, I, No. 3 (August, 1973), p. 342.

2. Louis H. Feldman, "Tho Romans and the Jewish Question," *Midstream*, XX, No. 1 (January, 1974), p. 80.

3. Baron, *History*, II, p. 57f.

4. There are differing views concerning the origin of the term, *Sadducee*. Most scholars seem to feel that it is derived from the priestly house of Tzadok, the name of a biblical high priest. The *Sadducees* represented the higher echelons of the priesthood and aristocracy and were, for the most part, accommodating toward Rome, cosmopolitan and generally more assimilated into Hellenistic culture. See Baron, *History*, II, p. 342, Note 43.

5. For the term, *Pharisee*, see Baron, *History*, II, p. 342, Note 43. According to Lauterbach the name was a result of being thrown out of the Sanhedrin after a power struggle. See Jacob Z. Lauterbach, *Rabbinic Essays* (Cincinnati: Hebrew Union College Press, 1951), p. 109.

6. Herford, *The Pharisees*, p. 44ff.

7. *Ibid.*, p. 48.

8. E. E. Urbach, "Class-status and Leadership in the World of the Palestinian Sages," *Israel. Academy of Sciences and Humanites Proceedings* (Jerusalem, 1969), II, p. 37.

9. Gedalya Alon, *Toldot Hay'hudim B'eretz Yisrael B't'kufat Hamishnah V'hatalmud* (Tel Aviv: Hakibbutz Ham'uchad Publishing House, Ltd., 1958) I, p. 9. Hereafter cited as *Toldot*.

10. *Ibid.*, p. 10.

11. *Ibid.*, p. 335.

12. Gedalya Alon, *Mehkarim b'Toldot Yisrael* (Tel Aviv: Hakibbutz Ham'uchad Publishing House, Ltd., 1957) I, p. 28f. Hereafter cited as *Studies*. He cites as an example of early rabbinic political activity, the pharasaic law that limited the actions of the king in fighting certain kinds of wars. It required the king to have the consent of the Sanhedrin before he could engage in an offensive war to acquire territory. Alexander Yannai nullified the court because he could not make it submit to his will, and did not want any unity set against his rights as king. See especially p. 31f.

13. *Ibid.*, p. 44f. See also *Talmud Bavli Shabbat* 33b, *Avodah Zarah* 2b.

14. E.g., statement of Rabbi Shimon ben Lakish in *Genesis Rabbah* 9.

15. Alon, *Studies*, p. 45.

16. *Ibid.*, p. 46.

17. Baron, *History*, II, p. 110.

18. *Ibid.*, p. 111.

19. Jacob Neusner, "The Religious Uses of History: Judaism in First Century A.D. Palestine and Third Century Babylonia," *History and Theory*, V, No. 2 (1966), p. 159.

20. *Ibid.*, p. 160.

21. *Ibid.*, p. 162.

22. *Ibid.*

23. Yigael Yadin, *Bar Kokhba* (New York: Random House, 1971), pp. 17-27.

24. See *Song of Songs Rabbah* 2:5,3 and *Talmud Bavli B'rakhot* 63b. Even though the sources state that the synod met in Yavneh, it most likely was convened at Usha. See *Encyclopedia Judaica*, XVI, p. 17f. The following rabbis are recorded as present: Yehudah, Meir, Yose, Shimon bar Yohai, Eliezer ben Yose Hag'lili, Eleazer ben Ya'akov. The patriarch, Rabban Shimon ben Gamliel, is not mentioned, probably reflecting a struggle for power between the sanhedrin and the office of the partiarch (*nasi*). The sanhedrin had tried to limit Shimon ben Gamliel's power which was, rather strengthened when Rabbis Natan and Meir unsuccessfully attempted to unseat him.

25. Jacob Neusner, *From Politics to Piety* (Englewood Cliffs: Prentice-Hall Inc., 1973), p. 124.

26. *Ibid.*

27. *Ibid.*, p. 136.

28. Ginzberg, *On Jewish Law and Lore*, p. 19.

29. Saul Lieberman, *Palestine in the Third and Fourth Centuries* (reprinted from *Jewish Quarterly Review* (new series), XXXVI, No. 4 and XXXVII, No. 1, Philadelphia: The Dropsie College of Hebrew and Cognate Learning, 1946), p. 341. Lieberman cites *Talmud Bavli Ketubot* 111a and *Song of Songs Rabbah and Zuta to Song of Songs*, 2:7.

30. *Ibid.*, 344.

31. Ginzberg, *On Jewish Law and Lore*, p. 12; Baron, *History*, II, p. 207ff.

32. Baron, *History*, p. 190.
33. Salo W. Baron, *The Jewish Community* (Philadelphia: Jewish Publication Society of America, 1948), I, p. 139f.
34. Erwin R. Goodenough, *Jewish Symbols in the Greco-Roman Period* (New York: Pantheon Books, Inc., 1954), IV, p. 24.
35. *Ibid.*, p. 44.
36. *Ibid.*, p. 54.
37. Gershon Cohen, "The Talmudic Age," *Great Ages and Ideas of the Jewish People.* Edited by L. Schwartz (New York: The Modern Library,1956), p. 164.
38. *Ibid.*
39. *Ibid.*, p. 165.
40. *Ibid.*, p. 166.
41. Gedalya Alon, "Concerning the History of Juridical Authorities in Palestine During the Talmudic Period," *Zion*, XII, No. 3-4 (July, 1947), p. 105f.
42. Baron, *History*, II, p. 200.
43. *Ibid.*, p. 203
44. *Midrash Tanhuma, Mishpatim*, 2 on Exodus 21:1 (with reference to Proverbs 29:4) as quoted by Baron, *History*, II, p. 203.
45. From the Hebrew, *mashiah*, which means anointed.
46. Jacob Neusner, "The Religious Use of History: Judaism in First Century A.D. Palestine and Third Century Babylonia," p. 166f. He cites *Talmud Bavli Sanhedrin* 93b as an example.
47. *Ibid.*, p. 167.
48. *Ibid.*, p. 169.
49. Alon, *Toldot*, I, p. 334f.
50. *Ibid.*, p. 335.
51. *Ibid.*, p. 338f.
52. Baron, *History*, II, p. 139.
53. The *p'shat*.
54. Baron, *History*, p. 144.
55. *Ibid.*, p. 120.
56. *Ibid.*, p. 216.
57. *Ibid.*, p. 235.
58. Cohen, "The Talmudic Age," p. 151.
59. *Ibid.*, p. 164.
60. Moore, I, p. 399.
61. Norman Bentwich, *Hellenism* (Philadelphia: Jewish Publication Society of America, 1919), p. 39f.
62. *Ibid.*, p. 40f.
63. *Ibid.*, p. 49.
64. *Ibid.*, p. 346.
65. Saul Lieberman, "How Much Greek in Jewish Palestine?" *Biblical and Other Studies.* Edited by A. Altmann (Cambridge: Harvard University Press, 1963), p. 130.
66. *Ibid.*, p. 129.
67. *Ibid.*, p. 130.
68. *Ibid.*
69. *Ibid.*, p. 135.
70. Julius Guttman, *Philosophies of Judaism.* Translated by David W. Silverman (Philadelphia: Jewish Publication Society of America, 1964), p. 40f.
71. Lieberman, "How Much Greek in Jewish Palestine?", p. 124.
72. Cyrus H. Gordon, "Homer and Bible, The Origin and Character of East Mediterranean Literature," *Hebrew Union College Annual*, XXVI (1955), p. 101.
73. *Ibid.*, p. 91.
74. *Ibid.*
75. *Ibid.*, p. 92.
76. Boman, p. 19f.
77. *Ibid.*, p. 206. Plato regards sight as a divine-like quality (*Republic*, VI, p. 307).

78. *Ibid.*, p. 19f.
79. *Ibid.*, p. 206.
80. *Ibid.*, pp.31,51.
81. *Ibid.*, p. 51f. He came from Ephesus which had a significant Jewish population which may have had some influence on his thought.
82. Similarly, it is difficult to fit Greek expression into Hebrew language without utilizing the terminology.
83. Boman, p. 53.
84. *Ibid.*, p. 54.
85. *Ibid.*, p. 67.
86. *Ibid.*, p. 113.
87. C.H. Dodd, *The Bible and the Greeks* (London: Hodder and Stoughton, 1954), p. 6.
88. *Ibid.*, p. 7. The dichotomy between Greek and Jewish thought continues in the hereafter. Charles, *Eschatology*, p. 80f, notes that Plato's concept of immortality is completely outside of the framework of the community and is for the individual who leads an aesthetic life. Civic and social virtues had no independent value, even in his *Republic*. However, in Judaism the individual could attain the highest only within the community both in this world and in the next.
89. Ginzberg, "The Religion of the Jews at the Time of Jesus," p. 308.
90. E. E. Urbach, "The Talmudic Sage — Character and Authority," *Journal of World Religion*, XI, No. 1-2 (1968), p. 135.
91. David Daube, "Rabbinic Methods of Interpretation and Hellenistic Rhetoric," *Hebrew Union College Annual*, XXII (1949), p. 240.
92. *Ibid.*, p. 246. See Notes 23 and 24 for citations.
93. *Ibid.*, p. 247. See Notes 25 and 26 for citations.
94. *Ibid.* See Notes 27 and 28 for citations. Daube points out the same rhetorical method was used in Roman law.
95. *Ibid.*, p. 248, Note 30.
96. *Ibid.*, Note 31.
97. *Ibid.*, p. 249f. Notes 33-37.
98. *Ibid.*, p. 250. For Rabbi Yishmael's view see *Talmud Bavli Sota* 37b, *Hagigah* 6a and *Zevahim* 115b, and the contrary idea of Rabbi Akiba that all law was given at Sinai. This seems to have been the type of discussion that could have occurred in Greek rhetorical schools.
99. *Ibid.*, p. 251f.
100. *Ibid.*, p. 257.
101. *Ibid.*, p. 258.
102. Henry A. Fishel, *Rabbinic Literature and Greco-Roman Philosophy* (Leiden: E.J. Brill, 1973), p. 54.
103. *Ibid.*, p. 89.
104. *Ibid.*, Chapter 1.
105. Barker, p. 425f.
106. *Ibid.*, p. 426f.
107. *Ibid.*, p. 428.
108. *Ibid.*, p. 195
109. Dodd, p. 242.
110. *Ibid.*, p. 247.
111. Cyrus Gordon, "Homer and Bible. The Origin and Character of East Mediterranean Literature," p. 95.
112. Wolfson, p. 9. But David Winston, in a lecture given in Berkeley on April 7, 1975, stated that Philo did accept the eternity of matter.
113. *Ibid.*
114. *Ibid.*
115. *Exodus Rabbah* 12:4 and *Deuteronomy Rabbah* 10:2 as quoted by A.J. Heschel, *Theology of Ancient Judaism* (London and New York: The Soncino Press, 1962), I, p. 67 (my translation).
116. Cited by Heschel, I, p. 131.

117. Perhaps they were discussing the rite of circumcision which was abominable to the Greco-Roman mind and was regarded as a mutilation of the flesh. Rabbi Akiba defends circumcision by declaring that man completes God's act of creation, just as making bread completes the creation of wheat.

118. Heschel, I, p. 131.

119. Louis Ginzberg, *Students, Scholars and Saints* (New York and Philadephia: Meridian Books and Jewish Publication Society of America, 1958), p. 40f.

120. R. Travers Herford. "The Influence of Judaism Upon Jews in the Period From Hillel to Mendelsohn," *The Legacy of Israel.* Edited by E.R. Bevans and C. Singer (Oxford: Clarendon Press, 1953), p. 103.

121. David Daube, "Rabbinic Methods of Interpretation and Hellenistic Rhetoric," p. 242.

122. *Ibid.*

123. Jacob Neusner, *There We Sat Down* (New York: Abingdon Press, 1972), p. 102.

124. *Ibid.*

125. *Ibid.*, p. 106.

126. *Ibid.*

127. *Ibid.*, 130.

128. According to Bacher this text should read Rabbi Yohanan ben Nuri since ben Gudgadah lived during a later generation. See *Talmud* (Soncino edition). *Horayot*, p. 71, Note 3.

129. *Talmud Bavli Horayot* 10a.

130. Lieberman, *Palestine in the Third and Fourth Centuries*, p. 344.

131. *Talmud Yerushalmi Peah* 8, 7, 21a, line 29.

132. Marmorstein, *Doctrine*, II, p. 31f.

133. *Ibid.*, p. 31ff. He indicates in which school specific rabbis should be placed. See also page 108 for a list of terms used by literalists or allegorists.

134. *Ibid.*, p. 126.

135. *Ibid.*, p. 111.

136. *Torah nitnah b'lashon b'nay adam.*

137. Marmorstein, *Doctrine*, p. 194. He cites *Exodus Rabbah* 12:4.

138. *Ibid.*, II, p. 140. See Note 24. See also, David Daube, *Collaboration with Tyranny in Rabbinic Law* (London: Oxford University Press, 1965), p. 39.

139. Louis Finkelstein, "Midrash, Halachot V'agadot," *Yitzhak F. Baer Jubilee Volume*, Edited by S.W. Baron, et al. (Jerusalem: The Historical Society of Israel, 1970), p. 45. He cites *Torat Kohanim, B'hukotai* (end of Chapter 8).

140. Heschel, II, p. 7.

141. *Ibid.*, p. 76.

142. *Ibid.*, I, p. 14.

BIBLIOGRAPHY

Biblical

Torah N'vi'im K'tuvim. Jerusalem: Koren Publishing Co., Ltd., 1965.

Rabbinic

Mishnah and Talmud

Shishah Sidray Mishnah. 6 vols. Edited with Commentary and Introduction (separate volume) by H. Albeck. Jerusalem: Mosad Bialik, 1959.

Mishnayot. 6 vols. with Commentary by Rambam, Obartinura, Tosfot Yom Tov. New York: M'fitzay Torah, 1954.

The Mishnah. Translated by H. Danby. London: Oxford University Press, 1933.

Goldin, Judah. *The Living Talmud: The Wisdom of the Fathers.* New York: New American Library, 1957.

Herford, R. Travers. *The Ethics of the Talmud: Sayings of the Fathers.* New York: Schocken Books, 1962.

Tosefta Z'raim. Edited by S. Lieberman. New York: The Jewish Theological Seminary of America, 1955.

Talmud Bavli. 20 vols. New York: M'orot Publishing Co., 1959.

Epstein, I., Editor, *The Babylonian Talmud.* 18 vols. London: The Soncino Press, 1948 (English translation).

The Fathers According to Rabbi Nathan. Translated by Judah Goldin. New Haven: Yale University Press, 1955.

Midrash

Mekilta de Rabbi Ishmael. 3 vols. Translated and edited by Jacob Z. Lauterbach. Philadelphia: The Jewish Publication Society of America, 1949.

Midrash Rabbah. 10 vols. Edited by H. Freedman and M. Simon. London: The Soncino Press, 1961 (English translation).

Midrash Rabbah. 2 vols. Edited by E. Zundil. New York: Hotzat Anafim, 1957.

Sh'mot Rabbah. 5 vols. Edited by T. Mirkin. Tel Aviv: Yavneh, 1959.

Vayikra Rabbah. 5 vols. Edited with introduction by M. Margoliot. Jerusalem: Academy or Jewish Research, 1960.

Midrash Tanhuma. Edited by E. Zundil. Jerusalem: Lewin-Epstein, 1960.

Midrash Tehillim (Sokher Tov). Edited by S. Buber, New York: Ohm Publishing Co., 1947.

Pesikta Rabbati. Edited by M. Friedman. Vienna, 1880.

Pesikta Rabbati. Translated by W.G. Braude. New Haven: Yale University Press, 1968.

Pesikta D'rav Kahanah. Edited by S. Buber. Zyck: Silberman, 1868.

Pesikta D'rav Kahanah. Edited by B. Mandelbaum. New York: The Jewish Theological Seminary of America, 1962.

Sifra D'bay Rav-Torat Kohanim. Edited by I.H. Weiss. New York: Ohm Publishing Co., 1947

Sifre D'bay Rav. Edited by M. Friedman. Vienna: 1864.

Yalkut Shimoni. 2 vols. New York: Pardes Publishing House, 1944.

Reference Works

Bacher, W. *Erkhay Midrash.* 2 vols. Translated from the German by A.Z. Rabinowitz. Jerusalem, Karmiel, 1923 (Hebrew).

Berlin, Charles. *Index to Festschriften in Jewish Studies.* Cambridge and New York: Harvard College Library and KTAV Publishing House, Inc., 1971.

Encyclopedia Judaica. 16 vols. Jerusalem: Keter Publishing House, Inc. 1971.

Ginzberg, Louis. *The Legends of the Jews.* 7 vols. Philadelphia: The Jewish Publication Society of America, 1968.

Goodenough, Erwin R. *Jewish Symbols in the Graeco-Roman Period.* 13 vols. New York: Pantheon Books, Inc., 1954.

Gross, M.P. *Otzar Ha'agadah.* 3 vols. Jerusalem: Mosad Harav Kook, 1961 (Hebrew).

Hyman, A.M. *Torah Hak'tuva V'ham'sorah.* 3 vols. Tel Aviv: D'vir, 1965 (Hebrew).

Jastrow, M. *A Dictionary of the Targum, the Talmud Babli and Yerushalmi and the Midrashic Literature.* 2 vols. New York: Pardes Publishing House, Inc., 1950.

Kosovsky, B. *Otzar L'shon Hatana'im (Mekhilta).* 3 vols. Jerusalem: The Jewish Theological Seminary of America, 1966 (Hebrew).

Otzar L'shon Hatana'im (Sifra-Torat Kohanim). 3 vols. Jerusalem: The Jewish Theological Seminary of America, 1968 (Hebrew).

Otzar L'shon Hatosefta. 5 vols. Jerusalem: The Jewish Theological Seminary of America, 1958 (Hebrew).

Kosovsky, C.Y. *Otzar L'shon Hamishnah.* 3 vols. Jerusalem: Masada Publishing Co., 1956 (Hebrew).

Mandelkern, Solomon. *Concordancia L'tanakh.* Tel Aviv: Schocken, 1962 (Hebrew).

Margoliot, M. *Encyclopedia L'hokhmay Hatalmud V'hag'onim.* 2 vols. Jerusalem: Mosad Harav Kook, 1960 (Hebrew).

Natan ben Yehiel. *Arukh Hashalem.* Edited by A. Kohut. 9 vols. New York: Pardes Publishing House, Inc., 1955 (Hebrew).

Zevin, S.Y. (Editor) *Encyclopedia Talmudit.* 14 vols. Jerusalem: Yad Harav Herzog, 1973.

General Bibliography

Abelson, J. *Immanence of God in Rabbinical Literature.* New York: Hermon Press, 1967.

Aberbach, Moshe. "Educational Institutions and Problems during the Talmudic Age," *Hebrew Union College Annual,* XXXVII (1966), 107-120.

Adler, Michael. "The Emperor Julian and the Jews," *Jewish Quarterly Review* (old series), V (1893).

Agard, Walter R. *The Greek Mind.* Princeton: P. Van Nostrand Company, Inc., 1957.

Agassi, J. "Convention of Knowledge in Talmudic Law," *Journal of Jewish Studies,* XXV, No. 1 (July, 1974), 16-34.

Agus, Jacob. *The Evolution of Jewish Thought.* New York: Abelard-Schuman, 1959.

Albright, William F. *From the Stone Age to Christianity.* New York: Doubleday and Co., 1957.

Alon, Gedalya. "Concerning the History of Juridical Authorities in Palestine during the Talmudic Period," *Zion,* XII, No. 3-4 (July, 1974), 101-135, 193 (Hebrew).

Studies in Jewish History in the Times of the Second Temple, the Mishnah and the Talmud. 2 vols. Tel Aviv: Hakibbutz Ham'uchad Publishing House, Ltd., 1957, I (Hebrew).

Toldot Hay'hudim B'eretz Yisrael Bit'kufat Hamishnah V'hatalmud. 2 vols. Tel Aviv: Hakibbutz Ham'uchad Publishing House, Ltd., 1958, I (Hebrew).

Aristotle. *The Politics.* Translated and introduction by Ernest Barker. New York: Oxford University Press, 1962.

Auerbach, Erich. *Mimesis.* Translated by T. Tragle. Garden City: Doubleday Anchor Books, 1953.

Bacher, W. "The Church Father, Origen, and Rabbi Hoshaya," in *Jewish Quarterly Review* (old series), III (1891), 257-360.

"The Origin of the Word Haggadah (Agada)," *Jewish Quarterly Review* (old series), IV (1892). 406-429.

Baeck, Leo. *The Pharisees and Other Essays.* New York: Schocken Books, 1947.

Baer, Yitzhak F. "Social Ideals of the Second Jewish Commonwealth," *Journal of World History.* XI, No. 1-2 (1968), 69-91.

Baltzer, Klaus. *The Covenant Formulary in Old Testament, Jewish and Early Christian Writings.* Translated by David E. Green. Oxford: Basil Blackwell, 1971.

Bamberger, Bernard J. *Proselytism in the Talmudic Period.* Cincinnati: Hebrew Union College Press, 1934.

"Revelations of Torah after Sinai," in *Hebrew Union College Annual,* XVI (1941), 97-113.

Barker, Ernest. *Greek Political Theory.* New York: Barnes and Noble, Inc., 1960.

Baron, Salo W. *The Jewish Community.* 3 vols. Philadelphia: Jewish Publication Society of America, 1948, I.

A Social and Religious History of the Jews. 2 vols., second edition revised. New York and Philadelphia: Columbia University Press and Jewish Publication Society of America, 1958.

and Blau, J.L. (editors). *Judaism: Postbiblical and Talmudic Period.* New York: The Liberal Arts Press, 1954.

Bentwich, Norman. *Hellenism*. Philadelphia: Jewish Publication Society of America, 1919.

Berkovits, Eliezer. " 'Conversion According to Halachah' — What is it?" *Judaism,* XXIII, No. 4 (Fall, 1974), 467-478.

Bevan, E.R. "Hellenistic Judaism," in *The Legacy of Israel* by E. R. Bevan and C. Singer. Oxford: Clarendon Press, 1953, 29-67.

Bickerman, Elias J. "The Historical Foundations of Postbiblical Judaism" in *The Jews,* Edited by L. Finkelstein. 2 vols. New York: Harper and Row, 1960, I, 70-114.

Blau, Joseph L. "Tradition and Innovation," in *Essays in Jewish Life and Thought Presented in Honor of Salo Wittmayer Baron,* Edited by J.L. Blau et al. New York: Columbia University Press, 1959, 95-104.

Bokser, Ben Zion. *Wisdom of the Talmud*. New York: the Citadel Press, 1962.

Boman, Thorlief. *Hebrew Thought Compared with Greek*. Translated by J.L. Moreau. Philadelphia: The Westminster Press, 1960.

Bright, John. *A History of Israel*. Philadelphia: The Westminster Press, 1959.

Buber, Martin. "Biblical Leadership," in *Israel and the World*. New York: Schocken Books, 1948.

Moses, the Revelation and the Covenant. New York: Harper and Brothers, 1958.

The Prophetic Faith. New York: Harper and Brothers, 1960.

Buchler, A. *The Political and the Social Leaders of the Jewish Community of Sepphoris in the Second and Third Centuries*. London: Jews' College (no date given).

Studies in Sin and Atonement in the Rabbinic Literature of the First Century. New York: Ktav Publishing House, Inc., 1967.

Types of Jewish-Palestinian Piety from 70 B.C. to 70 C.E. The Ancient Pious Men. New York: Ktav Publishing House, Inc., 1968.

Cassuto, U. *A Commentary on the Book of Genesis*. Translated by Israel Abraham. 2 vols. Jerusalem: Magnes Press, 1961.

Chajes, Z.H. *The Student's Guide Through the Talmud*. Translation and introduction by Jacob Schachter. New York: Phillip Feldheim, Inc., 1960.

Charles, R.A. *Eschatology: The Doctrine of a Future Life.* New York: Schocken Books, 1963.

Childs, Brevard S. *Memory and Tradition in Israel.* London: SCM Press, 1962.

Myth and Reality in the Old Testament. London: SCM Press, 1960.

Clarke, M.L. *The Roman Mind.* Cambridge: Harvard University Press, 1960.

Clements, R.E. *Prophecy and Covenant.* London: SCM Press, 1965.

Cohen, Boaz. "Letter and Spirit in Jewish and Roman Law," in *Mordecai M. Kaplan Jubilee Volume,* Edited by M. Davis. New York: The Jewish Theological Seminary of America, 1953, 2 vols. I, 104-135.

Cohen, Gershon. "The Talmudic Age," in *Great Ages and Ideas of the Jewish People,* Edited by L. Schwartz. New York: The Modern Library, 1956, 143-212.

Cohen, Naomi G. "Rabbi Meir: A Descendant of Anatolian Proselytes," *Journal of Jewish Studies,* XXIII, No. 1 (Spring, 1972), 51-60.

Cohon, Samuel S. "Authority in Judaism," *Hebrew Union College Annual,* II (1936), 547-631.

"The Name of God: A Study in Rabbinic Theology," *Hebrew Union College Annual,* XXIII, Part 1 (1950-51), 579-604.

"The Unity of God," *Hebrew Union College Annual,* XXVI, (1955), 425-479.

Cornford, F.M. *From Religion to Philosophy.* New York: Harper and Brothers, 1957

Daube, David. "Alexandrian Methods of Interpretation and the Rabbis," in *Festschrift Hans Lewald.* Basel: Verlag Helbing und Lichtenhahn, 1953, 27-44.

Civil Disobedience in Antiquity. Edinburgh: The University Press, 1972.

Collaboration with Tyranny in Rabbinic Law. London: Oxford University Press, 1965.

"Covenanting Under Duress," *The Irish Jurist,* II (new series), Part 2 (Winter, 1967), 352-359.

"Dissent in Bible and Talmud," *California Law Review.* 59, No. 3 (May, 1971), 784-794.

"The Influence of Interpretation on Writing," *Buffalo Law Review,* No. 1 (Fall, 1970), 41-59.

"*Kerdaino* as a Missionary Term," *Harvard Theological Review,* XL, No. 2 (April, 1957), 109-120.

"Limitations of Self-Sacrifice in Jewish Law and Tradition," *Theology,* LXXII, No. 589 (July, 1969), 29-34.

"Princeps Legibus Solutas," in *Studi in Memoria di Paolo Koschaker.* Milan: Multa Paucis, 1954, 463-465.

"Rabbinic Methods of Interpretation and Hellenistic Rhetoric," *Hebrew Union College Annual,* XXII (1949), 239-264.

"Texts and Interpretation in Roman and Jewish Law," *The Jewish Journal of Sociology,* III, No. 1 (reprint), 3-28.

Dodd, C.H. *The Bible and the Greeks.* London: Hodder and Stoughton, 1954.

Eichrodt, W. *Man in the Old Testament.* Translated by K. & R. Gregory Smith. London: SCM Press, 1959.

Theology of the Old Testament. Translated by J.A. Baker. Philadelphia: The Westminster Press, 1961.

Feinberg, B.S. "Creativity and the Political Community: The Role of the Law Giver in the Thought of Plato, Machiavelli and Rousseau," *Western Quarterly Review,* XXIII, No. 3 (September, 1970), 471-485.

Feldman, Louis H. "The Romans and the Jewish Question," *Midstream,* XX, No. 1 (January, 1974), 76-81.

Finkelstein, Louis. *Akiba: Scholar, Saint and Martyr.* New York and Philadelphia: Meridian Books and Jewish Publication Society of America, 1962.

Ha-Perushim ve-Anshe Keneset Ha-Gedolah. New York: Jewish Theological Seminary of America, 1950 (Hebrew).

Mabo le-Massektot Abot ve-Abot d'Rabbi Natan. New York: Jewish Theological Seminary of America, 1950 (Hebrew).

"Midrash Halachot v'Agadot" in *Yitzhak F. Baer Jubilee Volume,* Edited by S.W. Baron, et all. Jerusalem: The Historical Society of Israel, 1960, 28-47 (Hebrew).

The Pharisees: The Sociological Background of Their Faith. 2 vols., 3rd ed. Philadelphia: Jewish Publication Society of America, 1962.

"The Ten Martyrs," in *Essays and Studies in Memory of Linda A. Miller*, Edited by Israel Davidson. New York: Jewish Theological Seminary of America, 1938, 29-55.

Fishel, Henry A. *Rabbinic Literature and Greco-Roman Philosophy*. Leiden: E.J. Brill, 1973.

Frankfort, H. *Ancient Egyptian Religion*. New York: Harper and Row, 1961, et al. *Before Philosophy*. Baltimore: Penguin Books, 1959.

The Birth of Civilization in the Near East. New York: Doubleday and Co., 1956.

Freeman, Gordon M. "Political Theory in the Bible: A Study of Covenant," (unpublished Master's Dissertation, Department of Government, New York University, 1966).

Gandz, Solomon. "Oral Tradition in the Bible," *Jewish Studies in Memory of George A. Kohut*. Edited by S.W. Baron and A. Marx. New York: The Alexander Kohut Memorial Foundation, 1935, 248-269.

Gavre, Mark. "Hobbes and His Audience: The Dynamics of Theorizing," *American Political Science Review*, LXVIII, No. 4 (Dec., 1975), 1542-1556.

Ginzberg, Louis. *On Jewish Law and Lore*. New York and Philadelphia: Meridian Books and Jewish Publication Society of America, 1962.

"The Religion of the Jews at the Time of Jesus," *Hebrew Union College Annual*, I (1924), 307-321.

Students, Scholars and Saints. New York and Philadelphia: Meridian Books and Jewish Publication Society of America, 1958.

Glatzer, Nahum N. *Hillel the Elder: The Emergence of Classical Judaism*. Washington: Hillel Little Books, B'nai Brith Hillel Foundations, 1959.

Goldin, Judah. "The Period of the Talmud," in *The Jews*, Edited by L. Finkelstein. New York: Harper and Row, 1960, I, 115-215.

Goodenough, Erwin A. "The Political Philosophy of Hellenistic Kingship," in *Yale Classical Studies*, Volume 3. New Haven: Yale University Press, 1925, 55-102.

Gordis, Robert. "Democratic Origins in Ancient Israel — The Biblical Edah," in *Alexander Marx Jubilee Volume* (English section). Edited by S. Lieberman. New York: Jewish Theological Seminary of America, 1950, 369-388.

"The Lord Out of the Whirlwind," *Judaism,* XIII, No. 1 (Winter, 1964), 48-63.

Gordon, C.H. "Hebrew Origins in the Light of Recent Discovery," in *Biblical and Other Studies.* Edited by A. Altmann. Cambridge: Harvard University Press, 1963, 3-14.

"Homer and Bible: The Origin and Character of East Mediterranean Literature," *Hebrew Union College Annual,* XXVI (1955), 43-108.

The World of the Old Testament. New York: Doubleday and Co., 1958.

Graetz, H. *History of the Jews.* 6 vols. Philadelphia: Jewish Publication Society of America, 1893. Vol. II.

Grant, Michael. *The Jews in the Roman World.* New York: Charles Scribners's Sons, 1973.

Gray, John. *I and II Kings: A Commentary.* Philadelphia: The Westminster Press, 1963.

Greenberg, M. "Some Postulates of Biblical Criminal Law," in *Yehezkel Kaufmann Jubilee Volume.* Edited by M. Haran. Jerusalem: Magnes Press, 1960.

Guttmann, Alexander. "Akiba, Rescuer of the Torah," *Hebrew Union College Annual,* XVII (1942-1943), 395-421.

"Eliezer ben Hyrcanus — A Shammaite?" in *Ignace Goldziher Memorial Volume.* Edited by S. Lowinger, et al. Jerusalem: Rubin Mass, 1958, Part II, 100-110. "Foundations of Rabbinic Judaism," *Hebrew Union College Annual,* XXIII, Part I (1950-1951), 453-473.

"The Patriarch Judah I — Birth and Death," *Hebrew Union College Annual,* XXV (1954), 234-261.

"The Significance of Miracles for Talmudic Judaism," *Hebrew Union College Annual,* XX (1947).

Guttman, Julius. *Philosophies of Judaism.* Translated by David W. Silverman. Philadelphia: Jewish Publication Society of America, 1956.

Hadas, Moses. "The First Encounter of Judaism with European-ism," in *The Menorah Treasury*. Edited by Leo W. Schwartz. Phila-delphia: Jewish Publication Society of America, 1964, 43-49.

Hahn, Herbert. *Old Testament in Modern Research*. Philadelphia: Muhlenberg Press, 1954.

Harrelson, W.J. "Law in the OT," in *The Interpreter's Dictionary of the Bible*. 4 vols. New York: Abington Press, 1962, II, 80-86.

Hartom, A. "B'rit," in *Encyclopedia Mikra'it*. 4 vols. Jerusalem: Mosad Bialik, 1954, II, 347-349 (Hebrew).

Hatch, Edwin. *Essays in Biblical Greek*. Oxford: Clarendon Press, 1889.

Heidel, Alexander. *The Babylonian Genesis*. Chicago: The University of Chicago Press, 1963.

Gilgamesh Epic and Old Testament Parallels. Chicago: The University of Chicago Press, 1963.

Heinemann, Isaac. *Darchay Ha'agadah*. Jerusalem: Magnes Press, 1954 (Hebrew).

Heinemann, Joseph. "Early Halakhah in the Palestinian Targumim," *Journal of Jewish Studies*, XXV, No. 1 (February, 1974), 114-122.

Herford, R. Travers. *The Effect of the Fall of Jerusalem Upon the Charac-ter of the Pharisees*. London: The Society for Hebraic Studies, Publication No. 2, 1917

"The Influences of Judaism Upon Jews in the Period from Hillel to Mendelssohn," in *The Legacy of Israel*. Edited by E.R. Bevan and C. Singer. Oxford: Clarendon Press, 1953, 92-128.

Judaism in the New Testament Period. London: The Lindsey Press, 1928.

The Pharisees. Forward by Nahum N. Glatzer. Boston: Beacon Press, 1962.

"The Problem of the 'Minim' Further Considered," in *Jewish Studies in Memory of George A. Kohut*. Edited by S.W. Baron and A. Marx. New York: The Alexander Kohut Memorial Foundation, 1935, 359-369.

Heschel, Abraham J. *The Prophets*. Philadelphia: Jewish Publication Society of America, 1962.

Theology of Ancient Judaism. 2 vols. London and New York: The Soncino Press, 1962 and 1965 (Hebrew).

Hesiod. *Theogony.* Translated and introduction by Norman Brown. New York: The Liberal Arts Press, 1953.

Hillers, Delbert R. *Covenant: The History of a Biblical Idea.* Baltimore: The Johns Hopkins Press, 1969.

Hoenig, Sidney B. "New Light on the Epoch of Akabiah B. Mahalalel," in *Studies and Essays in Honor of Abraham A. Newman.* Leiden: E.J. Brill, 1962, 291-298.

Hoschander, Jacob. *The Priests and Prophets.* New York: Jewish Theological Seminary of America, 1938.

Huffman, H. B. "The Covenant Law-Suit in the Prophets," *Journal of Biblical Literature,* LXXVIII (1954), 285-95.

Jacobsen, T. "Primitive Democracy in Ancient Mesopotamia," *Journal of Near Eastern Studies,* II, No. 3 (July, 1943), 154-172.

James, Muriel M. *the Development of Hebrew Adult Education as Related to National Crisis from 1800 B.C. to 220 A.D.* (Unpublished Doctoral Dissertation. The School of Education, University of California, Berkeley, September, 1964).

Jonas, Hans. *The Gnostic Religion.* Boston: Beacon Press, 1963.

Josephus. *Jerusalem and Rome: The Writings of Josephus.* Selected and introduced by Nahum N. Glatzer. New York: Meridian Books, 1960.

The Jewish War. Translated by G.A. Williamson. Great Britain: Penguin Books, 1959.

Kadushin, Max. "Aspects of the Rabbinic Concept of Israel. A Study in the Mekilta," *Hebrew Union College Annual,* XIX (1945-1946), 57-96.

A Conceptual Approach to the Mekilta. New York: Jonathan David Publishers, 1969.

"Heinemann, I., The Methods of Agada," (book review) *Jewish Social Studies,* XIII, No. 2 (April, 1951), 181-184.

"Introduction to Rabbinic Ethics," in *Yehezkel Kaufmann Jubilee Volume.* Edited by M. Haran. Jerusalem: Magnes Press, 1960, 88-114.

Organic Thinking, A Study in Rabbinic Thought. New York: Jewish Theological Seminary of America, 1938.

The Rabbinic Mind. 2nd ed. New York: Blaisdell Publishing Co., 1965.

The Theology of Seder Eliahu: A Study in Organic Thinking. New York: Bloch Publishing Co., 1932.

Worship and Ethics: A Study in Rabbinic Judaism. Evanston: Northwestern University Press, 1964.

Kaufmann, Yehezkel. *Golah V'nekar.* 2 vols. Jerusalem: Mosad Bialik, 1960 (Hebrew).

Toldot Ha'emunah Hayisraelit. 4 vols. Jerusalem: Mosad Bialik, 1960 (Hebrew).

Klausner, Joseph. *From Jesus to Paul.* Translated by William Stinespring. Boston: Beacon Press, 1961.

Krauss, S. "The Jews in the Works of the Church Fathers," *Jewish Quarterly Review* (old series), V (1893), 122-157; VI (1894), 82-99, 225-261.

Lauterbach, Jacob Z. "The Belief in the Power of the Word," *Hebrew Union College Annual*, XIV, (1939), 287-302.

Rabbinic Essays. Cincinnati: Hebrew Union College Press, 1951.

Lieberman, Saul. *Greek in Jewish Palestine.* New York: Jewish Theological Seminary of America, 1942.

Hellenism in Jewish Palestine. New York: Jewish Theological Seminary of America, 1962.

"How Much Greek in Jewish Palestine?" in *Biblical and Other Studies.* Edited by A. Altmann. Cambridge: Harvard University Press, 1963, 123-141.

Palestine in the Third and Fourth Centuries. Reprinted from *Jewish Quarterly Review* (new series), XXXVI, No. 4 and XXXVII, No. 1. Philadelphia: The Dropsie College of Hebrew and Cognate Learning, 1946.

Lipson, Leslie *The Great Issues of Politics.* Englewood Cliffs: Prentice Hall, Inc., 1957.

Loewe, R. "Joshua ben Hananiah: Ll.D. or D.Litt?" *Journal of Jewish Studies.* XXV, No. 1 (February, 1974), 137-154.

McCarthy, Dennis J. *Treaty and Covenant. Analecta Biblica*, XXI, Rome: Pontifical Biblical Institute, 1963.

Mantel, Hugo. *Studies in the History of the Sanhedrin*. Cambridge: Harvard University Press, 1961.

Mann, Jacob. "Rabbinic Studies in the Synoptic Gospels," *Hebrew Union College Annual*, I (1924), 323-355.

Marcus, Ralph. "The Hellenistic Age," in *Great Ages and Ideas of the Jewish People*. Edited by L. Schwartz. New York: The Modern Library, 1956, 95-139.

Marmorstein, A. "The Background of the Haggadah," *Hebrew Union College Annual*, VI (1929), 14-204.

The Doctrine of Merits in Old Rabbinical Literature. New York: KTAV Publishing House, Inc., 1968.

"Ha'Emunah B'netzah Yisrael B'darshot Hatana'im V'ha'amoraim" in *Studies in Jewish Theology*. London: Oxford University Press, 1950, 1-16 (Hebrew).

"The Introduction of R. Hoshaya to the First Chapter of Genesis Rabba," in *Louis Ginzberg Jubilee Volume* (English section). Edited by A. Marx et al. New York: The American Academy for Jewish Research, 1945, 247-252.

"Judaism and Christianity in the Middle of the Third Century," *Hebrew Union College Annual*, X (1935), 223-263.

The Old Rabbinic Doctrine of God. 2 vols. New York: KTAV Publishing House, Inc., 1968.

"The Unity of God in Rabbinic Literature," *Hebrew Union College Annual*, I (1924), 467-499.

Martin, Rex. "The Two Cities in Augustines's Political Philosophy," *Journal of the History of Ideas*, XXXIV, No. 2 (April-June, 1972), 195-216.

Mendelsohn, I. "Canaan-Israel," in *Authority and Law in the Ancient Orient* (supplement to *Journal of the American Oriental Society*, No. 17, 1954).

Mendenhall, George E. "Covenant," in *The Interpreter's Dictionary of the Bible*. 4 vols. New York: Abington Press, 1962, I, 714-721.

Law and Covenant in Israel and the Ancient Near East. Reprinted from *The Biblical Archaeologist*, XVII, No. 2 (May, 1954) and No. 3 (September, 1954) by the Presbyterian Board of Colportage of Western Pennsylvania, 1955.

"The Relation of the Individual to Political Society in Ancient Israel," in *Biblical Studies in Memory of H.C. Allerman*. New York: Augustin Publishers, 1960.

The Tenth Generation. Baltimore and London: the Johns Hopkins University Press, 1973.

Mihaly, Eugene. "A Rabbinic Defense of the Election of Israel," *Hebrew Union College Annual*, XXXV (1964), 103-143.

Montefiore, C.G. and Loewe, H. *A Rabbinic Anthology*. Philadelphia: Jewish Publication Society of America, 1960.

Moore, George F. "The Idea of Torah in Judaism," in *The Menorah Treasury*. Edited by L. Schwartz. Philadelphia: Jewish Publication Society of America, 1964

Judaism in the First Centuries of the Christian Era. 3 vols. Cambridge: Harvard University Press, 1927-1930.

Muilenberg, James. "Form and Structure of the Covenantal Formulations," *Vetus Testamentum*, IX (1959), 347-365.

The Way of Israel: Biblical Faith and Ethics. New York: Harper and Brothers, 1961.

Nahmani, H.S. *Human Rights in the Old Testament*. Tel Aviv: Joshua Chachick Publishing House, 1964.

Neusner, Jacob. *From Politics to Piety*. Englewood Cliffs: Prentice Hall, Inc., 1973

History and Torah: Essays on Jewish Learning. New York: Schocken Books, 1965.

A History of the Jews in Babylonia. 5 vols. Leiden: E.J. Brill, 1965-1970.

A Life of Rabban Yohanan ben Zakkai Circa 1-80 C.E. Leiden: E.J. Brill, 1971.

"Rabbis and Community in Third Century Babylonia," in *Religion in Antiquity, Essays in Memory of Erwin Ramsdell Goodenough*. Edited by J. Neusner. Leiden: E.J. Brill, 1968, 438-459.

"The Religious Uses of History: Judaism in First Century, A.D. Palestine and Third Century Babylonia," *History and Theory*, V, No. 2 (1966), 153-171.

There We Sat Down. New York: Abingdon Press, 1974.

"The Traditions Concerning Yohanan ben Zakkai: Reconsideration," *Journal of Jewish Studies*, XXIV, No. 1 (Spring, 1973), 65-73.

Newman, J. *Halachic Sources from the Beginning to the Ninth Century.* Leiden: E.J. Brill, 1969, 1-32.

Noth, Martin. *Exodus: A Commentary.* Translated by J.S. Bowden. Philadelphia: The Westminster Press, 1962.

The History of Israel. New York: Harper and Brothers, 1958.

Oesterley, W.O.E. *A History of Israel.* Oxford: Clarendon Press, 1932.

Orlinsky, Harry. *Ancient Israel.* Ithaca: Cornell University Press, 1954.

Pedersen, J. *Israel: Its Life and Culture.* 4 vols. London: 1959.

Plato. *The Republic.* in *Great Dialogues of Plato.* Translated by W.H.D. Rouse. New York: New American Library, 1956.

Von Rad, Gerhard. *Genesis: A Commentary.* Translated by John Marks. Philadelphia: The Westminster Press, 1956.

Old Testament Theology. Translated by O. Stalker. Edinburgh: Oliver and Boyd, 1963, Vol. 1.

Radin, Max. *The Jews Among the Greeks and Romans.* Philadelphia: Jewish Publication Society of America, 1915.

Ramsey, Paul. "Elements of Biblical Political Theory," *Journal of Religion*, XXIX, No. 4 (October, 1949), 258-283.

Robinson, T.H. "Covenant in the Old Testament," *Expository Times*, LII, No. 9 (June, 1942), 298-299.

Rosenthal, Erwin I. J. "Some Aspects of the Hebrew Monarchy," in *Studia Semitica Vol. 1: Jewish Themes.* Cambridge: University Press, 1971, 3-20.

Roth, Cecil. *History of the Jews.* New York: Schocken Books, 1961.

Sabine, G. *A History of Political Theory.* New York: Henry Holt and Company, 1959.

Safrai, S. "Elementary Education, Its Religious and Social Significance in the Talmudic Periods," *Journal of World History*, XI, No. 1-2 (1968), 148-169.

Schechter, Solomon. *Aspects of Rabbinic Theology.* New York: Schocken Books, 1961.

Document of Jewish Sectaries. 2 Vols. New York: KTAV Publishing House, Inc., 1970.

Studies in Judaism: A Selection. New York and Philadelphia: Meridian Books and Jewish Publication Society of America, 1958.

Scholem, Gershom G. *Jewish Gnosticism, Merkabah Mysticism, and Talmudic Tradition.* New York: Jewish Theological Seminary of America, 1960.

Major Trends in Jewish Mysticism. New York: Schocken Books, 1954.

The Messianic Idea in Judaism. New York: Schocken Books, 1972.

On the Kabbalah and Its Symbolism. Translated by Ralph Manheim. New York: Schocken Books, 1973.

Schurer, Emil. *A History of the Jewish People in the Time of Jesus.* Edited by Nahum N. Glatzer. New York: Schocken Books, 1961.

Selb, Walter, "*Diatheke* im Neuen Testament," *Journal of Jewish Studies*, XXV, No. 1 (February, 1974), 183-196.

Sicker, M. "Rabbinic Political Thought: A Study of Fundamental Concepts." (Unpublished Doctoral Dissertation, The New School of Social Research, New York, June, 1971).

Skinner, John. *Prophesy and Religion.* Cambridge: The University Press, 1963.

Slonimsky, Henry. "The Philosophy Implicit in the Midrash," *Hebrew Union College Annual*, XXVII (1956), 235-290.

Smith, Roger W. "Redemption and Politics," *Political Science Quarterly*, LXXXVI, No. 2 (June, 1971), 205-231.

Sonne, Isaiah. "The Schools of Shammai and Hillel Seen From Within," in *Louis Ginzberg Jubilee Volume.* Edited by A. Marx et al. New York: The American Academy for Jewish Research, 1945, 275-292.

Speiser, E. "Mesopotamia," in *Authority and Law in the Ancient Orient* (Supplement to the *Journal of the American Oriental Society*, No. 17, 1954).

Strack, Hermann. *Introduction to the Talmud and Midrash.* New York and Philadelphia: Meridian Books and Jewish Publication Society of America, 1959.

Strauss, Leo. *What is Political Philosophy?* Glencoe: the Free Press, 1959.

Suelzec, A. *The Pentateuch*. New York: Herder and Herder, 1964.

Tadmor, Hayim, " 'The People' and the Kingship in Ancient Israel: The Role of Political Institutions in the Biblical Period," *Journal of World History*, XI, No. 1-2 (1968).

Talmon, Jacob L. *The Unique and the Universal*. London: Secker and Warburg, 1965, 64-90.

Tarn, W.W. *Hellenistic Civilization*. 3rd edition, revised by the author and G.T. Griffith. Cleveland and New York: Meridian Books, 1952.

Tcherikover, Victor. *Hellenistic Civilization and the Jews*. Philadelphia: Jewish Publication Society of America, 1959.

Tinder, Glenn. "Transcending Tragedy: The Idea of Civility," *American Political Science Review*, LXVIII, No. 2 (June, 1974), 547-560.

The Torah: The Five Books of Moses. A new translation of the Holy Scriptures according to the traditional Hebrew text. Philadelphia: Jewish Publication Society of America, 1962.

Towner, W.S. "Form Criticism of Rabbinic Literature," *Journal of Jewish Studies*, XXIV, No. 2 (Autumn, 1973), 101-118.

Urbach, E.E. "Class, Status and Leadership in the World of the Palestinian Sages," *Israel Academy of Sciences and Humanities Proceedings*. Jerusalem, II (1969) 31-54 (Hebrew).

Hazal: Pirke Emunot V'de'ot. Jerusalem: Magnes Press, 1969 (Hebrew).

Perakim B'toldot Ha'emunot Ve'Ha-De'ot Shel Hazal. Jerusalem: Hebrew University, 1958-1959 (Mimeo-Hebrew).

"Studies in Rabbinic Views Concerning Divine Providence," in *Yehezkel Kaufmann Jubilee Volume*. Edited by M. Haran. Jerusalem: Magnes Press (1960), 122-148 (Hebrew).

"The Talmudic Sage - Character and Authority," *Journal of World History*, XI, No. 1-2 (1968), 116-147.

De Vaux, Roland. *Ancient Israel*. New York: McGraw-Hill Book Co., 1961.

Vermes, Geza. *Scripture and Tradition in Judaism*. Leiden: E.J. Brill, 1961.

Ward, Robert E. "Culture and the Comparative Study of Politics, or the Constipated Dialectic," *American Political Science Review*, LXVIII, No. 1 (March, 1974), 190-201.

Weber, Max. *Ancient Judaism*. Translated and edited by H. Gerth and D. Martindale. Glencoe: The Free Press, 1952.

Weinfeld, Moshe. "Manhegut B'Yisrael Hak'duma," *Nativ Irgun*. Reprint. 1959 (Hebrew).

Weiss, David. "Towards a Theology of Rabbinic Exegesis," *Judaism*, X, No. 1 (Winter, 1961), 13-20.

Wilson, John. *The Culture of Ancient Egypt*. Chicago: The University Press, 1958.

"Egypt," *Authority and Law in the Ancient Orient* (supplement to the *Journal of the American Oriental Society*, No. 17, 1954).

"Egyptian Culture and Religion," in *The Bible and the Ancient Near East: Essays in Honor of William Foxwell Albright*. Edited by G.E. Wright. New York: Doubleday and Co., 1961.

Wolfson, Harry Austryn. *Religious Philosophy*. Cambridge: Harvard University Press, 1961.

Wolin, Sheldon S. *Politics and Vision*. Boston: Little, Brown and Co., 1960.

Wright, G.E. *Biblical Archaeology*. Philadelphia: The Westminster Press, 1957.

"How Did Early Israel Differ From Her Neighbors?" *The Biblical Archaeologist*, VI, No. 1 (February, 1945).

The Old Testament Against Its Environment. London: SCM Press, 1960.

"The Terminology of Old Testament Religion and Its Significance," *Journal of Near Eastern Studies*, I (1942), 304-414.

Wood, Neal. Review of *History of Political Philosophy*. Edited by Leo Strauss and J. Cropsey. *Political Theory*, I, No. 3 (August, 1973), 341-343.

Yadin, Yigael. *Bar Kokhba*. New York: Random House, 1971.

Yaron, Reuven. *Gifts in Contemplation of Death*. Oxford: Oxford University Press, 1960.

Masada, Herod's Fortress and the Zealots' Last Stand. London: Weidenfeld and Nicolson, 1972.

Zeitlin, Solomon. "Proselytes and Proselytism During the Second Commonwealth and the Early Tannaitic Period," in *Harry Austryn Wolfson Jubilee Volume*. Jerusalem: The American Academy for Jewish Research, II, 1965, 871-881.

Yeivin, S. "The Administration of Ancient Israel," in *The Kingdoms of Israel and Judah*. Edited by A. Malamat. Jerusalem: Israel Exploration Society, 1961.

Zunz, Y.L. *Hadrashot B'Yisrael*. Translated by M. Zak. Jerusalem: Mosad Bialik, 1954 (Hebrew).

GENERAL INDEX

INDEX OF RABBIS CITED FROM THE TALMUD AND MIDRASH

INDEX OF AUTHORS CITED

INDEX OF GREEK AND LATIN
TERMS